THE GOD
I BELIEVE IN

THE GOD
I BELIEVE IN

Conversations about Judaism with the Bostoner Rebbe,
Rachel Cowan, Emil L. Fackenheim, Louis Jacobs, Steven T. Katz,
Norman Lamm, Philip Leder, Yeshayahu Leibowitz,
Cynthia Ozick, Arno Penzias, Norman Podhoretz, Chaim Potok,
Natan Sharansky, and Adin Steinsaltz

JOSHUA O. HABERMAN

THE FREE PRESS
A *Division of Macmillan, Inc.*
NEW YORK

Maxwell Macmillan Canada
TORONTO

Maxwell Macmillan International
NEW YORK   OXFORD   SINGAPORE   SYDNEY

The Free Press
A Division of Macmillan, Inc.
866 Third Avenue, New York, N.Y. 10022

Maxwell Macmillan Canada, Inc.
1200 Eglinton Avenue East
Suite 200
Don Mills, Ontario, M3C 3N1

Macmillan, Inc. is part of the Maxwell Communication Group of Companies

Printed in the United States of America

printing number

1 2 3 4 5 6 7 8 9 10

Library of Congress Cataloging-in-Publication Data

Haberman, Joshua O.
    The God I believe in / Joshua O. Haberman.
        p.   cm.
    ISBN 0-02-931716-9
    1. Spiritual life—Judaism. 2. Jews—Interviews. 3. God (Judaism) 4. Judaism—20th century. I. Title.
BM723.H25   1994
296—dc20
93-46992
CIP

Contents

By Way of Introduction: A Confession

The saying of the Talmudic sage Ben Azzai, There is no person that has not his hour and not a thing that has not its place, applies to the religious development of many men and women. In almost every person's life there are situations in which religion has its hour of awakening. Take my case. My belief in God did not come in a single leap of faith, but in the course of various experiences first in Vienna, later during my Americanization in Cincinnati, and then close to fifty years as a rabbi in Mobile, Buffalo, Trenton, and Washington, D.C. (since 1969). Sabbatical studies in Jerusalem and worldwide added new dimensions of religious experience and understanding.

Born into a secularized, religiously unobservant family in Vienna, I was a most unlikely prospect for religious leadership. Both my parents had rebelled against their Orthodox Jewish upbringing in Galicia. Both substituted Zionism for the faith and piety of their families. I never heard my father recite personal prayers at home. My mother never lit Sabbath candles. When, in the spring of 1937, exactly one year before the Nazis invaded Austria, I told

1

my parents that I wanted to become a rabbi, their shocked reaction was, "He must see a psychiatrist."

What possessed me to turn my back on our affluent family business and choose a profession for which I seemed totally unqualified? Besides, the declining Jewish community of Austria had a large surplus of unemployed rabbis, not to mention that remuneration was meager. The fact that I was the only Austrian to enroll in Vienna's rabbinical seminary before it was closed down in 1938 after Hitler's Anschluss seemed to confirm the misgivings of my parents, who argued, "Who would be so crazy as to want to be a rabbi at a time such as this?" In a compromise with them, I entered the University of Vienna for doctoral studies in philosophy along with my rabbinic training at the Israelite Theological Institute, on the understanding that after graduation I would enter the family business.

By all appearances, I was a thoroughly secular and assimilated young Jew. An avid reader of German literature, I was at home in the writings of Goethe and Schiller, the novels of Thomas Mann, and the poetry of Rilke. Friedrich Nietzche was my favorite philosopher. For recreation I attended the theater and the opera. Rigorously prepared for academic studies at the Real Gymnasium Stubenbastei, I had been exposed to only two hours a week of ineffective religious classes offered by an exasperated rabbi to bored and inattentive Jewish students, while a priest and a Protestant minister fared no better with my Christian classmates. I can only describe my formal Jewish education as minimal and dismal. I picked up a smattering of Hebrew from a private teacher, reading without comprehension prior to my perfunctory bar mitzvah ceremony. It was all over within minutes after I recited two Hebrew benedictions at a weekday morning service in Vienna's Seitenstettengasse Tempel. I attended synagogue for only short visits on high holidays and on those very few occasions during the year when my father took me "to hear the cantor." Our religious observances at home were confined to the annual Passover seder with my father skipping through the Haggadah in Hebrew which none of us understood, and the lighting of the menorah on one of the eight nights of Hanukkah.

Yet there were also several persons and events whose influence sharpened my sense of Jewish identity and led to my religious awakening. Grandmother Dvoirele gave me a demonstration of prayer that I have never forgotten. She had come to live with us when I was about eight years old. Devoutly Orthodox, she prepared her own kosher food and spent long hours in daily meditation and prayer. I used to watch her early in the morning when, with eyes closed and her body swaying, she chanted most of the service from memory. Here and there she broke into sobbing as she opened up her heart to God with all her needs. To this day, whenever I wonder if God really pays attention to us, I think of Dvoirele and her unquestioning faith in the Almighty who hears our prayers.

From my first year in primary school to my last year as a student in Vienna, there was hardly a day without some anti-Semitic experience—insults, threats of violence and anti-Semitic graffiti on walls and billboards. All of this not only reinforced my Jewish consciousness but aroused increasing curiosity about my people's history and culture. What enabled the Jews as the only people of antiquity to survive? What made our religion so precious and important that we endured two thousand years of persecution for its sake? What truths did so many Jews of brilliance, scholars and philosophers, see in Judaism?

At the age of sixteen, precisely when I could begin to appreciate mature insights into the nature of Judaism, I got my first answers from Uncle Arje, an ordained Reform rabbi in Berlin with a university degree in philosophy. Driven out of Germany by Hitler, he found temporary refuge in our home in Vienna in the mid-thirties. While living with us, Uncle Arje initiated me into the systematic study of Hebrew so that I might read the Bible in the original. He made the Bible come alive for me, gave me glimpses of its greatness, made me aware of the profundity of rabbinic interpretations, and introduced me to contemporary Jewish philosophy, helping me to identify some of those biblical ideas and moral principles which have become part of the foundation of Western civilization. These biblical discussions prompted three fundamental questions which were to confront me with ever-growing insistence through my life: What does it mean, "God said" or "God commanded"?—the problem of revelation; Does

God really reward and punish?—the problem of divine justice; and Does God hear and help us in our needs?—the problem of prayer and divine providence.

I came to the Hebrew Union College in Cincinnati in 1938 with all of these questions. No, I did not have a call from God. I was not even sure that there was a God. But I had the burning desire to find out and thought that a commitment to the search was sufficient to enter a rabbinical seminary, on the assumption that I could become a believer at the time of my ordination. Seven years later, I was ordained as a rabbi, no longer questioning the existence of God but in doubt of everything else. Every sermon I gave in the ensuing decades became a challenge to rethink my beliefs. I overcame many doubts and grew in faith except for the question of divine revelation. The authority of virtually every page in the Bible hinges on belief in God as the ultimate source of the Biblical message. I undertook graduate studies on this question and wrote "The Validation of Revelation in Modern Jewish Theology," my doctoral dissertation. Twenty-five more years of reflection on the problem of revelation resulted in my book *Philosopher of Revelation: The Life and Thought of S. L. Steinheim.*

When I reached the age of seventy, I thought the time had come to make an inventory of the religious beliefs I had arrived at after forty-five years in the rabbinate, twenty-five of which I also spent teaching Jewish studies as adjunct professor at four universities and two theological seminaries. Knowing how my own ideas had grown when challenged to teach or preach, it occurred to me that nothing would clarify my own thinking better than some serious discussions on religious beliefs with a diverse group of prominent Jews, not merely rabbis and theologians but a cross-section of Jewish intellectuals.

The fourteen men and women interviewed here include three eminent scientists, two acclaimed novelists, two philosophers, the only American-born Hasidic leader, Soviet Jewry's most famous resistance hero, a university president, a convert, a leading theologian, the editor-in-chief of an influential magazine, and the world's best-known talmudist.

They responded candidly to the questions of faith which are on the mind of many Jews, though their answers are a far cry from textbook theology. Not unexpectedly, many a statement of belief is punctured by doubt. Nearly all confess wrestling with one or several articles of faith.

The discussions focus on God and the reasons which either support or inhibit faith, and the role of teachers, family, books, and personal experiences. Among the questions from various angles are: What is the evidence for faith? What is meant by an experience or encounter with God? What is revelation? What happened at Mount Sinai? How can messages from God be verified? Does faith in God affect one's moral life? What does prayer accomplish? Is there a soul and a life hereafter? Are Jews the chosen people? Where was God at the Holocaust? What about the Messiah? Does God act in history? What is the religious meaning of the State of Israel?

Will the reader find surprises in this book? I think so. To cite but a few: The most rigid halakhicist* among the Orthodox members of the group, the ninety-year-old biochemist and philosopher Yeshayahu Leibowitz, most sharply rejects the idea of divine guidance in history, has no use for the Messiah, and professes agnosticism concerning the immortality of the soul, resurrection, and the hereafter. On the other hand, the highly sophisticated editor-in-chief of *Commentary*, Norman Podhoretz, for whom God is the source of cosmic and moral law, unexpectedly speaks of a deeply personal, mystical encounter with God, and even more surprisingly, has a theory about the devil. The astrophysicist and Nobel laureate Arno Penzias makes the strongest argument on behalf of religion's equal credibility with science. Rachel Cowan, raised in a family of New England WASPs only to discover Judaism, convert, and be ordained as a Reform rabbi, ardently upholds the doctrine of Jews as the chosen people. The novelist Cynthia Ozick, a thorough rationalist, finds highest meaning in the Jewish dietary laws (*kashrut*) even though the Bible offers no reason whatever for mandating these rules. Rabbi Levi Isaac Horowitz, better known as the Bostoner Rebbe, head of America's first native Hasidic dynasty and probably the most parochial-minded of the group, nevertheless has the keenest insight into the mentality of secular Jews and

---

*Expert in Halakhah, Jewish law.

explains why so many of our intellectual elite are now flocking to Jewish traditionalism.

It should be readily apparent that this book is not a systematic presentation of Jewish doctrines in their historic development of 3,500 years. Its focus is today's faith. The sources for this book are not other published writings but personal thoughts and beliefs spontaneously expressed in face-to-face interviews of from one to three hours. Subjectivity is the key note of each of these conversations, and yet together they are fairly representative of the religious state of mind among contemporary Jews. The men and women in this group were drawn from virtually every branch of Judaism. However, none voiced official doctrine. Each spoke as an individual.

The "Bostoner Rebbe"
(Levi Isaac Horowitz)

The "Bostoner Rebbe" is the first American-born Hasidic leader. He is unique among Orthodox leaders in his openness and outreach to all sorts of Jews, and has a following far beyond his own community including the unaffiliated and agnostic. The Rebbe divides his time between Boston and Jerusalem, where many of his Hasidim have settled around the synagogue and study center which he built on the outskirts of the city. Now about seventy years of age, he was a mere youth of twenty-three when, upon his father's death, he took charge of his congregation in Boston. Over the years he has attracted thousands of followers, especially college students and academicians, who relish the joy and enthusiasm of the communal Shabbes meal with the amiable rebbe leading them in song. In conversation he appears not awesome but calm and wise, with a sense of humor. His warm personality and practical outlook make him a much sought-after counselor. He is known to exert extraordinary efforts to help desperately ill patients obtain treatment and to mount fund-raising campaigns for their medical expenses. Frequent contacts with the medical community have made him sufficiently knowledgeable to act as an adviser on health problems. His three sons are rabbis and his two daughters are married to rabbis.

I wanted to find out what made this authentically Orthodox Hasidic leader attractive to so many academic youths and professionals who, under his influence, have turned to an observant Jewish way of life. He contradicts the stereotype of the Orthodox rabbi as a self-segregating outsider who rebuffs secular society and clings to a world that has passed. True to Hasidism, he perceives God's presence in the everyday. He often answers a perplexing question with a parable or analogy drawn from ordinary experience. Thoroughly American, he is an effective organizer and a pragmatist who favors the experiential approach to religion over theological speculation and argument. He knows that people who share a Shabbes meal with song and laughter will be more receptive to prayer and the religious message than an audience in a lecture hall treated to a theological discourse. A personality such as his is part of the explanation for the Orthodox Jewish revival in the western world. We spoke at Har Nof in Jerusalem, November 17, 1991.

Q: With reference to Shimon ha-tzadik's statement, *al ha-torah, al ha-avodah, v'al g'milut khasadim* [upon three things the world exists: on foundations of Torah, worship, and good deeds] I ask you: Why not add *al emunah* [upon faith]? Is faith less important than *Torah, avodah, g'milut khasadim*? How important is *emunah* [faith] on the scale of priorities of Judaism?

BOSTONER: When you are saying *al shloshah d'varim ha-olam omed* [upon three things the world exists . . .] you are talking to a Jew. You are not talking to a heathen; you are not talking to a person who believes in a different faith. You are talking to a person who is seeking a way of being able to complete his function in this world and that person is a *Yid*, a Jew. Once you know you are dealing with a Jew, obviously emunah would have to be the built-in factor in the three priorities of torah, avodah, and g'milut khasadim [Torah, worship, and good deeds]. If the person is going to be doing g'milut khasadim [good deeds] just because it is a moral responsibility, it is a different type of g'milut khasadim.

The g'milut khasadim that Shimon ha-tzadik speaks of is g'milut khasadim in the life of a Yid. There are *halakhot* [rules] in g'milut khasadim, which tell you how one should go about it. It is not just how a person feels about it. It is assumed that he has already reached a point of faith in the *ribbon shel olam* [the Almighty] and faith in that which in this world represents the Almighty.

Q: In the context of Pirke Avot [Sayings of the Fathers] where the words were spoken in a circle of sages who were seeking the best way of serving God, faith could be taken for granted. But, in the context of the twentieth-century American Jewish community, largely faithless or wavering and shot through with doubt, can we omit emunah from the highest priorities of the Jewish way of life today?

BOSTONER: It depends on whom you are addressing. If you are addressing a Yid, there is no need to stress the fact that a person has to have emunah; it is assumed that he has it.

Q: Suppose he doesn't have it?

BOSTONER: If he does not have emunah?

Q: What do you do?

BOSTONER: Then you have to start *aleph-beit* [i.e., from the beginning]. But it is not a person you are going to be able to teach the *darchei ha-Shem* [the ways of God], of torah, avodah, g'milut khasadim. If the *ikar* [the fundament] is missing, then you have to sit down and teach him and learn with him what that ikar is. If you go to medical school, you are not going to say, I have to make sure that I know that medicine is a very important part of life. It would be ridiculous. A person who is in medical school knows that medicine does that. To tell a Yid that you have to believe in *ha-Shem* [God] is superfluous.

Q: You have had remarkable success in bringing people back to Judaism, in fulfillment of the *mitzvat kiruv* [command of attracting others to Judaism]. What do you consider the most important single element in bringing Jews back to faith?

BOSTONER: I am asked many times what is the formula by which, with God's help, I am successful in being able to get people to find *derekh ha-Shem*, the way of God. There is no special formula for success in reaching out. Years ago I felt that, if I was going to speak to a philosophy major in a university, I had to be prepared philosophically to challenge his ideas. However, after a while, I learned that the person is not interested in the philosophy part. Philosophy he has at school, whether it is at Harvard or Brandeis or wherever he attends. What he wants to hear is the *d'var ha-Shem* [the word of God]. That is what the person who comes to talk to me is anxious to listen to, not a philosophical discussion, Kant or whatever. The word of God is what the people are after, even if, at times, it is not what people think they're after. You wonder how should I address that person who comes from the outside? Should I give him the elementary facts of life for a Yid who believes in Torah? But that's exactly what he wants to hear. You have to tell him what you represent, and not talk about what he already has wherever he is coming from. So you have to give him that which is you, without coloring it and making it look attractive.

There is no such thing as preparation in reaching out for people. I think that *ta'amu u're'u* [taste and see] is the main factor: taste and see. It is to be able to get the person to observe, to experience, and thereby to appreciate what *Yiddishkite* is. You can write the best book on Shabbes; it might have some impact, but not the same impact that the person has experiencing a Shabbes with a family that is traditional and seeing how Shabbes starts from the moment you *bench lecht*, when you light the candles until you do *Havdalah* ["separation" of Sabbath from ordinary days]. That unity of purpose, the unity of the family, as experienced on Shabbes is not something you can discuss or portray in an essay. So ta'amu u're'u refers to experiences which can affect people. But to prepare, to have a certain standard speech, or a certain standard approach to a newcomer to faith, is wrong; it is impossible.

There was a girl who wrote me a note from Israel saying that she's happy to inform me that she just recently became a *kallah* [bride] to a yeshivah boy. She said, I don't know whether you remember me, but my first Shabbes I experienced with you: Shabbes morning after Kiddush you called me into your study and you asked me what I did, and my response was that I am a sculptress. And you told me, "Why don't you sculpt yourself? And this is what did it." Now this was the first time I had a sculptress who came to see me from the university and I had no opportunity of planning the way by which I could reach her. The ribbon shel olam gives you the right words at the right time and you are successful. A plan of reaching out is not the answer. You have to be with it and you have to be able to understand human beings, their weaknesses and their strengths, and you have to tell it as it is. When she told me she was a sculptress, I just looked at her and imagined how she would take a stone and try to sculpt it; so my response was, "Why don't you sculpt yourself?" That was not a planned answer. That is what I am saying.

Q: The passage from Psalm 34.9, ta'amu u're'u, i.e., first taste or experience—does it mean we should seek an experience of God? Or does this refer to examples of Jewish living?

BOSTONER: To me, it is the experience of mitzvot. Through mitzvot, we experience Torah. Torah and mitzvot represent in this world the elements of ha-Shem, the elements of faith. These are the instruments by which we are able to experience what ha-Shem means. You're from Washington, right?

Q: Yes.

BOSTONER: When people take the tour of the White House and they walk through, whether it is the East Room or whatever, they are basically going into a building that is no different from any other building, but they realize that this is where the president of the United States is and where policy is set for the United States and the world. Being there, the people have a sense of awe and appreciation of what it is to be an American citizen, what it means to be the president of the United States. They have a certain sense of the importance of what is happening. Some parts of the White House, e.g., the president's living quarters, are not open to the public. In that same vein, a Yid can certainly not drop in on the inner sanctum of God, no more than, when in the White House, one would go into the president's living quarters. Very few people have the privilege of being able to do that.

For a person to say that the only way to appreciate the United States or the president, is to inspect his private quarters, such a person would have chutzpah [insolence]. That is not where you belong. You have to be able to start in kindergarten and move up to first grade, second grade, and so forth. When people come in to tell me that they want to learn Kabbalah, I turn them down. I say, "This is not for you. Kabbalah is after you finish. If you train to be a physician, you must first go to medical school, then into the operating room, and finally surgery. You can't go into the operating room or surgery when you are in elementary school." My feeling is that through the elementary, simple experience of mitzvot a person will gain insight into what it means to be a Yid, what it means to be having faith.

Q: So, you see the religious life as a process of stepping up?

BOSTONER: It is stepping up within the framework of Torah and mitzvot. That is the way of discovering the ha-Shem, that special feeling of being connected, of being linked up. And again there is no such thing as a plan: "I'm going to link up by being able to observe and do a certain thing." Some people, for instance, were turned on to Yiddishkite by the Havdalah service which impressed them; another by the *l'cha dodi* ["Come, my beloved"— a popular Sabbath eve song]. For another person, the Kiddush [Sabbath sanctification prayer] made it. Now, there is no planned way of being able to reach that which is in the highest sphere. We are talking about an understanding of God, blessed be His name, what it means to have faith and the experience of it suggested in the phrase "taste and see."

Q: What does it mean to know God? Do we know God either through the ways of men, of human beings, "in all your ways," in all your doings, "you shall know God"? [Prov. 3.6] Or, do we come to know God in some mysterious ways? Or, by recognizing the works of God, maybe in the cosmos or maybe in the interior life of the individual? How does one come to know God?

BOSTONER: *Moshe rabbenu* [Moses, our teacher], when he asked to know God, he got the answer that every Yid ought to realize. Moses said that he wanted to experience more than he had been experiencing and the Eternal said, *v'ra-ita et akhorai ufanai lo ye-aru* ["you shall see my back-side but not my face" Exod. 33.23]. Moses had wanted insight into the riddle of the suffering of the righteous and prosperity of the wicked. God responded, I can't let you into the inner sanctum; I can't let you into that which is my domain. You as a human being are finite, and the finite and the infinite cannot mix. One cannot comprehend the other. Therefore, "You shall see my back-side but not my face," meaning that you can only understand the workings of God, by *hindsight*, by appreciation of that which happened after the fact, but you cannot understand it at the time it happens. Therefore, a person who says that he is going to try to understand and reach great heights by his efforts, he is full of chutzpah. It is chutzpah to feel that we have a right to see the doings of ha-Shem.

If Moses was turned down, we certainly would be turned down. All we have a right to do is to hope that through our spiritual experiences, God might enter, in a very minute way, into the sphere of life that we live. But we only need that little light to illuminate and give us the understanding and appreciation we seek. In that sense every Yid has the opportunity of experiencing God. "In all your ways you shall know Him" is a statement somewhat easier to understand than the answer to Moses' question. "In all your ways you shall know Him" means that a person can see the greatness of God in every creation, in every creature, in everything that happens, not just in the cosmos and all the great things that occur. The Kotzker rebbe said of the ten plagues of Egypt: "Miracles are for people who are the sons of Ham," i.e., the lowest. A human being does not have to understand God only by the great miracles that happen. We have to appreciate God by the very sight of a baby born and just look at that baby and realize the greatness of the creations of ha-Shem: *ma rabbu ma-asekha* ["How great are your works, O Lord," Ps 104.24]. You can see God in everything: it just depends on how you look at it.

Q: This is what you mean by "in all your ways you shall know Him"?

BOSTONER: Exactly. People who travel where there is beautiful scenery, if they have a camera with them, they have a chance maybe to catch a few glimpses of those great moments and, then, they are able to look back at it. If they don't have the camera to preserve what they have seen, it will be very hard for them to recall what they have seen. However, the camera, the shutter has to be open and the opening of the shutter is for a split second. It is not to be overexposed. A split-second view is that which makes the picture real and this is what the picture of life with ha-Shem is.

Q: With all our apparatus of perception ready for that moment or split second.

BOSTONER: A split second; a moment is a lot.

Q: You suggested the thought that we come to know God only as we prepare ourselves and that, at a certain moment, there might be a breakthrough. We may get an insight, but we have to be prepared. Now, what happens when we think such a moment has come and we feel the presence or the word of ha-Shem? Is there any criterion by which we can tell that God has now spoken to us or God is present or with us?

BOSTONER: This is not simple. We don't have a voice recorder to be able to tell if it is God or not. Maybe, at the moment, we are mixed up, but there would come a time, when the person would realize that he is spoken to by God; if he has an insight into that which is God, he would realize that it was God that spoke to him. Of course, we are not talking about ordinary people. It would be something a person would come to realize, if not at the moment, perhaps later in the sense in which we interpreted the words "you shall see my back-side," i.e., when we look back, we shall recognize the doings of God and say, "That was a great moment!"

Q: Let me turn to questions of faith and doubt for most Jews today, the question of *t'chiat ha-metim* [resurrection of the body] and the survival of the soul or spirit after death. The restoration of the body at some future point is, to some people, simply fantastic. They consider it a fairy tale. But at one time we know that this was a central belief in Judaism.

BOSTONER: It still is.

Q: How do you understand death and the possibility of surviving death?

BOSTONER: First of all, we have to understand that life and after-life are two different planes and the person who is alive cannot understand death and the dead cannot understand life. It is a common question and I think my common answer to it is the parable of the king who wanted to give a treat to his workers, in an African country where there was a diamond mine. He told them that for the next three hours all the diamonds anyone could pluck from the ground would be theirs to keep. The workers went down into the mine and then there were some workers who, as soon as they found a diamond, polished it off, cleaned it off, and ran around to all the others that were plucking diamonds and said all excited, "I found this six carat diamond." There were others who, when they found a diamond, put it in a little box, and didn't clean it up. They knew they had the diamond there and intended to clean the diamond off after the three hours were up. Meantime, they thought, "I have to try to put as many diamonds as I can into my little bag." After the three hours, the fellow that ran around showing off his great find, ended up with one or two diamonds, whereas the others were able to fill their bags with many diamonds. Why? Because they used the time for what the time was meant to be.

Life is not meant to investigate what is going to happen afterwards. If you spend time on that which happens afterwards, you'll miss the opportunities that are here in life. There is so much to do while you are alive that while thinking about what is going to happen afterwards, you will be missing great opportunities of what is happening here at the moment. The greatest moments are the moments that a person is alive. Concentrate on what you can take here; pluck as many diamonds as you can. One hour of this world is worth more than all of the *olam habo* [hereafter] in which to collect the dividends. This is the way we see it and investigating and thinking about the hereafter is not really our business.

Q: Our chief concern, you are saying, is to be this-worldly in our attention.

BOSTONER: Right. What is going to be happening afterwards, we shall experience when we get there. I'm not worried about it at all.

Q: Is t'chiat ha-metim a doctrine or is it a symbol?

BOSTONER: It is a doctrine. The *Rambam* (Maimonides) says it is one of the thirteen fundamentals of our faith and for a believing

Jew it is a very simple doctrine. The Gemara suggests an argument in support of the idea of t'chiat ha-metim. If God can create man from nothing, then He can certainly recreate man from that which was.

Q: The idea of the Messiah has tremendous political weight now; it is explosive. On the other hand many Jews today feel that belief in the Messiah is not important to them. Would we be just as well off without even thinking about the Messiah?

BOSTONER: The thirteen principles of faith of the *Rambam*, include: "I believe with perfect faith in the coming of the Messiah." We believe in the Messiah and each day await his coming. But there is a difference between believing in the coming of the Messiah and what we must do about it. Do you stand by the front door and wait for the Messiah instead of doing the job you are supposed to do? Just as we must fully live, even while believing in the hereafter, so, must we go on working even while waiting for the Messiah. Get yourself ready to be worthy of the coming of the Messiah and expect that he will come because of what you are doing. The Messiah is not a political issue for the believing Jew. It is a question of faith in the ultimate perfection of life. If we try to perfect ourselves, if we do what we are supposed to do, if we make the world a better place to work or live in, then the Messiah will come because we are deserving a better world. But if we don't, then it is chutzpah for us to think that our generation will merit the coming of the Messiah when the generation of the Ba'al Shem [founder of Hasidism in the eighteenth century] did not merit his coming.

Q: Do you think of the Messiah as a person or as a supernatural being?

BOSTONER: It is what the *Rambam* says, a person but with supernatural qualifications. It is not something we are going to figure out.

Q: You prefer to leave it open?

BOSTONER: Yes, I believe that whenever the Messiah is going to come, I believe that everyone is going to be able to say, "*Hinney,* here he is!"

Rachel Cowan

R aised in a New England family whose roots go back to the Mayflower, Rachel Cowan converted to the faith of her late husband, Paul Cowan, with whom she had coauthored *Mixed Blessings: Untangling the Knots in an Interfaith Marriage*, a helpful book for intermarried couples. Ordained as a rabbi at the Hebrew Union College-Jewish Institute of Religion in New York, she is currently Program Director for Jewish Life at the Nathan Cummings Foundation in New York. Formerly, she served as Program Director of Temple Ansche Chesed and now teaches Introduction to Judaism classes and workshops for interfaith couples in New York.

In view of the growing number of converts in the Jewish community it seemed important to include a Jew by choice in our religious conversations. Rachel Cowan converted not for the purposes of facilitating a marriage or for other extrinsic motives but out of real conviction. What was it that drew her to Judaism? Like many other liberals, she found the Jewish accent on justice appealing. But that alone would not have brought her into the Jewish fold. The decisive factor, it seems, was the intensely personal prayer experience she had as a member of a *Havurah* (Jewish Fellowship group). The highly participatory informal worship setting of the *Havurah* enabled her to sense the immediacy of God's presence, something she had felt neither in earlier church visits nor later in formal synagogue services.

I was struck by an uncommon openness in her religious beliefs. She is not yet doctrinally set in her ways; she is still groping for deeper religious insight. Even as we talked about the possibility of God intervening in human history, she changed her mind. After first denying God's involvement in human affairs she concluded with an affirmation of divine participation in history. Several other partners in dialogue, among them seasoned theologians, also acknowledge significant changes in their religious views (Fackenheim), or confess to uncertainty about Jewish doctrines (Jacobs, Lamm). Absolute certainty about all religious doctrines may therefore indicate lack of reflection more than strength of faith. We spoke in Cowan's office at the Nathan Cummings Foundation in New York, February 3, 1992.

Q: What was your own religious home background before your conversion?

COWAN: The strongest religious influence on me was my grandmother. She was a devout Episcopalian. My parents were totally secular. Completely. They saw religion as the opiate of the masses and had no use for it whatsoever. So I didn't have many early memories of being very awed by being in church, but never liking the idea that Jesus was the Son of God or that he had been crucified. It never made any sense to me and so I never developed a Christian faith. I did develop a sense of appreciation for the power of God.

Q: God's awesomeness?

COWAN: Awesomeness, and also that faith could move you. My grandmother's nickname for me was Rashi.

Q: You mean Rashi, the commentator?

COWAN: She never heard of the commentator, that was just what she called me.

Q: Were there any kind of religious practices at home when you grew up?

COWAN: No. We went to Sunday School. At home we had Christmas every year—but our Christmas was very secular—and on Easter we only had the Easter eggs. When I was in Junior High, we moved to Wellesley, Mass. We joined the Unitarian church because Wellesley was a town where you needed to belong to a church. The family just had to belong somewhere and so from my parents' perspective, the Unitarian Church was the least objectionable. They had an intellectual minister. He was very liberal, very progressive. His preaching was intelligent, and I loved it. I loved the church; I taught Sunday School; I was president of the Youth Group. What I liked was that this community of people came together for something transcendent and there was some teaching to pass on. When Paul and I were married, we were very secular. Our religion was the civil rights movement. For many interfaith couples like us, the Unitarian church serves as a compromise, but I didn't want it because I felt it had no mystery. There was no ritual, there was no tradition: it was all rational. I also went to Quaker summer camps, and for me the experience of the silent meeting was something I found very powerful. I had a very strong sense of God being in nature, but no vocabulary for it at all.

Q: No theology?

COWAN: No theology. Seeing this butterfly or this sunset, I thought, there must be a God.

Q: A response to grandeur or beauty? Or something else?

COWAN: Being in awe. What Heschel* would have called radical amazement.

Q: What brought you into Judaism? Was it something prior to your marriage or after marriage? Was it Paul? Some other person? Or was it some book? What really gave you that initial push?

COWAN: What I had brought from before my marriage were my values. Judaism, I found, expressed those values better than any-

---

*Abraham Joshua Heschel (1907–1972), one of the leading Jewish thinkers in America.

thing else. I mean a real commitment to social justice and a real sense that our role in life is to make the world a better place. I found that embodied in Judaism. Being a WASP in New England can be so dry, with a sense of duty motivating everything. In Judaism the commitment to social justice seemed to be so much more a part of a full life. My parents also were very respectful of Jews and concerned about anti-Semitism. They taught us early how wrong anti-Semitism was.

Q: Was your mother also born into the Episcopalian tradition?

COWAN: Yes.

Q: So, your parents were homogeneous in their religious upbringing and in their social status?

COWAN: Yes, old New England families. When I met Paul, I was more interested in the fact that he was Jewish than he was. One of the first things that I wanted to know from him was what is the meaning of the first Jewish holiday that we encountered. It was Yom Kippur.

Q: Did he know anything?

COWAN: No, he didn't have a clue. When I met him, he had just graduated from Harvard. He had dropped out in his junior year and gone to Israel and that had made a huge impression. He loved Israel and it made him feel very proud of being Jewish, but had taught him nothing about Judaism.

Q: It was a strong affirmative response to his Jewish roots without knowing really what it was all about.

COWAN: Exactly. We met the first time through the civil rights movement in Cambridge, Maryland. Then we drove together to the U. of Chicago where we were going to graduate school, just by chance. We sort of fell in love en route. At sunset, Paul said, "Let's get dinner"—but then he added, "I'm not going to eat for another twenty-four hours." I said, "How come?" He said, "It is Yom Kippur. Jews do not eat on Yom Kippur," and I said, "How come? Why not?" Paul said, "I think it's because of solidarity with Israel."

Q: I suppose his parents didn't observe Yom Kippur?

COWAN: His father had been Orthodox as a child but, later, his parents had no affiliation with the organized Jewish community, although my father-in-law, *alav ha-shalom* [may he rest in peace], once taught at Brandeis and was instrumental in founding the Oral History Library at the American Jewish Committee.

Q: They rejected the tradition?

COWAN: His mother had been raised as a Christian Scientist, but she was Jewish. She never knew the tradition. His father had known it as a child, but it had been associated with an orthodoxy that he completely rejected. Anyway, we went to Israel on our honeymoon. When we came back, I bought him a Haggadah for his birthday, because it was my sense that here is a treasure and I want it. Paul was disappointed. What would we do with this? I was ready for it, but it really took the birth of our children to focus us on what we were going to do.

It seemed to me again that the initiative was coming from me and not from Paul. I felt that if the children grew up as ignorant about Judaism as he had, it would be a crime. It would be erasing their history and a great loss to them not to know where the Jewish half of them was coming from. The process of teaching them about Judaism brought us into situations where we had to do some learning ourselves. Simultaneously, Paul's sense of deracination had become intolerable to him and he needed to find out where he came from. And then, as our marriage went on, as we got older, we realized that the spiritual questions that had concerned us as children were still important questions and that Judaism was the arena where we could look for a spiritual pathway. We happened to live on the Upper West Side where we were lucky to find a lot of teachers and more learning opportunities than there are in most communities.

Q: Did you join some Havurah?

COWAN: There was a Havurah in our neighborhood. Some of its members taught at the religious school which we started for our children and called the Havurah School. One of them, Isa Aron, who is now a professor of education at HUC [Hebrew Union College–Jewish Institute of Religion] in Los Angeles, said to us at the time, "We can't make your kids Jewish for you. They will only be Jewish if you want them to be Jewish. So you have to figure out what we're going to teach and you have to come help us teach it." That challenge got us involved.

Q: So both of you grew together Jewishly.

COWAN: Paul had learned nothing of the religion till then.

Q: It was new territory for you too. But hadn't you been, at least, Bible-literate beforehand?

COWAN: In college I had read the New Testament.

Q: You probably knew more than Paul, then?

COWAN: No, because he had gone to Choate. He had more of a Christian education than I did. He used to go to chapel every day. He knew Christianity both from Choate and from Harvard as an American studies major.

Q: But he knew virtually nothing of Judaism, except that the Bible was originally a Jewish book?

COWAN: He knew the Bible was a Jewish book and accepted the supreme ethical idea that the role of a Jew in the world is to bring about *tikkun olam* [world perfection]—a term he would not have known at that time.

Q: Was the pursuit of justice and perfection in the ethical sense the extent of his Jewishness at that time?

COWAN: He probably would not then have phrased it that way. Rather, Jewishness meant to him at that time that you had to make sure that another Holocaust does not happen here. That meant you had to fight racism and you had to fight anti-Semitism.

Q: You went through some kind of formal conversion, did you not?

COWAN: I did fifteen years after Paul and I were married. Rabbi Wolfe Kelman was on my *beth din* [rabbinic court].

Q: Was he the sponsor?

COWAN: Yes. We had worked together in the revitalization of the synagogue in our neighborhood and we had become very good friends and he became an important teacher to me.

Q: Was it within the Conservative movement then that you took up the Jewish faith?

COWAN: Within the Havurah movement, really.

Q: Which in the long run were your most significant or meaningful religious experiences before or since your conversion?

COWAN: One was going to the Havurah on Rosh Hashana when I knew very little about the holiday. I walked into this room and there were all these people sitting on the floor—this was in the early '70s. We were using the Harlow Machzor [Holy Day prayerbook]. It has a really nice section of reflections in English on the theme of *teshuvah* [repentance]. Somehow I sensed that there was in Judaism a wisdom that said we were not expected to be all perfect. There was a wisdom about the process of personal growth and a ritual to stimulate and encourage that. Another experience occurred in Jerusalem in the summer of '79. I went to the Wall and I had a horrible shock. It was very painful going there and being segregated into the women's section, with the women all peering over to the men on the other side. How could I convert to this religion? How deeply rooted is sexism in it? How could I stand it? I just started to weep and ran away from the Wall. I felt as if I had been robbed of something.

I had a friend who now is a rabbi here in the States but lived in Israel at the time, Jonathan Omer-Man. Jonathan at that time was living in Jerusalem and he said to me, "Rachel, for you, God is not at the Wall. That is not where God lives. The Wall is just a national monument. You will find God in many other places." It was such a comfort to me when he said that. Then, I realized that in any spiritual tradition, there are some ways that are difficult to accept or that need to be changed. And one of the things that I had been really moved by in Judaism was the way people got so engaged and took ideas seriously and struggled with them. There seemed to be room for discussion and different strains of thought.

Q: How do you identify yourself at the present time? Are you comfortable in Reform or are you drawn toward Conservative or Orthodox Judaism?

COWAN: I think of myself as being post-denominational, like many in the Havurah movement. I am comfortable in Reform and I am comfortable in Conservative Judaism. I have important teachers who are Orthodox. In Reform, what suits me is the idea that you should practice Judaism with informed choice.

Q: The freedom to choose is very important to you?

COWAN: Very important.

Q: When you say "informed choice," it sounds more like a prayer to me. I only wish all my fellow Reform Jews acted according to an informed choice. Unfortunately, very often it is an ignorant choice.

COWAN: That is true.

Q: More often, it is *convenient* choice.

COWAN: Yes, convenient choice. I tell you what makes me uncomfortable in any synagogue. Since I came through the Havurah movement, I like a more informal worship setting. I like it when the congregation participates. Sometimes it is very esthetic when the cantor sings beautifully. But I prefer the spirit when everybody sings. That doesn't happen very often in Reform congregations. And in many Conservative congregations it doesn't happen either. When I come back into a congregation, it would be one of my goals to develop a more creative, egalitarian, and participatory worship service.

Q: Heschel once said that the problem with Reform and Conservative congregations is that there are no surprises; it is so predictable, page by page; it gets boring. What is thrilling in the Orthodox congregation, despite much tedium, is the unpredictable element. People are each on their own and sometimes reach crescendos of fervor in prayer.

COWAN: I don't like it when everyone does exactly the same thing at the same time. I've had some very important prayer experiences. Apart from the communal aspect of Judaism, which I like, is this sense of intensely personal communication with God, the sense of being in the presence of God.

Q: The directness and immediacy of God in Jewish worship?

COWAN: It's absolutely overwhelming. I was talking about it with Wolfe Kelman one time. When you have an experience like that, how do you trust it, how do you know that that was real? He said no person of faith lives on that level. You create a spiritual discipline so that between this moment and the next something carries you along and you are sort of ready and you are speaking to God when these moments happen.

Q: When I entered the Hebrew Union College, every freshman had to go through an interview and one of the questions, upper classmen warned us, was, did you have a call? We wondered how we knew. Did God speak to us? I now ask you this question. Did you ever have that sense of being called?

COWAN: What I had the sense of was having been transformed by this experience so that I saw the world differently. I felt I am on this path. I can't prove it, but I know it. I no longer see the world the same way. I no longer want to be a community organizer, organizing about secular issues. I honor people who do and I think it is wonderful, but I need to be, my work needs to be somewhere on a religious path. I would never have imagined that happening to me. It just wasn't what I'd ever planned. I have a social work degree, but all of a sudden I just felt this is what I need to be doing. It wasn't God saying, Rachel, go become a rabbi, not in the way the prophets felt called by God, but just a little shift in vision. It was the same when I decided to convert.

Q: How long after your conversion did you enter the Hebrew Union College?

COWAN: I think three or four years. I had been married fifteen years already and my conversion was sort of like a wedding after you'd been living together for a long time. We were already keeping kosher.

Q: It confirmed what you had already been for some time. Do you still keep kosher?

COWAN: Yes.

Q: Do you have children?

COWAN: Two, twenty-one and twenty-three.

Q: And what pathway are they going?

COWAN: My son is a junior at Wesleyan. My daughter lives in Boston. They strongly identify as Jews. My favorite courses at rabbinic school were in theology. I am very close to Eugene Borowitz. It was really important for me to work out some theology so I could talk to people about why I was there. I had come to a sense of living in relationship with God. I like the idea of covenant theology. But when Paul became sick, the night I came home from the hospital after his diagnosis of leukemia, I just wept the whole night and I said, "God, save him, please save him." I then stopped to think, Rachel, what are you praying here? You don't believe in a God who makes sick or cures. What do you mean? That whole year I was really struggling with that question. Could I stay a rabbi? Did I still have a belief that could sustain me? And then, when Paul died, I was again working through that question and I didn't come back to the same place I was before.

Now I feel much more comfortable with the idea of a God who comforts, who can accept rage and alienation, and remain steadfast. I wrote my thesis on two psalms of grief and I studied all the commentaries which were written in a time when people believed that illness was a consequence of sin, something I completely rejected. So, of course, I couldn't accept these commentaries as the final interpretation of those psalms. They were just making me angry. I still don't believe that God punishes or that Paul was sick and died because of anything he did. He just had a bad gene. Life is really hard and God is there as a source of strength. That was a further dimension of religious experience, knowing that in spite of his illness, Paul and I were on a path together. When he died, it was if he had fallen over the edge of the cliff, but I kept going.

Q: I asked about your son and daughter, whether they followed more or less the same path.

COWAN: The year that Paul died, Matt took off from school, so he is a year behind. The kids are very strongly identified as Jews. They are not particularly religious. Matt is still very angry. He keeps saying Paul was so religious, what good did it do him? But, interestingly, he took Jewish Studies that he liked a lot in college and he is now taking a Buddhist class. What he objects to in Buddhism is a very Jewish objection: "What is wrong with attachment? What is wrong with this world? We should live in it and be present in it and try and change it." I'm glad because I was a little worried he might go off.

Q: Now, with reference to your own view of God. You got into something close to an experience of God: the reading of the psalms, the illness of Paul, the desperate attempt to invoke God's help with a question in your mind whether there can be any response from God to either this prayer or any other prayer. Have you come to terms with God on any level?

COWAN: One level certainly is that I believe we are in a relationship. I pray a lot and I don't feel as if I'm deluded or praying to a blank wall. But I am angry a lot of the time also. I hurt so much, and often prayer brings me comfort, diminishes my loneliness. Sometimes, though, it doesn't. But I wait and it works another day. As for the idea of God's love being real? Mine is a personal God.

Q: You are not speaking of any evidence, are you? It is just an inner certainty and no more than that?

COWAN: It is just the inner certainty and it is based on my really existential leap of faith. Like Buber, I would say this is real, these very intense I-thou moments which are very, very brief and quite far between. I was walking with Isa on a vacation we took together the year Paul died. We went to the state of Washington, to some lake in the middle of the wilderness. We got off the boat and I looked up at these mountains and I said to myself, "Paul, where are you? These mountains are cold; they are stone; this earth is stone; we are just these little bits of flesh passing by. What is the point of all this and what happened to you?" I started to cry. It just seemed so overwhelmingly bleak. Then the next morning, I was out walking and all of a sudden I absolutely knew that Paul was with me and I absolutely knew that he was part of God. His presence was real, but it was a presence that was linked to the presence of God. Nobody said anything, but I felt incredible relief and comfort. When I am feeling really lonely, really sad and depressed, the memory of that experience gives me strength to go on.

Q: It seems that the religious experience you speak of is the sense of the most intimate kind of connectedness, isn't it?

COWAN: Yes.

Q: When you say "I-thou," you mean relationship, connectedness, a sense of being with and within the whole universe and having a sense of interaction of some sort?

COWAN: Yes. There is a sense of reality. I remember Eugene Borowitz saying something about the footprint in the sand. A funny analogy comes to mind. When I was small, in second grade and living in Newton, Mass., I remember once looking out the window, and there was snow. It was Christmas morning and on the roof of the porch there was a footprint. "Oh, Santa Claus is here," I was so excited. Clearly my father had done that and it was proof of the existence of Santa Claus. Well, what happened to me there by that lake, was like the invisible footprint—just some emotional reality which I can intellectualize and put into the framework of Borowitz's covenant theology.

Q: Have you pursued theological studies systematically?

COWAN: Not since school. I would like to, but I haven't. I was just ordained two-and-a-half years ago. Paul had died in September and in March I was looking for jobs. And I just wasn't ready for it at all.

Q: Are you ready for it now?

COWAN: I've become involved with a project here related to healing. What would really interest me is to do more than congregational work; it is something I hope to do in a couple more years, when I feel like I am more fully healed, which is to bring Jewish insight and wisdom and tradition to people who are ill or to their families who are feeling spiritually abandoned. Very few of our people are close enough to a rabbi to feel comfortable talking. Most Jews don't have a rabbi. Maybe the hospital chaplain comes by every once in a while. I'm interested in developing ways of bringing to people that kind of spiritual comfort.

Q: Wouldn't the Book of Psalms be of enormous value? In Jewish tradition, saying *tehillim* [psalms] has always been used for healing purposes.

COWAN: When I finished my thesis I talked to Gene Borowitz about one thing I would love to do. The commentaries to the psalms still reflect the theology of the all-powerful God who punishes. I would like to take the commentaries forward from there.

Q: Let me ask you about the Bible. You were raised in New England which is not quite the Bible Belt. But the Bible is fundamental to the culture of New England. When you began to read the Bible seriously, not just routinely in public school, did you then have a sense of the Bible being God's word? Have you developed a new understanding of the Bible? How do you read the Bible today?

COWAN: I read the Bible every week. But when I taught Sunday School in the Unitarian church, the Bible was an interesting myth, a human product. At Bryn Mawr I studied New Testament and I knew all the comparative analyses of the Gospels, but I didn't read much of the Bible. It wasn't in my family tradition.

Q: How about your grandmother? Did she read the Bible regularly?

COWAN: If she did, she pretty much kept it to herself. Occasionally in Sunday School, we would have to memorize verses, but the first time I really read it was when I began to be active in the Havurah. On Saturday mornings a few parents would get together and read the Torah portion in English. I remember taking a class on Shemot [Book of Exodus] taught by Ed Greenstein who teaches Bible at J.T.S. [Jewish Theological Seminary] What was so extraordinary about it was that in reading this text you would, on the one hand, see in it an ancient Near Eastern code structure and, on the other hand, a sacralized Judaized interpretation of that code. As a modern Jew you would know that both were in some sense true. So I read the Bible attentively, conscious of its centrality.

Q: Do you treat the Bible as a springboard to your own reflections or do you look for a message from God?

COWAN: Our people have teased out of the text such layers of meanings. What is sacred is what was woven into it and what is read back out of it. God is infused in it, but I don't think the Bible is God's word.

Q: Heschel once said, "When I pray, I speak to God; when I study Torah, God speaks to me." Do you have that sense of God speaking to you when you read the Torah or hear it read?

COWAN: When I read Torah, I feel people speaking; I feel history; I feel tradition and I feel the wisdom of the ages; but I think underneath is God. God gave us this Torah, in whatever way it happened, and so it is imbued with God's presence. All this is relevant to a learners' service I lead every other Shabbat for about twenty-five people.

Q: Where do you do that?

COWAN: At Ansche Chesed Congregation. Many of the people who come haven't read the Torah since they were in Hebrew School. These are adults whose problem isn't so much that they don't know Hebrew (although that is a problem), but that they don't know why they should come to synagogue. But something has drawn them so they are there struggling with the meaning of it all. When we read the text, they will react, "Ugh! What kind of a story is this?" Or, "Why are these our heroes?" They take it all so literally. Each time I try to explain or interpret the text, I see the deep wisdom that's in it.

Q: You mentioned the learners' service. Do you personally pray regularly at certain times?

COWAN: I don't. I went to the minyan [quorum for public worship] every morning when I was saying Kaddish [doxology recited by mourners], but now I don't. I find the service has too many words for the morning so I pray alone at home. I always say the *birchot ha-shachar* [morning benedictions] and the Sh'ma [affirmation of God's oneness, Deut. 6.4]. I always wake up and I say *modah ani lefanekha* [I thank you . . .]. Then I put my head out of the bathroom window so I can see if the sun is up at the end of the block, and I say the blessing of *Yotzer ha-me-orot* [Creator of lights]. Then I say the Sh'ma [Deut. 6.4] and some of the morning blessings.

Q: Every morning?

COWAN: Yes. I also love the *Elohai, neshamah* [My God, the soul Thou gavest me . . .].

Q: Are you a regular Friday evening or Saturday morning worshipper?

COWAN: Yes, Saturday mornings, at Ansche Chesed or B'nai Jeshurun Congregation, or wherever I am. Friday nights I observe more at home.

Q: With the children?

COWAN: Or with invited friends.

Q: You stressed your own and Paul's strong commitment to social justice and to the betterment of the world. Do you take the Messiah concept seriously? Do you expect a Messianic Age?

COWAN: To me, the idea of the Messiah is what is relevant to the difference between my commitment and my mother's to social justice. I learned my values from my parents. They are secular, rooted in this world. The welfare of people is the end. But events in history are often so discouraging. It is easy to give up on the struggle. I think we need a Messianic "view," to keep at it for the long run, but I don't believe in the Messiah.

Q: You see the Messiah functionally, like setting a goal or standard?

COWAN: Right. Something always ahead of us to achieve. This Messianic view implies prayer and the faith that we aren't just people acting on our own and doomed to die, because, if we are just acting on our own, I think we'll all kill ourselves. The Messianic belief gives me hope that we can redeem this world.

Q: Can you imagine God intervening in the flow of events of history?

COWAN: This is a hard one for me.

Q: Is the opposite possible? Could God be totally detached from the events of our life and our history?

COWAN: If I believe in a God who exists in relationship with me personally, then I believe that God exists in relationship with the whole world. Therefore, I guess I have to believe that somehow there are times when God's spirit and humanity connect, which is what we pray for in the Alenu, that God's name will be one, i.e., that we will connect. I guess that there will be a sort of a merging. Yes, I do believe in God's coming into the world.

Q: You obviously believe in the freedom of human beings. When a moral impulse sways human beings to move toward a higher moral level—is it all man's own doing? Or can you see the initiative coming from God? Would you say with Heschel that God seeks out man? That God is in search of man?

COWAN: I love that idea. It is a very appealing idea to me. When I read the Torah I think here God creates this splendid world and immediately it goes wrong and God is trying to intervene. So, I guess, I don't believe that God stopped.

Q: The Bible strongly affirms the belief that there is divine initiative. God monitors the world.

COWAN: My problem is that I can't see any pattern in a series of historical events. For example, I could never say that there was some higher plan which would justify the Holocaust so that it might lead to the creation of the State of Israel. Is there a sign that God's plan is being worked out in history? I think there has been much progress, but concomitant with the progress has been our increasingly powerful capacity for destruction. So, I don't know the answer to the question. I think about it, but I haven't worked it out.

Q: You are a Jew by choice and you found a kind of affinity with the Jewish people in terms of culture and ethical aspirations. How do you react to the idea of the Jews as a chosen people? A people to whom God has assigned a special role? Is it something that still rings true in some way or the other?

COWAN: It rings true for me. It rings true in the sense of Jews being a people with a destiny, with a role in the world. It doesn't mean being a better people or that other people don't also have roles. But I believe that what we have been given, this tradition, calls upon us to live it. I think we have yet to realize our potential, but this idea of being a light to the nations I take very seriously.

Q: But is it a *divinely* given task? Or is it something that high minded prophets and teachers proposed?

COWAN: Rationally, I would say that it was good rhetoric for some prophets, trying to project a national purpose for a disparate, disobedient people to rally around. It was a tactic. But I think it has a deeper meaning. It comes back to your question about God intervening in history that I can't really answer. As for the connection between God and His people, it doesn't mean to me that God doesn't care as much about everybody else. But the idea of Jewish chosenness, I do take seriously.

Q: So you do believe that there is a special function for the Jewish people. Is this function primarily moral or does it extend to other dimensions?

COWAN: Well, that raises the question if the purpose of the Jews is merely to survive? Survival for survival's sake? I really don't like this survivalist rhetoric. The sort of people who heed that view, the survivalists, remind me of the settlers' mentality on the West Bank. They are very Messianic, but I feel that survival is meant for a purpose; on the one hand it is ethical, and, on the other, it involves being in relation with God, developing our understanding of the meanings of our tradition, teaching and passing it on.

Q: The task of teaching the monotheistic faith?

COWAN: Yes.

Q: You told me of a moment in the mountains when you had a strong sense that Paul was with you. Do you believe in the hereafter? In soul survival? And if you do believe in an enduring spiritual self, does that belief include resurrection?

COWAN: Resurrection, that's beyond my limit.

Q: You won't go as far as that.

COWAN: I could say Paul is dead—he had forty-eight years on this earth and they were great because he was a wonderful person and leave it at that. I don't. But then half of me wonders if, whatever belief I hold, may have come out of my need, since I can't bear the absolute separation. After saying all that, I still believe in Paul's presence because it has happened to me a couple of times, not like in those movies, an apparition at night, but just this sense of his being there.

Q: A sure feeling?

COWAN: His *neshamah* [soul] somehow being there and so I do believe that. I can't prove it at all, but I am comforted by it. I don't see a world to come, but a spiritual continuing.

Q: You see some kind of continuity. Could you be more specific about it?

COWAN: I was talking to Shlomo Riskin, the Orthodox rabbi who is now in Israel. He said, and Gene Borowitz said the same thing, "Rachel, I just can't believe that a person, such as Paul, that smile, that energy, has all been snuffed out. That sort of spirit must be continuing." When you see a person reduced to being just a body, you know that something is missing. What is missing must have gone somewhere. I remember when I walked out of the hospital after Paul died, at about 5 in the morning, the day of Sukkot. We walked out to where the car was and the sun was just rising on the East River and I absolutely felt that his spirit came right by and went up. I just suddenly intuited that it had occurred and, to this day, I know that it happened.

Q: You believe that he remains part of the universe we all inhabit?

COWAN: Right, and not just molecules dispersed, but as a particular spirit.

Q: The person or the essence of his personality still is. We probably will never go beyond that.

Emil L. Fackenheim

B orn in Halle, Germany, in 1916, Professor Emil L. Fackenheim studied at the *Hochschule für die Wissenschaft des Juden-
tums** in Berlin before World War II. On *Kristallnacht* (November
9, 1938) he was dragged off to the Sachsenhausen concentration
camp. After his release he received rabbinic ordination and in
1939 emigrated first to Scotland and then to Canada. There he
earned his Ph.D. and became professor of philosophy at the University of Toronto. Following his retirement in 1983, he moved to
Jerusalem where he is now a Fellow of the Institute of Contemporary Jewry at the Hebrew University of Jerusalem.

If the Holocaust novels of Elie Wiesel may be condensed into
one searing question about God's response to the Holocaust, Emil
L. Fackenheim's writings might be considered the answer of a
philosopher. No one has wrestled more profoundly and longer
with the theological ramifications of God's part in history. This is
not to say that Fackenheim has not dealt with other major issues

---

*Seminary for the training of Jewish scholars and Reform rabbis founded in 1872 in
Berlin.

of faith. He is constantly rethinking his beliefs. A religious liberal, he has been critical of the theological shallowness of liberal Judaism; he has moved beyond Martin Buber and Jewish existentialism to the more profound thought of Franz Rosenzweig and back to the classics of Jewish medieval philosophy, especially Maimonides' *Guide to the Perplexed.* He has challenged the non-Orthodox intelligentsia to rethink fundamental Jewish beliefs, including the idea of revelation, and has made God the focus of much of his writing and lecturing. He is a modernist imbued with the philosophies of the modern age and at the same time an ardently believing Jew. His is a faith deepened and refined by reason.

Recognized internationally as "our leading contemporary existentialist philosopher," Fackenheim is the author of a shelf of books which include: *God's Presence in History, Encounters Between Judaism and Modern Philosophy, To Mend the World: Foundations of Future Jewish Thought*, and the popular summary of Jewish beliefs, *What Is Judaism?* We spoke at Fackenheim's home in Jerusalem, November 10, 1991.

Q: Strange that I should interview you on the anniversary of *Kristallnacht*. You have wrestled philosophically and theologically with the problem of the Holocaust and the new theology which must respond to it. Which were the major changes in your view of God in the post-Holocaust era?

FACKENHEIM: Just fifty-three years ago today, I was grabbed by the Gestapo and together with about twenty or twenty-five others, put into a cell. There we sat, our future unknown. After a while an older man asked me, "Fackenheim, you have studied Judaism, we haven't. You tell us what Judaism is now." I had nothing to say because I was not going to say that we are being punished for our sins or that we're all responsible for each other, and some of us responsible for the sins of others. I wasn't even going to say this has a meaning in the mind of God that is unknown to us. Other such things I would have found obscene and an insult to those harmless people. We were sitting there not knowing what was going to happen to us. Almost fifty years later

I wrote a book *What Is Judaism?* I remember how I began the book and I say now, there are two things to be said. One is that Judaism must not be destroyed by what was happened. The other thing is that the Holocaust is such an enormous catastrophe that things cannot go on the way they did before. And this is what I've been wrestling with all these years.

In the book itself I made an additional point and I learned this in Sachsenhausen, the prewar concentration camp. Once I was walking outside the Hebrew Union College in Jerusalem with one of the professors. Our conversation turned to the former dean, Professor Jakob Petuchowski. My friend said to me, "The trouble with Jakob is that he loves Judaism too much and Jews not enough." I said, "There is one difference between him and me. We come from the same religious background, but I was in a concentration camp and he was not." I learned some enormous lessons in those three months in that camp, namely that *amcha*, the ordinary people, is not to be dismissed as thoughtless or shallow. Then, there was also this. The only person whom I heard complaining how God can do this to me and feeling sorry for himself, was a Czech rabbi who should have been the leader of his congregation. He was a coward and a weakling. But the ordinary people didn't blame God at all. They said very simply, "These Nazis are bastards and we have to try to do what we can to survive." Much later, after the Holocaust, I came upon learned rabbis who said this is not a time of *kiddush ha-shem* [sanctification of God], it's a time of *kiddush ha-chayim* [sanctification of life]. Ever since I have not wanted to address myself only to professors. Some University of Toronto Jewish professors used to drive me up the wall when they said things like, One man's terrorist is another man's freedom fighter, platitudes which passed for wisdom.

Q: When people lose the power of distinction, they lose their morality. There is no morality without the ability to distinguish between what is a terrorist and what is a freedom fighter. What you are telling me then, is that in the concentration camp you experienced not so much a revelation of God, but of the people of Israel.

FACKENHEIM: Yes. I believed firmly in God. I had studied Buber, a tremendous influence; later, Franz Rosenzweig became an even greater influence. I learned from them that all this modern business of having ideas of God and the experience of God but not God Himself did not do justice to the great tradition of Judaism. When Buber talks about dialogue, he means "the real other."

Q: Would you go so far as to say that *am Yisrael*, the people of Israel, is in a way an incarnation of God?

FACKENHEIM: No, I will try to keep a sharp distinction from Christianity. Some of my best friends are Christians, those who are taking their own testament seriously. Bonhoeffer* is a grand example. Bonhoeffer, if he had lived, would probably be the greatest theological friend we have today. But he died a martyr. He, more and more, came to take the Old Testament seriously.

Q: Seriously in what respect?

FACKENHEIM: First of all, there is very little ethics, very little community, very little understanding in the New Testament that *this* world needs redemption. You just jump across the world in order that the meek shall inherit the earth. "I have overcome the world" strikes me as a most Christian statement in John.

Q: It's an escape from the world, isn't it?

FACKENHEIM: Still, I take Christianity and Christian theology seriously because they face up to a very fundamental problem which we, too, must face. If God is God and man is man, how can there be a relation between them? Hegel gave this question the most profound theological or philosophical treatment in modern times and, up to a point, tried to do justice to Judaism. But I have dealt with this in my book.†

Speaking of modern philosophy, where must there be for Jews a parting of ways with Kant? Kant says a righteous man loves God without being afraid of Him. A righteous man is one whose soul is so pure that his will is at one with God. But the rabbis never say that. They said the greater your closeness to God, the greater the

---

*Dietrich Bonhoeffer (1906–1945), German Protestant Theologian, executed by the Nazis.
†*Encounters Between Judaism and Modern Philosophy* (New York: Basic Books, 1793; Reprint, New York: Schocken Books, 1978).

fear of Him, too. And love does not drive out fear when it comes to a relationship with God, meaning the fundamental understanding of human creatureliness.

Q: And you persist in the Jewish understanding of the total otherness of God and the separation of God and man?

FACKENHEIM: Yes. But, then, if you insist on that to such an extent, how is it that God, from Abraham on, establishes relationships with man? It is a fundamental problem, relevant to the Holocaust. I have reached a new understanding, and it is a kind of desperate thing. When Buber says there is an eclipse of God, I accepted this for a long time, but at length found it inadequate because you could say, if, of all times, God is not at Auschwitz, who needs Him anywhere else? The psalmist is much more helpful because he complains to God about His absence. He says, "Where are You, why aren't You present now?" The Psalms have become very important to me. One says that the Lord is My Shepherd and even in the Valley of Death, He is with me; as Heschel said, "Man is not alone." But if that is really a profound affirmation, shared by Christians, then, when you come to the Holocaust, you have to speak of abandonment, a divine abandonment.

Now, I ask myself retroactively, how come the Jewish people collectively have, throughout history, affirmed God so firmly? Through the ages, maybe this required not just faith, but a most extraordinary resistance to despair. Socrates, he can die alone; it doesn't bother him. Heidegger thinks everyone who is authentic dies alone. But the twenty-third Psalm says precisely that no evil is to be feared, not even death, because God is with me. If this is Judaism's fundamental affirmation, then, with reference to Auschwitz, we may have to speak of our abandonment by God. If we Jews collectively had to say that, then how can the individual Jew today still recite the twenty-third Psalm, "The Lord is My Shepherd," at a funeral? Or, for that matter, how can we, collectively, say God has returned to us at Zion?

Q: Do you have any further comments on the "abandonment of the Jews"?

FACKENHEIM: A Christian theologian in Manchester in discussion with me said that Christian sentiment abandoned the Jews from

1935 on. In 1935, when human beings were being separated between Aryans and non-Aryans, if the Christian world had then said, "Now we are Jews," the Third Reich would have collapsed.

Q: You mean if they had done what the Danish people did, and put the yellow star on their clothes?

FACKENHEIM: They didn't do it. What can Christianity do now that it has failed the greatest test since its origin?

Q: You affirm, as you always have, that God is present. Would you then say, to put it in the simplest terms of a pious Jew, that God is not only present, but that He also cares? Is it possible for us to say that God cares about what happens to you and to our people? Recently in *Reform Judaism*, Alex Schindler* makes a theological point: God hears each individual heartbeat. Is this rhetoric or is it a statement of faith?

FACKENHEIM: That is a good statement because the notion that each individual counts and each individual moment counts is really pushing the Jewish affirmation of the Twenty-third Psalm to its logical conclusion. Because of that people become religious in the trenches.

Q: They find God, so to speak, "in the foxholes."

FACKENHEIM: Yes. What would you say about a god who becomes relevant only at the point of death? That is why I had to abandon Buber's notion of an eclipse of God at the Holocaust. There is a wonderful statement by Kierkegaard who has always been my favorite Christian thinker. He thinks about the first destruction of Jerusalem. And he says many innocent people died then, women and children, and so on. Then he lambastes the conventional Christian theologians and the ministers who say all this happened only once and it happened so long ago, so it doesn't really matter. Kierkegaard responds that the scandal is not that it happened only once, but that it happened at all. And the fact that it was long ago makes no difference. His answer is one which cannot be a Jewish answer. He says there is something edi-

---

*Rabbi Alexander Schindler is president of the Union of American Hebrew Congregations and one of Reform Judaism's most prominent leaders.

fying about always being wrong over against God. This is not a Jewish statement.

God's otherness, if you take this in the Barthian sense, in the Kierkegaardian sense, means that we are always wrong against God. But that's not how it is understood in our Bible. Note the surprising fact that the same Abraham, who does not protest that he has to sacrifice Isaac, protests the destruction of Sodom and Gomorrah. As Abraham protests, so does Jeremiah, so does Job. God gave us a covenant, which certainly means that He cares. In the name of this covenant He wants us to observe mitzvot. He, as it were, needs our help.

A Hasid once called me, "I want to see you." I asked, "Why?" He said, "I have something to teach you." So, he showed up, about twenty-five years old, in his black garb and *payot* [side curls]. What I remember was this question: "Did it ever occur to you that the God who asks Abraham to do the *akeda* [binding of Isaac as a sacrifice] sends an angel to stop it?" And he said, "God was fed up with Abraham; when he asked him to sacrifice his son—that was the test—He wanted Abraham to say no!"

Q: That's a beautiful lesson.

FACKENHEIM: That's a tremendous thing. I did not ask the man where he got it from. Is it traditional, or post-Holocaust?

Q: You refer to the covenant. Is the word covenant a synonym for relationship? Do you understand the covenant in Buber's sense of a dialogue, or as an actual set of reciprocal obligations?

FACKENHEIM: I don't know whether it needs to be such a strong either/or. I would probably follow Rosenzweig. Rosenzweig is the greater thinker, certainly as a philosopher, and the fact that he lived only half as long as Buber really makes his work all the more astounding. Rosenzweig was deeply involved in Hegel and I got deeply involved in Hegel. When he had to turn against Hegel, it was for very profound reasons, as I turned against Hegel, too. Now the reason I mention Buber and Rosenzweig is I think that Rosenzweig would take a middle course between those two [the either/or of covenant as dialogue or contract]. I wrote a piece about Rosenzweig in my youth which was all wrong. I said he was an existentialist, that everything depends on personal commitment. Now that is true for Kierkegaard, but it is not true for Rosenzweig because for Rosenzweig everything depends on the commitment of the Jewish community in their historical continuity. Buber, on the other hand, rejecting the Halakhah [traditional Jewish law], says, I understand what God wants of me for this hour, only in this hour.

Q: Doesn't Buber see his so-called encounter with God in a strictly personal, individual sense?

FACKENHEIM: Buber is really antinomian. Now Rosenzweig was never antinomian. His key faith is that the law is there; what happens individually is that it turns for the individual into a command. That concerned me in the first thing I ever wrote when I was just twenty-two years old. It excited me greatly because how can you say that what generations and generations of Jews have practiced was now simply to be cut up into personal commitments? The fact that Buber never went to synagogue has something to do with it. In this he was followed by my late friend Will Herberg.

Q: He never went to synagogue?

FACKENHEIM: Very rarely. I used to preach in the New York German synagogue and Herberg once showed up, looking very much out of place. He wore a hat—he never did otherwise—maybe he had borrowed the hat. He followed Buber much more than Rosenzweig.

In contrast, Rosenzweig, when he was bedridden, people came for Sabbath services in his home, to read the Torah and pray with him. For Rosenzweig, there is no change in Jewish history. And this is where I part company with him—or, I did, once I began facing up to the Holocaust. But for him Judaism rests on the continued commitment in history of the Jewish people to the same thing. Now if it is the same thing, how come he didn't become Orthodox? In the first place, he, of course, believed in Biblical criticism, and he couldn't understand how anybody could reject it and I can't understand it either. I don't take Biblical criticism too seriously, but you can't ignore it and, in principle, reject it. In the second place, in his study of history before he became a Jewish philosopher, he could not maintain the fiction that Halakhah has remained unchanged and was given to Moses during the forty days at Mount Sinai.

Q: So, the mitzvot [commandments] were without authority for him?

FACKENHEIM: That is true. According to him, modern Jews are in the position of outsiders who may try to come "back in,"—into Jewish religious life, that is. We all are that way except for the ultra-Orthodox. We should get in from the outside, but we can't jump in, so what I do is what is doable for me.

Now what do you mean by doable? For myself I light Sabbath candles just when I feel like it; it is just "custom and ceremony." If I practice it only as law, it is dead. But if it becomes mitzvah [commandment], and not just law, then I do it. And what is the difference? In the mitzvah you feel addressed by God who is behind the command. When there is just law, God is, so to speak, absent. But once it is a commandment, you are in the circle of commandments. That doesn't mean that you have a religious experience every Friday night. So I think if Rosenzweig had lived thirty years longer, he might very well have become completely Orthodox. Then you are practicing everything with the proviso that the law never is merely law. It is law that is potential mitzvah and the fundamental task of *mitzvoth bein adam u'vein ha-makom* [commandments between man and God] is to draw the two closer to each other.

Q: For Rosenzweig, much of Torah was our people's record of mitzvot; each could become mandatory for him personally, after testing them out in practice, one by one. But Buber considered the mitzvot as part of someone else's religious experience which he could not use in his quest for a dialogue with God.

FACKENHEIM: Buber, in a ground-breaking essay which really changed my life, and I read it many, many times when I was eighteen or nineteen years old, *The Man of Today and the Jewish Bible*, opens with a question about the Jewish Bible. What makes the many books *one* Book? It is the record of the encounter between a people in history and the Nameless One. I came to question it after the Holocaust because I asked, does this apply to Esther? You could hardly apply it to Esther.* Exodus would have to be the center. Now I reached the conclusion in my last book that maybe the center has to be shifted to Esther. The absent God is alluded to. There is a threat. But who averts the threat? Instead of God, you have Mordecai and Esther, assisted by luck. One interpretation, the traditional one, may merit the presence of the unmentioned God. But the "secular" reading cannot be ignored.

Q: The people becomes the redeemer.

FACKENHEIM: It's not quite as strong. In my most recent book, which is on the Bible, I became very cautious about theology. I asked the question, how, after the Holocaust, does a Jew read this book? Well, he has to reject many things. Only then can he accept many things and see them in an entirely new light.

I said after the Holocaust *the* fundamental principle in the light of the Hebrew Bible is the survival of the children. For example, the murmurers, after the Red Sea experience, are quite right. The children are dying of thirst. It's different from Korach. So then I reached a climactic scene which almost bowled me over. What is Moses' relationship to God through the whole desert experience? When the Israelites commit their second worst sin, namely, trusting the negative spies and the slander of the land, the punishment is that the whole generation would be killed. Moses goes along with it, but the children are not to be killed. They get into the promised land. In contrast, after the sin with the Golden Calf, God wants to commit a Holocaust and wipe out everybody and start with Moses all over again. Moses then, as it were, blackmails God. He says if you want to kill them all, you kill me too. And what will the Egyptians say? So God relents and the children live. I've never seen the contemporary significance of that before. Why do I see it now? Because I say, "Look what happened to the children of Auschwitz."

---

*The Book of Esther, the most secular Biblical book in which God's name is not even mentioned, tells how the Jews of Persia by their own efforts, i.e., without waiting for divine intervention, turned tables on their enemies and escaped. Fackenheim's point is that the Book of Esther, contrary to Buber's understanding of the Bible as the record of Israel's historical encounter with God, represents history without God and, thus, conforms to the Jewish sense of abandonment by God in the Holocaust.

Q: You refer to the Bible as Israel's dialogue with God. We have in the Bible the voice of the people, as individuals and as a collective community. Where do you hear the voice of God? To what extent is God present in the Bible? How do you understand the Bible as revelation?

FACKENHEIM: Well, you know I learned from Rosenzweig and on this point, I would give Rosenzweig's answer. The first thing that Rosenzweig wrote after his return to Judaism was an essay called *Atheistic Theology*. Nowadays, after the God-is-dead theology nobody would worry about the title of that essay, but then it was a shocker and was meant to be a shocker. It is quite possible that the object of this attack was his friend, Buber, because Buber in those days did not yet speak of dialogue. He spoke of three main ideas of Judaism and then he changed in 1922. When we saw Buber, my wife and I, a very amusing thing happened. He said, "Do you know that I didn't start thinking until I was forty years old?" That's what he said. I was forty-one at the time and Rose was twenty-five; then he turned to Rose and said, "Mrs. Fackenheim, have you started thinking yet?" I think what he referred to was *I and Thou*. It was a fundamental and revolutionary thought, i.e., the otherness of God and yet God is in relationship with us.

Now Rosenzweig called these earlier passages that talk about the great Jewish idea of God as one, *Atheistic Theology* because, he says, paganism, both ancient and modern, finds itself insulted by the idea of a higher, divine content entering into a vessel, namely the human being who is unworthy of it. That was Rosenzweig's definition of revelation, and he didn't have to change it, since he holds that nothing happens in Jewish history between Sinai and the Messianic days. The great Jewish task is to be the eternal people and forever reaffirm the same thing, climactically, on Yom Kippur. On Yom Kippur there is really a divine presence according to Rosenzweig. There is divine forgiveness, and that is why he can say that there is one reality which transcends death and that is the Jew on Yom Kippur. However, Rosenzweig had a fundamental problem with revelation. In the event of revelation, when a divine incursion occurs, one might ask, how do you get any content out of the revelation? He says somewhere in a letter "and

God descended on Mt. Sinai . . . and spoke." Rosenzweig remarks, "The word 'spoke' is already interpretation because, if there is this enormous thing of a divine reality which the human being encounters, one infinite and the other finite, where does communication come in?"

I want to tell you of an incident with Heschel. I once visited him and he had just found in the Mekhilta [Midrashic Commentary to the Book of Exodus] an enormous *midrash* regarding Mount Sinai, specifically on the passage "and they *saw* the voices" (Exodus 20.15). Any Biblical critic would say this is a mistake, but the midrash says they saw what was audible and heard what was visible. Heschel, who was philosophically well trained, was absolutely ecstatic about it. "When I try to explain this to my students, I say, human knowledge is limited to five senses. Do you suppose that if there are angels and they communicate with God, they would be hearing things with human ears and seeing things with human eyes? Therefore, if a divine revelation comes to humans and not to angels it must confuse all their senses." So how do you get out of the confusion? Of course, we organize our thoughts. So there is a human interpretation. Then the question arises, what if our interpretation is arbitrary? The midrash says the six hundred thousand Israelites at Mount Sinai all heard it differently. Rosenzweig would accept all this and say, "We don't want any arbitrary Torah interpretation. How do we get unity of understanding and the unity of the Jewish people? Through study, through founding a *Lehrhaus!*" Rosenzweig did all this very well.

Q: You refer to Rosenzweig's stress upon two high points in the Jewish experience of God: Sinai and the reconstitution of Sinai on Yom Kippur when the people again faces God and experiences in some way the presence of God. Do you think the word "experience" is meaningful or applicable to God? In what sense does a human being experience God? Can you point to a personal experience of God? What would that be?

FACKENHEIM: Well, the word "experience" is, in the first place, a slippery word because it can mean at least two different things. It can mean something purely subjective. The opposite meaning is that the "Other" somehow encounters me. Now Rosenzweig thought that it would be presumptuous, even an aberration, for individuals to claim that. The prophets claim that, but as the Talmud says, "When prophecy ceased it was given to fools and children." What happened to Rosenzweig personally when he went on that Yom Kippur to Petuchowski's father's synagogue? It will always be a secret. But he emerged from that saying that he had considered baptism yet decided to remain a Jew. If I want to find out what he might have experienced, the best thing to do is to read the Machzor [High Holy Day prayerbook].

Recently I went to shul [synagogue] on Rosh Hashanah and my mind wandered, and I was seeing all these Russian *olim* (immigrants) who had come. I was told only ten percent of them go to shul. So they handed the Machzor with the Russian translation to them, and I wondered what they could make of it? They read, "God is king." Where is God king? Not in Russia, not in Iraq, not even in Israel. Here, *pekidim* [bureaucrats] are kings. Alright, "God remembers." These passages always move me, passage after Biblical passage is quoted, as if we were afraid it might not be true. God remembers? He has forgotten us for seventy years, the Russian Jews might say. Then comes the section of the redemption. The exiles will be ingathered and the shofar [ram's horn], God's symbol of redemption, will be sounded. They can make something of that. Although it is not quite clear when the redemption will come, here they are, in Jerusalem, amazingly, and that has become a very central part of my religious view.

Q: Rosenzweig doesn't say he experienced God. He had *an* experience which turned him around.

FACKENHEIM: But you see, what has always moved me from the time I was a small child, is the inscription on the synagogue wall which says, *da lifne mi atta omed* [know before whom you stand]. It is a profound statement for me. Does "standing before God" mean that you have to experience His presence? I don't think it does. If prayer means that God is addressed as "Thou," does that mean I must have a personal experience of God? I don't think it necessarily does. When Rosenzweig considered the siddur [the traditional prayerbook] it was for him a handbook of Jewish theology. He took prayer seriously, especially the liturgy of Yom Kippur.

Q: But the statement to which you refer says *da*, "know." Is knowing the inner certainty of being in the presence of God—the equivalent of experience?

FACKENHEIM: Yes. Your question is a very good one, because all this emphasis on experience can lead you very badly astray. Let me give you a ridiculous example. I was once at one of those summer camps for youth. A friend of mine came for the weekend and we talked about Buber and so on and then someone asked, "Why don't you speak of your experience?" There was a moment of silence and then someone said, "God is my prune." I said, "What do you mean?" "Well, you know, if I have constipation, I take a prune and when the constipation is relieved I feel God." I think this is about the worst example of what experience can be and the subjectivity it implies. Rabbi Akiba used to say when people came to him for judgment, "You don't stand before me, Rabbi Akiba, you stand before God who is the ultimate Judge." Now I think that it would take quite a bit of analysis to determine whether this requires a God experience. I don't think so.

Q: Can you describe any point in your life when you either had an experience that turned you around or a moment of illumination? Anything that could be called a personal revelation of God?

FACKENHEIM: Yes, I would say so. I certainly have often stood in prayer, not very much in these last years.

Q: Why do you refer to the last years as being less prayerful than former years?

FACKENHEIM: I heard all sorts of enlightened people say we mustn't think of God as a man with a white beard. It always struck me as utterly silly, because I had never known a man with a white beard. There is a story by C. S. Lewis, whom I used to read quite a bit at one time, about an enlightened man who didn't want his child to think that God is a man with a white beard. So he said that God is the first substance and the child pictured a huge mountain of tapioca; what is worse, he didn't like tapioca. All of our terms for God are metaphors. Now what has happened to me in recent years, is that I was thinking of God as a person like a certain teacher of mine, a very lovely teacher but utterly ineffectual. In my old age, this silly image came to my mind as I wonder about God after the Holocaust.

Q: You cannot think of God as a person?

FACKENHEIM: No, no. This is not a serious argument against God as a "person." What I want to say is, that perhaps more telling than prayer have been those moments when something comes to me and I have no choice but to do this because this is my mitzvah.

Q: An unaccountable inner force telling you to act?

FACKENHEIM: Kant says in a famous passage that the goddess, before whom we bend a knee, may be the conscience within us or may be a force beyond us that merely stimulates the conscience, but it really doesn't make any difference what it is except for speculation, because the duty of a man is the same.

When several friends of ours decided we must leave Germany, one of us said we shouldn't just leave, we should make a theological statement. I made one and several others did too. It was as though you stood in the presence of God. You don't know what happens tomorrow; you might never get out of Germany; they might kill you. If you get out, you don't know where you would end up. In this context, we certainly spoke with conviction. And, then, in turn, in England and Scotland during the war we were sent away, we didn't know where, by boat. It turned out to be Canada. I had to speak at Friday night services on the boat. We had organized that. I had forgotten what I said. We knew that one of the two boats had been torpedoed by the Germans. They put us in the bottom of the boat and if there had been a torpedo, we wouldn't have had a chance. According to a guy I met about twenty years later, who remembered what I had forgotten, I said, "We don't know where we're going, but one thing we do know is that wherever we go, God is with us." I wouldn't have said that unless I believed it. The extremity of the crisis in this situation brought this out.

Q: So to you, the nearest thing to an experience of God is the sense of an absolute certainty of God's presence?

FACKENHEIM: Well, I would say, a commanding presence. When we celebrated the end of the Six-Day War and all our enemies said we celebrated our victory, we were, of course, celebrating our salvation from yet another Jewish disaster that did not come. When we came for the first time to Israel and that was in 1968, maybe then I had a religious experience. Rose and I had never been here. The first thing I saw were hundreds of Jews from all over the world. All Israel is a family; and I had an experience of a religious sort upon seeing the first store, with a Hebrew sign. For me, this sign and the presence here of Jews who, had they been elsewhere, might have been lost to the Jewish people, was a remarkable experience. We had been invited by the government. A taxi driver took us and his name was Elijah. I started talking about miracles and he said, "We Israelis don't believe in miracles." When I said there are no miracles without human action, he accepted my interpretation.

Q: Are you a believer in the Messiah? Hermann Cohen was so certain about the Messianic Age that he expected it to happen in his lifetime and was disappointed when Rosenzweig said it might take fifty to one hundred years. Rosenzweig also gave central place to the Messianic idea. Does that idea play an important role in your own Jewish outlook?

FACKENHEIM: I have become very dubious. I am actually writing a small piece for the Canadian Jewish Congress which wants to take the Ontario government to court for not paying money for Jewish education, since the province is paying money for the Catholics, but not for the Jews. So I have to write something about why education is indispensable for Jewish survival. I start out with the miracle at the Red Sea and I end up with the Messianic hope. But the Messianic hope has become very, very reduced. For example, the statement, "A person who saves one human being is as though he saved the whole world," is something shot through with skepticism: You can't save the whole world. On the other hand, don't wait for God to do it either. Who knows what is going to happen? This is a brutal world often threatened by catastrophe.

Q: Is the Messiah any person who does a good deed, who saves or helps a person?

FACKENHEIM: I think we have Messianic fragments. We just have to muddle through. I think at this point, to affirm the Messianic hope unaltered and tie it politically to Israel's current predicament, is utterly unwise. We cannot ignore the threat of destruction. The destruction could well happen as, little by little, the Arabs get their state while life gets tougher and people leave Israel again, and so on. It has become very problematic. So does that mean I give up on the Messianic hope? No, I think it has become much more precarious. There is still hope for Messianic fragments. But I think so many leftists abuse the Messianic hope as a stick with which to beat Israel, ignoring its precarious situation. I don't think when a person is promoting his peace idea, he should invoke Isaiah as a political principle.

Q: You draw a distinction, then, between Isaiah's Messiah vision and the ideological utopianism of leftist Jews who substitute their political agenda for the Messianic fulfillment?

FACKENHEIM: The traditionalist is much wiser than the modern Jew because the Messiah is either expected when the world is good enough to make his coming possible or wicked enough to make it necessary.

Q: If the world is good enough without the Messiah, then who needs him?

FACKENHEIM: I think however good the world is, it is never good enough. Ernst Bloch, who wrote the book *The Principle, Hope* (*Das Prinzip Hoffnung*), was in a way pro-Jewish, in upholding the Exodus God who moves forward as a revolutionary in Judaism but also in Christianity. But what's the consummation? He says the complete form of this is atheistic Messianism. But how wayward this is, is supremely manifest in statements of Bloch's like the one that Moses Hess would find his Jerusalem in Stalin's Moscow. That was said by a man who had taken refuge from the Nazis in capitalist New York.

I must take seriously the tragic things some Orthodox Hasidim say. They said, that the Holocaust is so full of wickedness that, after that, only the Messianic age is adequate. But it is tragic because the Messianic age did not come. This is not the *atchalta ha-geula* [the start of redemption] but, as the new prayer says, *reshit tzemichat geulatenu* [the beginning of the *sprouting* of our redemption]. I was told once that the Nobel prize winner, Shy Agnon, had something to do with the formulation of this prayer. Agnon was no mean stylist; so when he made this qualification, "beginning" *and* "sprouting," he meant something. I would say that, in the sense in which I can accept the idea that we live in the time of reshit tzemichat geulatenu, I don't even rule out the horrible possibility of destruction. The survival of the state is not negotiable for Jews, but that does not mean that it can be guaranteed. Then what is the point of *tzemichah* [sprouting]? It suggests that redemption is a process. I would say there is a little bit of *geulah* [redemption] in the Russian Jews' coming and even more so in the Ethiopians' coming, but all of this, as we read in the paper every day, is very precarious. There are also counter movements.

Q: Are you identifying current political events with the Messiah?

FACKENHEIM: No, but I think they are not unrelated. Especially if you have the State of Israel coming after the Holocaust. The relationship between these two events is extremely difficult, but a few things are clear: The founding of the state, at least, removes the utter obscenity of Jews being helplessly murdered by their enemies. We cannot rule out a future destruction, but at least it will not be a Holocaust. The Law of Return is holy to me because what it really means is that we decree the end of the exile. We can no longer say we wait for the Messiah to gather us in. This is the end of the exile and it continues to reverberate. Who would have said ten years ago that the Russians would be coming to Israel?

Q: Then, for you, the State of Israel is taking on the Messianic role?

FACKENHEIM: I would not quite say that, but it is central in the way Jewish destiny is working itself out.

Q: You speak in terms of Messianic development, a redemptive age, a time or series of events that lead to redemption, but you apparently leave out altogether the personification of the Messiah. Could the Messiah be a "son" of David?

FACKENHEIM: I think this idea would have to be greatly qualified. Let us speak of sparks of redemption. The last redemptive moment I have heard about was, when Sharansky came to the

Western Wall and an Ethiopian walked up to him, shook his hand and said, welcome from one *oleh* [immigrant] to another. I would say that a Messianic moment was in that handshake between those two persecuted Jews, one a secularist Jew and the other one whose people have been religious Jews for two thousand years.

Q: So you are not in need of a personal Messiah?

FACKENHEIM: No, not really. Unless you wanted to go with Maimonides whom I've never really been able to understand on this. He gets often quoted, but really misquoted, saying that there is no difference between the Messianic and the non-Messianic Age, except that Israel will have its own state and will be free from persecution. But if that were the case, maybe Ben-Gurion was a Messiah or, maybe Shamir is the Messiah.

Q: Is this a misunderstanding of Maimonides?

FACKENHEIM: Yes, you see, Maimonides adds something which is why, I think, the people don't understand him. He says, whatever else the Messiah will do, will be revealed only when he is there. Otherwise, Maimonides would have to ask the question, all right, here came Joshua and here came David and here came Solomon—and what happened? The State was destroyed. So here comes Ben-Gurion and here comes Shamir and the State can be destroyed again. So what is Messianic about it?

Q: So in your opinion, Maimonides still leaves the mystery of the Messianic fulfillment a mystery?

FACKENHEIM: Yes. I learned from Leo Strauss not to read the *Rambam* (Maimonides) simplistically. But lots of people haven't learned that. In that famous passage Maimonides also speaks about the lion lying down with the lamb, and calls it not a mystery, but a metaphor. But then he comes out with his statement about the nonmysterious political reality, to which however, he adds, "whatever else the Messiah will do." In other words, mystery may be there after all, not in the political dimension of the liberation of the Jewish people, but in what more there is. This is why he can believe it lasts forever. Without this, we would have to follow the alternative of Spinoza, who was a pre-Zionist Zionist, and said, "If the Jews had not been emasculated by their religion, i.e., no longer active but waiting, I firmly believe, for history is changing, that one day they would restore their state." They would restore their state and, then, as history is changeable, it might get destroyed again. Spinoza was a Zionist but no Messianist. A friend of mine, a lifelong Zionist, recently said to me, I get very depressed because whenever we came back to this place, it never ended well.

Q: Are you referring to historical events? If it never ended well, as you say, it follows that if you wait long enough, there will be a catastrophe sooner or later.

FACKENHEIM: If that is the case, then there is no Messianic redemption.

Q: That is exactly my question: Is there or is there not? You do believe there is?

FACKENHEIM: I think you have to hold on to it even if you can't say what is going to be. If you don't hold on to it, then the hope—and a Jew without hope is really a contradiction in terms—will always be a very limited one in the sense in which every person hopes. Where there is hope there is life. And when there is life there is hope.

Q: Do you believe we are a chosen people? What does that mean in today's world? Are we the only chosen people? Are there others? In what sense are we chosen?

FACKENHEIM: I don't use the expression "chosen." I use the expression "singled out." I think that is much more adequate to the Jewish experience. "Chosen" always raises questions about superiority and along those lines I have some trouble with the prayerbook. I think we are singled out.
    There is a wonderful story by Kafka which I like to tell my students. A man goes out in search of the law (the Halakhah). So he goes to a very lonely mountain pass and finally comes to two guards who guard the gate. Is this the gate to the law? May I pass through? They answer, only if you fight and defeat us, and there are more dangerous things to come. So he decides to wait. To make a long story short, he waits there day after day and year after year and he gets old and is almost dying, always asking, can

I pass and they always say no. But they are very friendly about it. So finally when he is at the point of death, he asks his last question, something he never thought of before: how come, all this time nobody else ever tried to pass here? Because this gate was for you alone, and now that you are dying, we'll lock the gate. All we have to do to make it a Jewish story is to say it applies collectively to us from Abraham on. It means that the most important problem for Jewish identity is that you are born into something. A Christian is baptized into his faith. If I am a Jew, by the mere accident of birth, then of course I have nothing to do with it. But according to Jewish custom, he becomes a bar mitzvah [responsible for the commandments] any way. Why he, why not someone else? We are singled out for it.

I said this when I went for my first postwar dialogue with German Christians in 1983. The Catholic said, "I could not be a Christian if there were no Jews practicing their Judaism." And then he went on to say, "But I have to tell you, that I feel I live in a more beautiful country." So I said to him, "I know your country is beautiful. I have often gone there for a visit, the Cologne Cathedral, for example; however, I only go there for a visit because I am not permitted to abandon my Jewish post." I used this military metaphor. The word "post" suggests nobody else is at that post, but it is ours. Now you see when you think that way, the most shocking aspect of the Holocaust comes out. If a Jew is born into the covenant, the one way to destroy it for him is murdering him because of his birth; not as past murderers have done, because he is an infidel, or a crook or a scoundrel or so on—he was killed because of his birth and that was the unique thing about the Holocaust.

Q: You would say then that the Holocaust in a sense confirms the singularity of the Jewish people?

FACKENHEIM: That is quite true. But of course, at Sinai Jews were singled out for life and here we were singled out for death and to wrestle with this is very important. I had some very good students this years. I explained to them Buber's concept of a miracle. It is not an intervention by God, but an event that has become the more astonishing the more it is explained. One of my students then said, "Isn't the Holocaust an anti-miracle?"

Q: That is an interesting question.

FACKENHEIM: I think we are in the midst of the most tremendous transition perhaps since Sinai. It has often been said that there are two epoch-making events in Jewish history, the Exodus and Sinai. Since then there has only been, at most, one at a time. Now we have two again, the Holocaust and the State of Israel. And how to relate the two adequately for future Judaism is not yet clear.

Q: But you are working at it.

FACKENHEIM: Yes, I firmly believe that, if we are still around in two hundred years from now, Jews will think that our generation was uniquely blessed because the fate of all Judaism hung in the balance and we were in this generation. We had to deliver it some way, just like the generation of Akiba.

Q: Then by remaining Jewish, we confirm the singularity of the Jewish people in its posture, standing at the post, no matter what?

FACKENHEIM: The post has changed.

Q: Has the task changed?

FACKENHEIM: Some of it has and, of course, about that there is a great struggle between Jews. I think Jews can't do anything unless they survive.

Q: We speak of the survival of the Jewish people. How about the survival of the human being? Is man a passing shadow? An accident? A speck of dust? Or is there something indestructible in man—the soul, the spirit?

FACKENHEIM: "Indestructible" is not a word for Jews. When I think of human beings whose spirits were destroyed by diabolical machinations in the Holocaust, I no longer can say "indestructible." But, the divine spirit is another thing. The Bible is always dialectical about this, "What is man and . . . yet, but little lower than the angels" (Psalm 8).

In the little article I am writing for the Canadian Jewish Congress, I am thinking of the last sentence being something like this: "Many Jews, without falling away, no longer believe in God, either when it comes to miracles and salvation or when it comes to commandments. For them there is no God, but they're still bidden to act as though human beings had been created in His image." I think that this is a fundamental affirmation that cannot be empirically verified, yet despite enormous contrary evidence, it's got to be affirmed. Jewish stubbornness must affirm it under all circumstances. And if you face, as Buber did, Joseph Goebbels, you shouldn't say about him what Buber said, that no human being is beyond redemption; in my book, Goebbels is beyond redemption. You should say he destroyed the divine image in himself. That is true of all those Nazis who tried their best, as Roy Eckhardt said, to make the holy people into feces. When people do that, they destroy the divine image in themselves.

Q: So when you speak of the soul, of the permanent value or sanctity of man, you are thinking primarily of the metaphor of man made in the image of God?

FACKENHEIM: Yes.

Q: And you think that this belief in "God's image" is something which overwhelms or overcomes death? Is it greater than death? Can we say that there is something in man that outlasts his physical existence?

FACKENHEIM: It is a very, very difficult thing to say. I think that perhaps the rabbis got this idea only because, looking for redemption only within history . . .

Q: They could not find it!

FACKENHEIM: Well, even if you can't find it, can you hope for it? Let us think, for a moment, about resurrection. Do you want that all souls should be resurrected, including the children who died of cancer and so on? I'm always amused by Saadia. He proves the *olam ha-ba* [the hereafter] on very doctrinaire premises. God exists; His existence is proved; God is just and His justice is proved. But the world is not just. Therefore, God can be just only if there is an olam ha-ba in which things are straightened out. Now I have often quoted this to my students. This is, of course, no solid proof because it rests on all sorts of unquestioned premises.

Consider also the dynamic of a curious thought from Pirke Avot [Sayings of the Fathers]: "Better is just one moment in the world to come, than the whole of this world, and better is one moment of mitzvah in this world, than the whole of the world to come." If you believe in the olam ha-ba, then of course one moment of the world to come is better than this world. That's not so difficult, once you have a notion of eternity at all. The other statement prompts the question, why should anyone think that mere flesh should be destined for olam ha-ba? Because there is the possibility of a moment of mitzvah. When a person does a mitzvah—I am using now somebody else's expression—the whole universe holds its breath. What a grandiose thing it is. If you do a mitzvah and there is a God, this has got something to do with God. Why does God need us to perform mitzvah?

I always found the objections to the olam ha-ba silly and superficial in Reform Judaism. It's the Age of Enlightenment. Why talk about eternity? The Enlightenment was pretty shallow religiously, though it was good for democracy. But what gave me pause is the Holocaust. I had a moment of truth when Michael Wyschogrod— I crossed swords with him quite often—once said at a meeting, "Nothing evil happened to the children at Auschwitz. They are all happy with God in heaven, and if I didn't believe that I would shoot myself." He is an honest person and I think maybe he would shoot himself.

But I said, My God, is this a flight from the horrors of this world? Is this escapism and pie in the sky and what Marx and all the others have to say? And I thought about it some more. And then, one of the horrors of the Holocaust hit me: Here are people who are as though they have never been, especially the children. They leave no memory; they have not been able to do anything; they were murdered. Therefore, they are human beings who are as though they had never been. Judaism says about death, you should repent the day before your death. That means that even if a human being dies in the ripeness of time, the last moment before death, the very affirmation that he makes, is not some kind of evidence or proof, but a commitment—can this really be the end? Now what if one were to say with Jewish tradition that all people who had the chance, not only Jews, of course, but others as well, to do something noble, worthwhile, it isn't just the deed which will be forgotten, it's the deed plus the doer. All these have a share in the world to come, but these six million have none? Now that would be a victory for Hitler beyond even the grave. Therefore, I raise this question, partly in response to Wyschogrod: If there is no hereafter for such as these, then the hereafter does not exist. In other words, for anyone thoughtful enough to say at a funeral, we remember that his soul is with God and God remembers his good deeds—for any such person to say that the six million victims of the Holocaust, or the children starving to death in Africa, are forgotten as though they had never been is a most shocking thought and contrary to everything in Judaism.

Q: So from your point of view, if there is to be any meaning at all to life, there has to be some meaning to the lives of millions of people who were annihilated, some in childhood, some even in infancy. All that cries out for some kind of hereafter. You also made the point that when you perform a mitzvah, at that point you transcend this world.

FACKENHEIM: Einstein was once asked (because he was not a believing Jew, but he was a very deeply religious person in his own way), the universe existed before there were human beings and presumably will remain after there are human beings, what is the difference of a world without humanity? He thought for a while and said, "Nobody could listen to the music of Mozart any more." That is, of course, a very profound point, coming from a basically agnostic person. It is easy to ask, what is human life anyway? People are born and die and they are a nuisance in old age and all these other horrible things. You might even ask, how many Mozarts were murdered in the Holocaust? But leaving Mozart aside, every human being is of infinite worth. That is what it says right in the Bible.

Q: If there is something infinitely precious in every human being, it cannot be totally annihilated.

FACKENHEIM: Except by the person himself. But what happened when they murdered the children before they could express themselves? The Holocaust continues to shock us and thoughts about it have to go on for a long time to come.

Louis Jacobs

Rabbi Louis Jacobs combines the qualities of a great rabbi, scholar, preacher and theologian. Born in Manchester, England, he received the best available yeshivah training, earning his Ph.D. at the University of London, and is the author of over twenty books on Jewish theology, law, and mysticism. He is keenly aware of the tension between traditional Jewish law and the changing conditions of Jewish modernity. After a long, bruising struggle with Great Britain's official religious establishment under its chief rabbi, Jacobs founded the independent New London Synagogue and created the movement of Conservative Judaism in Great Britain.

I have long admired Rabbi Jacobs as one of the most lucid interpreters of Jewish theology and ethics. Having exposed himself fully to modern science, general literature, and biblical criticism, he emerged unscathed in his basic Jewish beliefs.

Disavowing the fundamentalist view of the Bible's inerrancy and the dogma of the Pentateuch's Mosaic authorship, he nevertheless upholds belief in divine revelation, not in the simplistic sense of a dictation from on high, but as God's communication whose meaning must be expounded by rational interpretation. While aiming to strengthen every doctrine of Judaism with the resources of his learning and theologically trained mind, he has the candor to voice reservations or uncertainty about some beliefs to which he can no longer fully subscribe, notably the idea of the chosen people and the Messiah.

Modern Jews in quest of faith may confidently turn to him as an illuminating teacher and guide. His writings reflect the intellectual depth of Jewish philosophy, notably Maimonides, the spirituality of the Bible, Midrash, Kabbalah mysticism and Hasidism, as well as the moral sensitivity of *Mussar literature*.* His more recent books include *Religion and the Individual: A Jewish Perspective, Holy Living: Saints and Saintliness, Principles of the Jewish Faith, and Jewish Theology*. We spoke at his home in London, August 8, 1991.

Q: How did you arrive at the God concept such as you hold today? Was it primarily learning, speculative reasoning, an experience, or some significant event in your life which contributed most in the development of your belief in God?

JACOBS: I never had anything like a mystical experience. I've written on the mystics and I think I can have some glimmer of understanding of what they're talking about, but that's about as far as it goes. My belief in God (I do believe in God) has very little to do with experience, certainly not of a mystical nature. I was brought up with a belief in God. My parents believed in God; my teachers did. Although I've had my periods of Sturm und Drang and struggled with my beliefs, it's been chiefly with regard to the meaning of revelation and God's communication with man. But belief in God—I always had it. Obviously every person has periods of doubt, what the mystics call the dark nights of the soul. It might be evidence of superficiality, but I've never had any real, agonizing doubts about the basic belief.

Q: Do the words "encounter with God" and "dialogue with God" mean anything to you?

---

*See footnote, p. 239.

JACOBS: To be honest, I would say, not much. I could understand Wordsworth's "Intimations of Immortality" and what he's talking about; I can understand that everyone has experiences where something clicks and makes sense.

Q: When Buber or Rosenzweig speak of an encounter with God, do you find any meaning in it?

JACOBS: I'm not sure that I do. I find this a very Germanic way of thinking and it's not in the mood of the kind of philosophy I've read during my years.

Q: Do you conceive of God as a personal being or as some power or force?

JACOBS: I certainly believe in a personal God with all the qualifications that are required. I subscribe entirely to William Temple's idea that God is a he and not an it. But He's more than a he. He is more than personal. I find great difficulty with the naturalistic understanding of God, à la Kaplan* and others. This denudes the concept, as I see, of its whole meaning. I know there are difficulties about the notion of a divine mind, but the alternative of God as a "process" or God as a "power" that makes for righteousness, I find theologically inadequate and incomprehensible. It is as difficult to catch that as it is to catch the idea of a personal God. Human personality is the highest form of being that we know. Therefore, we describe God in terms of a person, meaning the incomprehensible One, Who brings the world into being and Who is the One with Whom we can communicate.

Q: Do you, at this point, reject Maimonides' negative theology?†

---

*Rabbi Mordecai M. Kaplan, professor at the Jewish Theological Seminary in New York and founder of the Reconstructionist movement, defined Judaism as an evolving religious civilization. Identifying theologically with religious naturalism and philosophically a pragmatist, Kaplan viewed God in nonpersonal terms as a "process" or "the power that makes for salvation." He repudiated supernaturalism, negated historic revelation, and rejected the idea of a divinely chosen people.

†In keeping with the doctrine of God's total otherness, Maimonides—and Christian scholastics following him—developed a method of suggesting the transcendent nature of God by negations rather than stating God's attributes in positive terms. This method of suggesting what God is *not*, e.g., God is not mortal, or God is not limited, etc., rather than what God is, came to be known as "Negative Theology" or by the Latin term, *via negativa* (the negative way).

JACOBS: No, I wouldn't necessarily. I have difficulties with Maimonides, but I don't think it's correct to understand Maimonides, or for that matter the kabbalistic doctrine of *ein sof* [infinite], the *via negativa*, as having anything to do with the naturalistic understanding of God. I could go along theologically with Maimonides and agree with him that you can't really say God is compassionate, but there is a God. Whereas, if you describe God in naturalistic terms, God is just a name you give to some vague something that is "out there"—and this I don't understand.

Q: The subject of revelation has engaged a great deal of your thought. In what sense would you say the Torah is God's word or that God's word is in the Torah?

JACOBS: After Biblical criticism has done its work, it's difficult to see the Bible as an infallible text. In view of the human elements in it, it would be rational to say that the Bible, and the whole of the Torah, is a human product, the work of human minds engaging themselves in the quest for the divine. But from another point of view, it would all be part of the divine process of revelation. I do believe in *torah min ha-shamayim* [Torah from heaven], in what I hope is a sophisticated way; I'm not a fundamentalist. I believe the important word there is not "torah" nor "ha-shamayim," but "min" [from]. What does it mean, torah min ha-shamayim? Does it mean when "the Lord spoke unto Moses saying" that those words themselves were spoken by God to Moses? And what about the whole question of all the evidence that so much of the Pentateuch is post-Mosaic? And what about rabbinical literature and what about the doctrine of *torah she b'al peh* [orally transmitted Torah] which itself had a history of development? I would go along with those theologians who say that revelation is an *event*, and then the spelling out of it, is what we call torah she b'al peh.

Q: Are you saying that revelation is a process in which some kind of intellectual message or spiritual impetus comes from God and is filtered through the human mind that translates it into words?

JACOBS: I wouldn't put it quite as boldly as that because revelation is a mystery. I mean, if you talk about God communicating His will to mankind, since there is a human element to be recognized, it's not simple transmission; as somebody once said in a controversy in which I was involved, when it says that God gave the Torah to Moses, it was not like the queen giving the football cup to the captain of Chelsea. It's not that, it is much more inter-action. I would put it this way: The Torah is the way in which my people in the past—and it is still going on—have interpreted what it is that God wants them to do. So it is to be understood in dynamic terms. And that's how we see, even in the most Ortho-dox view, rabbinic law. Rabbinic law wasn't given to Moses at Sinai; Hebrew wasn't given to Moses at Sinai; the synagogue wasn't; l'cha dodi [Sabbath hymn] wasn't. So what's the authority for it? Since it's part of Jewish worship, it is what God wants me to do.

Q: How do you understand, specifically, such terms as "God says," "God spoke," "God commanded?"

JACOBS: I would understand this to mean that various phases in the history of ancient Israel, certain institutions, and certain ideas and laws were seen to be the will of God. Therefore, those who wrote about it or perhaps initially spoke about it, said that this is *torat Mosheh* [Torah of Moses], this is what God said to Moses, just as you'll find in the later literature statements that say this is torat Mosheh; they don't mean literally "it was given by Moses," but they mean "it was given"—i.e., "it is true." After all, the whole doctrine of torah min ha-shamayim itself has a history. It is not something that dropped min ha-shamayim [from heaven]. One can see how it developed. It was a way of saying that Judaism is a true religion, a valid religion.

Q: However it is given, whether as fundamentalists would say—actually in writing or conveyed through the minds of those who speak for the Torah—in what sense would you believe that its source is in God?

JACOBS: Yes I would say, of course, everything has its source in God. So what would we mean by something being more sacred? I would interpret this as having a good deal to do with the doctrine of Jewish chosenness. In other words, since I am of the Jewish people and I accept the Jewish faith, I would say that in some special sense there is a meeting between humans and God in Judaism.

Q: You believe there is an essential thought or message from God which was received by the Jewish people gradually, perhaps understood better in the course of time?

JACOBS: I think so, with some qualifications, because it isn't just something that was conveyed in the past which would be a new kind of fundamentalism. I certainly wouldn't agree with those who say, "O.K., God did reveal it, but He did it through J, D, and P."*

Q: How do you react to the notion that the sincere pious scholar who studies Torah is thinking the thoughts of God?

JACOBS: He is thinking those thoughts after Him. I would go along with it except I would add, he is *attempting* to think God's thoughts after Him. I believe that if you give up the fundamentalist approach, you've got to invoke the idea of a quest. The quest for Torah is itself part of Torah.

Q: Is there any way, any criterion, by which to validate conclusions one may draw in this quest, other than that of an inner assurance?

JACOBS: Yes, but the inner assurance is the way in which we validate everything and I would say that there are two tests: one is what you call inner assurance or the conscience or whatever and the other is the total experience of the Jewish people and for that matter, to some extent, of other peoples as well. How do we validate anything? I don't mean mathematics, but moral questions to which we have to apply what we think is right. I would say that the Torah is marvelous and it works, but there are areas where it just doesn't work and where the tradition is not in accord with what many reasonable people consider to be justice, and then it has no authority.

Q: On what basis would you reject certain parts of the Torah as not being divine, as erroneous?

---

*J, D, P refer to various sources of the Bible according to the so-called Documentary Theory: J, Yahwist (spelled Jahwist in German); D, Deuteronomist; P, Priestly Code.

JACOBS: The obvious example is the law of *mamzer* [offspring of forbidden marriage].* This law seems to most reasonable people, and even to most fundamentalists, unjust. I think the fundamentalist Jew would say it isn't just, but then who says that God has to be just? And I would go on with that as well if I did not believe, on other grounds, that that could not be a divine law. For example, I would have to ask what did the word "mamzer" originally mean in the Torah? I would have to point out that in the whole rabbinic tradition there is the attempt to get rid of this law, as unjust law. So, therefore, if I am pushed into a corner and I have to say that this is what God wants, and I really believe that this is what God wants, I would have to submit. But since I don't believe God wants it that way, I think the Torah itself would call for a repeal, or at least an avoidance of this law.

Q: You would, in other words, find inconsistencies between the law of *mamzerut* [illegitimacy] and standards of justice as they are pronounced and upheld elsewhere in the Torah?

JACOBS: Elsewhere in the Torah and also elsewhere in the human brain and conscience.

Q: To you, the human conscience, then, is the authoritative source of moral judgments?

JACOBS: I don't see how that can be avoided.

Q: Is your sense of morality, of what is right or wrong, shaped by what you know to be the mitzvot or does your conscience have its autonomous source in something else, justice or right?

JACOBS: I think it is autonomous. I don't think there is any such thing as a Jewish ethic. Ethic is universal. There may be Jewish emphases. I'm not even sure about that, but I would put it this way: Judaism wants us to lead an ethical life. Or, God wants us to lead an ethical life. But I don't go to the Torah to find out what is

---

*A *mamzer*, worse than a bastard born out of wedlock, can never be legitimized since his parents are unmarriageable, such as adulterers or incestuous partners. Although the child itself is innocent of wrongdoing, it is afflicted with severe penalties on account of its parents (see Deut. 23.3). This fact already jarred the sense of justice of rabbis long ago who tried to mitigate the harshness of the law.

an ethical life. I don't go to the Torah in order to say that I have to be just. I would say it is in the Torah *because* it's right.

Q: How do you relate what you consider to be the principles of justice to God himself? Do you think God cares whether you do one thing or the other?

JACOBS: Well, "cares" is a loaded word. From one point of view, the Kabbalists in their doctrine of *ein sof* [the limitless God] say that there is a level where you can't say about God that He cares. But that level is of no concern to us. Our concern is with the God of religion. The God of religion cares. That's the only way in which humans can express their belief that to be in tune with the universe, one has to be just and compassionate.

Q: Do you say then that your caring and your sense of mandate in certain moral situations is directly related to the will of God?

JACOBS: It would be absurd to say that my conscience is my supreme guide, I really don't want to say that. But one can say that human reasoning is the angel between *God and man*. And, this is really why I take issue with the rationalistic view because the rationalistic view has to explain how moral consciousness arose. Ultimately, unless you have the idea of transcendence in which the moral sense is grounded, you come up with the idea, that, as Bertrand Russell said, in terms of logic there's no real reason for condemning Hitler for killing the Jews. Where, then, is this moral sense of duty grounded?

Q: And you feel that grounding is in God?

JACOBS: Yes.

Q: Probably the most imperiled, most jeopardized doctrine today relates to God's justice, especially divine retribution. In the light of the Holocaust, how would you respond to a person who says *eyn din v'eyn dayyan* [no justice and no judge], "I see no evidence of God's justice"?

JACOBS: But that expectation of justice must also come from somewhere. The very fact that we protest means there is something that cries out that this isn't as it should be.

Q: You see in the protest against injustice the rehabilitation of the force of justice?

JACOBS: Right, I could not put it better myself.

Q: Can we still speak of Jews as a chosen people?

JACOBS: I certainly don't go along with what I would call a qualitative basis of the doctrine by Jews like Judah Halevi and Chabad [Lubavitch Hasidim]. Yet there is something special about a Jewish soul: *dos pintele Yid* [the point of Jewishness]. There is something there which is different. Another view treats chosenness as a historical fact. It's interesting that Maimonides, because of his logic and his metaphysical approach, has very little use for the doctrine of the chosen people. He does not mention it as one of the thirteen principles of his faith. And when he talks about it in a little reference, he says, that he does not know why God chose the Jewish people. There are antecedents in Jewish thought for the view that chosenness is to be understood as noblesse oblige and sheer loyalty. I am not sure that I would want to make too much of a theological doctrine about it. I would say that it's part of our loyalty to the people to which we belong and I certainly wouldn't interpret the doctrine to exclude others from God's special care.

Q: Could you do without the doctrine or tradition of the chosen people?

JACOBS: I think I could do without it, and I think I would feel better without it. On the other hand, it's so deeply rooted that I'll probably keep it like every Jew, whether he likes it or not. So, what one has to do is to make something of it, I mean, to see it not in aggressive terms, but in terms of noblesse oblige.

Q: Are you more inclined to the concept of a *drafted* people, a people on whom a task has been placed?

JACOBS: Yes, it is often said that the choice is not for privilege but for service. But I think there is a point in Kaplan's retort that that in itself is a privilege. Also Geiger; you see even Geiger has the idea of a special Jewish genius. This is not my tendency. I've just written a book *Religion and the Individual*. The doctrine of the chosen people may well be stressed at the expense of the individual.

Judaism is also a religion for the individual soul. It's not just for the people.

Q: Are you looking toward Messianic times? Do you expect the Messiah?

JACOBS: I don't know. There again, I could do without both doctrines. I would be agnostic about it. I know it's a doctrine that has kept the Jewish people in existence. I also know that there were false Messiahs and that it could be a very dangerous doctrine. So I think it would be presumptuous for anyone to say, "I'm sure there's not going to be a personal Messiah." I don't know. This is one of the things that I would leave to God. Why do I have to decide this? Speaking personally, it doesn't have enough impact on my life that I've got to defend the doctrine. I can be agnostic about it, but I would not be agnostic about the doctrine of the hereafter. In other words, I would say that I would be agnostic only about t'chiat ha-metim [revival of the dead], bodily resurrection. But that the individual soul is immortal seems to me to be an essential part of religion.

Q: This is part of the eschatology of Judaism. Is that the part you would appropriate?

JACOBS: Yes—because the strongest argument to me for immortality, if I believe in God, is that otherwise the God Who creates and destroys is a wastrel! I don't believe in God Who is a wastrel. But how to understand it is something I don't know. Maimonides said it is like a man born blind trying to explain the nature of color. But it seems to be so much of the essence of Judaism that I couldn't believe in God and not accept the idea of immortality. Otherwise, what's it all for?

Q: You said something beforehand which I think goes to the core of the Jewish faith posture. You said, "This is something I would just as soon leave to God." Jews have been more than willing to leave many things open-ended. In their quest, they have not always pushed for the final answer. When you say, I'll leave this to God, are you not implying that God is involved in our history, in the events of this earth and in our lives? Can we still believe that God acts to help and save us?

JACOBS: That belief would have particular difficulties after the Holocaust. The question of divine providence is a very difficult thing because we can't trace it. It's impossible to say here is God and here He's not, since God is involved in everything. So, I don't know the answer to that. If, as I believe, the real heart of religion is the individual soul and God, then whatever salvation God is bringing relates to the individual soul. In this respect, I don't think there is much difference between Christianity and Judaism except that we don't need Jesus to carry out this role. Historically, *yeshua* [salvation] refers to the salvation of the Jewish people, but as a means to an end, I would say. It is not an end in itself. The Jewish people are midway between the individual and mankind as a whole. So, I think of the tensions between Jewish peoplehood and universalism and, on the other hand, Jewish people and the individual. Somehow, we have to live with these tensions. We can't get rid of any of the three parts of it.

Q: Are we back to the question of Job, God, where are you? Why don't you help us? Are we letting God off the hook for not performing in the present by giving Him a chance to come to the rescue?

JACOBS: I don't agree that God is not working in the present in human souls.

Q: How about such catastrophes as the Holocaust?

JACOBS: That would be the terrible question of evil. Why is there evil in God's universe? Nobody knows the answer to that. We can only see some glimmer of an answer. I would favor the free will defense. You have to have freedom for human beings to develop. You have to have an arena where there is a struggle between good and evil, in which people make their own souls, so to speak. Think of Keats's idea that this world is a vale of soul-making.

Q: Maybe God has done enough for us by giving us the will to overcome evil.

JACOBS: Or perhaps, one may say, God wants us to be God-like; but how can we be God-like unless we struggle with evil? However, this is like saying that God makes people sick so the nurses should be able to do their work of salvation. According to Leibniz, this is the best possible world.

Q: You don't believe that?

JACOBS: Could any other world realize the same goods? That's what is really involved here.

Q: What do you see ahead for the Jewish people and for the State of Israel?

JACOBS: I've no idea. I can only pray that it is going to be a good future.

Q: You have no question about the survival of the Jewish people in the coming decades?

JACOBS: Well, I'm not sure about the survival of the human race, but if the human race survives, the Jewish people will survive.

Steven T. Katz

S teven T. Katz, an Orthodox Jew and noted authority in modern Jewish philosophy with a Ph.D. from Cambridge University, is full professor of Near Eastern Studies at Cornell
University, having previously served as professor and chairman
of the Department of Religion at Dartmouth. He has been
appointed to visiting professorships at Hebrew University of
Jerusalem, the University of Toronto, Harvard, Yale, and the
University of Pennsylvania. Thoroughly committed to logic and
rational argumentation in the pursuit of philosophic truths, Katz,
in his personal religious outlook, relies on faith when reason falls
short of compelling evidence in support of his beliefs.

I approached Professor Katz with this question in mind: what
remains of the body of Jewish beliefs when a philosophically
trained thinker applies to it the scalpel of his analytic mind? Professor Katz, I learned, emerged from a prolonged intellectual tur-
moil, due to the clash of reason with faith, able "to deflect every
negative argument." Consequently, he "wound up in a position
where belief was at least a possible and respectable option." After

75

twenty-five years of disciplined philosophic studies, he wants to be counted as a witness *for*, not against, the verities of Judaism.

Avoiding philosophic jargon, he speaks of God and revelation not in terms of cerebral abstractions, but with the ardor of a believer. Yet, far from being a dogmatist he allows his sharply critical reason to examine every proposition of faith and is honest enough to confess that he has no satisfactory understanding of God's justice in light of the undeserved suffering of the righteous, especially in the Holocaust. Similarly, he candidly admits that some Jewish beliefs, such as the resurrection of the dead, are faith-statements which cannot be corroborated by any line of reasoning.

He is the author or editor of about a dozen books on Jewish philosophy and religious thought, including *Post-Holocaust Dialogues: Critical Studies in Modern Jewish Thought*. We spoke in Katz's office at the Oxford Center for Post-Graduate Hebrew Studies, Oxford, England, August 22, 1991.

Q: You are a recognized author and professor in Jewish philosophy and theology. I am not looking for textbook theology but your personal beliefs. What do you believe about God? Is God an idea, a power or a being with whom humans may have personal communication? Are you a theist?

KATZ: I've been wrestling most of my adult life with that issue, namely, how does one hold firm to a belief in a God who is providential and caring, a God who is involved in human life with the kind of personal intimacy and concern that is the hallmark of the God of Israel. That has always been the central point of my theological ruminations. What kind of being could that be and how does He manifest himself? What's the evidence for such divine concern in the world, especially in light of the Holocaust which has been my special problem theologically. It's not been easy.

Q: Are you a theist? That is, do you believe in God as a *personal* being?

KATZ: Yes, I'm very much a theist, very much of a Jewish theist. It seems to me that it's too easy just to be a theist, because one can be a theist of various types and avoid many problems by eliminating the personality of God in intimacy with humans, but that would make God irrelevant.

Q: Did you go through any stages in developing your view of God or have you thought about God in basically the same way through the years?

KATZ: Early on, I took these beliefs at face value and didn't pay much attention to them. Being raised in a yeshivah community and other Orthodox environments, one doesn't ask these theological questions. One doesn't ponder them. Only in graduate school here in England, in Cambridge, reading all of the philosophers of religion who were challenging all the premises, asking questions about verification and questions about the meaning of God-language, did I start to think about these things in what I would call a mature and adult way. That has now been going on for about twenty-five years since that point in time.

Q: Did you go through a crisis?

KATZ: Not a crisis. I never reached the point of not putting on my *t'fillin* [phylacteries] or not going to *shul* [synagogue]. I didn't reach that kind of rebelliousness where I said there is no God and there is no Judge. Perhaps more in keeping with my nature, it was a mellow process, something that didn't lead to the destruction of my lifestyle, but that very much unsettled me intellectually.

Q: Was there a major turning point for you, an encounter with a person, or a teacher or book that opened up new vistas?

KATZ: The decisive thing was that I came to realize, after very close study of the negative evidence, that is to say, the philosophical arguments against God and against the kinds of God-idea that I would like to hold, that I could, in effect, deflect all of those critical arguments. For any negative argument I could find a counterargument. I could not find a suitable proof in the traditional sense. I could not find a proof that was intellectually coercive in defense of God, that would provide knockdown arguments to the atheist or agnostic. But to my own satisfaction, I was sufficiently able to deflect every negative argument, and so I wound up in a position where belief was at least a possible and respectable option in face of very serious arguments for and against.

Q: Were there any formative experiences that stand out in your mind?

KATZ: I don't know about powerful religious experiences in the paradigmatic sense. As someone who's written extensively about comparative mysticism and studied Hasidism and Jewish mysticism with some intensity, I know that I have not had the kinds of experiences we would call mystical experiences or experiences of a peak sort, to use Margharita Laski's phrase. But, I've had sufficient comfort, a sufficient sense of well-being, and a sufficient awareness of continuity and community to make religion, Judaism, come alive in a way that is more than just ideas.

Q: What you're saying is that feelings that have developed in the course of your life, perhaps in connection with prayer, have been confirming what you were prompted to affirm intellectually.

KATZ: I think that is a good way to put it. If you take the view that there is no clear, decisive, evidence for or against the transcendental claims made by the tradition, then I want to be open to various possibilities. The practicing side of Judaic experience, t'fillah [prayer], Shabbat, the phenomena that go with the liturgical cycle and especially the family life cycle, have been very reinforcing, very supportive of the basic notion of providence.

Q: Your Judaism, then, developed as both orthodoxy and orthopraxis, teaching and practice, together.

KATZ: That's correct. Either without the other in Jewish terms is suicidal. Knowing the right thing in Judaism without practicing it in any way is, I would think, not very satisfying.

Q: In modern Jewish thought, Buber and Rosenzweig stand out. They gave currency in Jewish theology to the term "encounter with God" and "dialogue." Do those terms mean anything to you?

KATZ: Let me separate that into two parts. I wrote my doctoral dissertation on Martin Buber. I was extremely critical of Martin Buber and have continued to be perhaps his best known critic in a philosophical sense. And the reason is that I think Buber's particular formulation of those terms is really empty of content and turns out to be relatively puerile and meaningless. However, in a more constricted sense, particularly in the context of the circumstances of t'fillah, the term does make sense to me. In the performance of t'fillah, not all the time because that would be the ideal, but occasionally, one feels that one is in the presence—a transcendental presence—of one's maker, of one's keeper. There is a profound feeling of reciprocity, a sense of intimacy that comes in the performance of certain mitzvot, sometimes on Shabbat, sometimes Yom Kippur, but especially in t'fillah, on different occasions. It means something. Whether it has an objective ontological corollary, or it's only a psychological condition, that's the open question. But even if it has, in large part, a psychological aspect, I would argue for analyzing it as a distinctive ontological condition that is not reducible to a mere psychological state.

Q: "Encounter," to you, is the sense of God's presence, and "dialogue," a feeling that this presence is perceived in a reciprocal, mutual process.

KATZ: It's interactive, and the person with whom one is in interaction is, *kivyachol* [as it were], the divine person. The ultimate presence is interested and engaged. It's not just listening like some psychoanalyst who just listens but has, in effect, no personal involvement. It's someone who is deeply, genuinely interested and reciprocates that interest.

Q: And for that, of course, we can furnish no evidence other than subjective certainty.

KATZ: There is a subjective certainty. There is an old story about someone who asked Frederick II for the evidence of providence and he replied, "the Jews." And Karl Barth, when asked, what is your proof of the existence of God, said, "the Jews." And I would like to think that Jewish survival is objective evidence and the reconstructed State of Israel is objective evidence. However, I am well aware that none of these evidences are definitive.

Q: From what you've said it's obvious that you think of God or that you relate to God as a personal being. I must confess that I cannot possibly relate to an impersonal divine being. On the other hand, I also have great difficulty conceiving of God as a personal being. The only way we can pray to God is by imagining a personal being to whom we direct our prayers. But what does that really mean to you?

KATZ: There are two things to be distinguished here. First I think it is very important in this discussion of basic theological notions not to reduce God solely to the personal. The impersonal, which you've had a tough time relating to, just as I do, is still very much an aspect of divinity, of transcendence. As for the mystery of God, it has rightly been noted, if I could understand God, *I* would be God. And the Kotzker Rebbe once said, "A God that any Tom, Dick or Harry can understand, phooey, I don't need such a God." So there is always the mystery of the divine transcendence.

But when one conceives of the personal aspects of divinity, that is, God is not a person but has personal aspects, one desires a sense of security and a sense of the meaningfulness of life more than anything else. By security I mean that human life is not a random thing, that it is not absurd, that there is some kind of ultimate purpose into which we fit in some oblique way that is not clear to us. That our actions do matter, and that ultimately there will be a kind of squaring of the circle, that a divine personal being, God, knows how it all fits together. Meaninglessness is the ultimate enemy of Judaism. So for example, in your sermon last Saturday, you mentioned Job. I've always read Job in a confident way because what happens in the whirlwind is that out of the chaos and struggle the Almighty reveals Himself, not how He works—that is the mystery—but that He works. God acts as an agent who provides assurance that there is some ultimate sense to our being, and to the being of the world. In this we find the comfort to know that our life counts and that the world counts and that it's not all Sisyphus, pointlessly rolling the rock up the hill only to have it come back down again and crush us.

Q: I think it was Heschel who said, "When I pray, I speak to God, when I study, God speaks to me." When you read Tanakh [Bible] or hear the Torah read from the *bimah* [pulpit platform], do you understand that to be God's word? In what sense is the Torah God's word?

KATZ: That is a more troubling question than the nature of God in the sense that modern scholarship has brought a tremendous armory to bear on the question of *Torah mi-Sinai* [Torah given at Sinai], that is, a literal revelation of the Torah text as the encoded word of the divine. When I hear the Torah read and studied, having been trained to hear all the critical doubts and know all the critical problems, the challenges do surface and the literal text does become problematic. But there is something about the Torah text, a kind of uncanny quality, that always presses itself upon me. The more I study it closely, as I have done over many years, the more it comes back to redeem the situation, to undo, if not altogether, the doubts, I have. By uncanny I mean that there always seems to be more in the Torah text, a profundity, a depth of human wisdom and transcendental experience that defies ordinary expectation. In every passage, whether we find it explained in the Midrash [Commentary] or some kind of kabbalistic exegesis, there seems to be something quite extraordinary about the Torah text as it speaks to us in every generation. I have tried to wrestle with that. I have tried to make a study, a serious study, of the alternative theories of revelation.

You mentioned Buber. I think it's fair to say that Buber has been the most influential exegete of the modern nonpropositional interpretation of revelation that attempts to defend the theory of revelation in a post-Kantian age, that is, to defend the theory of revelation as not heteronomous, i.e., as not being the command of God, and not literal so that it is not subject to the criticisms of the higher Biblical critics. My own view, however, is that all of the nonpropositional reconstructions of revelation ultimately come to rack and ruin and one has to consider some kind of propositional reading. That helps me take the Bible in some more substantive sense. The other thing is that I always find that the "reductive" accounts of Torah, to use that term here, are inadequate. Reading the Torah purely as a psychological account, as a sociological account, as an historical account, as a Marxist account, never does justice to the richness and variety, to the extraordinary fecundity of the Torah as a source and document. All this reinforces, at least for myself, the notion that this is a text of sacred meaning, of sacred origin.

Q: Are you saying that the magnificence of the contents of the Torah is really its own evidence?

KATZ: Yes, that's a good way to put it; the message carries a lot of its own evidentiary weight. There seems to me to be some awareness, some disclosure of authority, of exceptional power, that is more persuasive than any alternative explanation of the text. And that overwhelming sense that the Torah is always more than we understand, that it transcends our effort to make it into something merely of our own design, that it is always the incarnation of a mysterious presence, is the compelling, or should we perhaps say more cautiously the near-compelling, evidence in itself.

Q: How do you answer Rosenzweig's point that the Torah speaks to him differently on Shabbat when he hears it read or chanted, than if he were to read it on a Monday out of a book? That on Shabbat the Torah speaks as though it were the word of God?

KATZ: I find that persuasive, though not unproblematic. The context in which one encounters the Torah is crucial. The questions you put to the text in different contexts will give you different responses. There is something else that Rosenzweig was pointing to that is extremely important, probably his greatest insight—the genius of Rosenzweig—and that is his larger understanding of the Shabbat experience. He would always say that Shabbat is a touch of eternity in time. When Rosenzweig heard the Torah on Shabbat, he felt that historical arguments, the historicity of the document, historicism as a philosophical problem, was not convincing. One experiences in Jewish life, one experiences Jewish life as, a sense of eternity.

Q: He stressed the experiential aspect of Judaism, didn't he?

KATZ: Yes he did; and he invoked an experience of a reality not touched by time. The Hegelian argument is that everything moves in time and, therefore, things grow old and are transcended by new things in time. But Rosenzweig contended that there were some realia, preeminently the Torah, that do not stand in that relationship to time, do not grow old, are not transcended by the movement of history. In so doing he perceived the basic meta-historical rhythm, despite the modern arguments that

Judaism is essentially a historical religion, of the Jewish tradition. He understood that Shabbat is, in a sense, not in history; that liturgical time is not linear but cyclical; that the festival calendar, the daily routine of *shakhrit* and *minkhah* [morning and afternoon prayers], the weekly routine of Shabbat, all these things are not really historical in any ordinary sense.

Q: The Shabbat, for him, was a kind of tuning into eternity.

KATZ: Eternity, timelessness.

Q: What relationship can you see between mitzvot and revelation or mitzvah and morality? I am thinking about a comment Rosenzweig made that the mitzvot revealed long ago may themselves become channels of fresh revelation. In the very act of performing them, we are not only responding to a divine command, we are again renewing the actual reception of the commands as though they were originally directed at us.

KATZ: There's the famous Midrash that all of Israel, all their *neshamot*, all the souls of Israel, stood at Sinai.

The other thing that might be suggested about mitzvot is this. There has been an on-going search among Jewish thinkers to provide what medieval philosophers called *ta'amey ha'mitzvot* [reasons for the commandments], an effort to explain all the mitzvot both individually and collectively by attributing to them some meaningful quality in terms of reason, for example—one immediately thinks here of the *Rambam*'s [Maimonides] monumental effort in this direction—or by ascribing to them some pragmatic or health benefits. But it strikes me that the essential meaning of mitzvot is, in fact, dialogical.

It was Saadia who in his Emunot-ve'Deot [Book of Beliefs and Opinions] made a very interesting point. He said there are two kinds of mitzvot. There are *mitzvot sikhliot* and *mitzvot shimiyot*, rational and nonrational commandments. And he asked, which are the most important? Most people would say the rational. Saadia said the a-rational, because they are the ones that we wouldn't possess if it weren't for the Almighty specifically giving them to us through the unique act of revelation. And in that he pointed out that there is something essential in the Torah that is not reductive. We don't keep the Torah because it is philosophically persuasive. We don't keep the Torah because it brings good health or because it leads us to be good citizens, though it may, in a secondary way, have such utilitarian consequences. Rather, the primary purpose of the mitzvot is relational. With every mitzvah comes an act of relation. We don't just keep the mitzvot; we attend to the *Metzaveh* (commander), that is to say, we're not interested in performing a ritual; we're interested in establishing a relationship with the commander of the mitzvot.

Q: It's our opportunity to respond to the Metzaveh.

KATZ: It's our opportunity to establish community.

Q: Do you think that mitzvot are the shapers of our morality or is our morality based on something else?

KATZ: That is a hard question. It raises an old debate whether there is a meta-Halakhic law, a meta-Halakhic ethic. And there is no one answer to that. And the reason I say that is this. There are some places in the Torah, and then later in the development of the *Halakhah*, where it is quite clear that the meaning of the mitzvah and Halakhah are shaped by certain notions of natural justice, natural law. On the other hand, there are other places where that clearly is not the case since we also find divine commands that run counter to our moral sense, for example, in some of the cases of war and their aftermath. We would also find this to be true, for example, with regard to something like the laws of slavery. While they are more humane than other laws of slavery, one would expect that there should be no institution of slavery in the Torah. In consequence of this textual complexity, one therefore, has to say that here is a regimen of mitzvot that is independently validated. That God's will is not bound by our moral constraints.

Q: Then your moral sense may have its roots elsewhere, is that it?

KATZ: There is something problematic about the form of your question. I don't think that morality for Jews is a separate category independent of tradition. I think that morality is a mitzvah, or rather a set of complex mitzvot. One does not perform immoral acts for the same reason that one adheres to the ritual law, because both are grounded in commandments and prohibitions.

Thou shalt not kill and Thou shalt not eat nonkosher food have the same status, odd as that may seem, in that both are grounded in revelation. An independent ethic, at least for Jews, is a very difficult proposition to maintain.

Q: Every mitzvah implies that we are commanded to do something, not only because of our duties toward others or to ourselves, but because God is affected by it. Can you really conceive of God caring one way or the other whether we give a tithe to charity?

KATZ: Yes. This notion of man affecting God is what the philosophers call "divine passibility," namely, God as susceptible to "feeling," so to speak, and thus, in a way, capable of change in interaction with man. Biblical evidence in support of this notion is overwhelming. Moshe prays to the Almighty and God changes His mind. Avraham has a conversation with the Almighty about Sodom which means He is open to influence, though Avraham doesn't prevail. It's a long tradition that has become extremely important in modern Judaism because of Kabbalah, the notion of men and women through their performance of the mitzvot exercising what technically is called theurgical power, the actual power to affect God Himself. I am prepared to say that it is a reasonable theological notion. And I do so for the reason I mentioned earlier, namely the two aspects of God, one of which is the mystery of God which entails that He operates according to a scale of His own benevolence and His own wisdom, the second of which is that, at the same time, as the Creator of all He is providentially involved with the community. He is interested in the behavior of those with whom He is in relation. This is the meaning of covenant.

Q: Even if that human being, in the perspective of the cosmos, is smaller than an ant in an ant hill?

KATZ: Exactly, even then. We can think of this in, among other ways, parent-child terms. In view of the fact that sentient beings like ourselves are concerned with the behavior of all those we come in contact with, we can readily conceive of some kind of benign rationality, some form of benevolent ultimate being concerned with those others with whom it comes into contact, especially when these others possess the qualities we associate with human beings.

Q: It's very hard for us, even for theologians or philosophers, to make sense of the attributes of God. We want to think of God as just. In the faith-system of Jews, retribution—reward for the good deed and penalty for the transgression—is fundamental. How can we fit that into our faith-system now in the light of the Holocaust?

KATZ: There is no doubt that what you say is correct and that the main spine of the tradition, from Biblical times to our own era, is that suffering is *mipne chata'enu*, because of our sins, we are punished. On the other hand, already in the Biblical period, people understood that the concept of mipne chata'enu had to be nuanced. The Book of Job repeats all the classical explanations. His friends tell him, you are a sinner, you did this, you did that, and we know from the prologue that that's not true, that there is something else at work. After the *khurban bayit sheni* [destruction of the second temple], actually already after the *khurban bayit rishon* [destruction of the first temple], prophets and sages introduced other notions, for example, of *yissurin shel ahavah*, afflictions of love, or alternative notions of an inexplicable kind of divine justice, or the idea of the suffering servant, or the expectation that the righteous will receive their rewards in the world to come. These are some of the many intriguing "explanations" that the tradition has spawned in order to deal with the fundamental problem of evil and the dilemmas of theodicy. I don't think any of them are satisfactory.

I know of no satisfactory effort to reconcile what happens on earth with a very strict theory of providence. Evidently there is more, or rather there needs to be more, to the universe than we comprehend. We don't understand all that happens here. If there is another kind of complementary existence, to which we will be heir, then there will be some kind of reconciliation. Of course, that is the role of the Messianic hope. But, frankly, I pretend to, and possess, no special wisdom here. It strikes me that the free-will defense (of God), the most often-used argument to decipher the problem of theodicy, is interesting but it's not persuasive. The idea that God had to allow evil so that man could demonstrate his freedom of will in making his choices has a lot of theological attraction, but it's ultimately not philosophically convincing. The readings that are deterministic, that invoke determinism, are worse. Other contemporary arguments, like Whitehead's contention—recycled by Arthur Cohen in his work on the Holocaust entitled *The Tremendum*—that God is not really all powerful, I find unattractive for other reasons. And so the problem of theodicy remains the weightiest theological problem for which I do not know any satisfactory solution.

Q: Would you put this problem on that famous shelf we call *Teku* (an acronym suggesting that we must await the reappearance of Elijah for a solution)?

KATZ: Yes, I think that it would have first place on that shelf. But, let me add something more on this question for you to consider. What I have to say is not meant to reconcile the fact of evil with God's goodness and justice, but to go back to something we talked about before. Evidence is very, very difficult to arrive at and to weigh in this area of concern. How do you quantify good and evil? And what counts as evidence here? For example, the *Shoah* [Holocaust] has raised the problem of evil with overwhelming urgency in our time. Now, however, consider that if you give negative metaphysical weight to the Shoah—which, of course, we must—one has to give positive metaphysical weight, I should think, to the re-creation of the State of Israel. So again you come to this peculiar conundrum: The Shoah was overwhelming evidence, but not decisive evidence, for the power of evil, i.e., for the nonexistence of God. Alternatively, the creation of the State of Israel, as well as the flourishing of the American Jewish community are, in this context, positive evidence for the existence of God. One is left, therefore, even allowing fully for Auschwitz and Treblinka, with conflicting, and finally indecisive, indicators. God never makes it easy. Had there been no State of Israel, it might have been much easier to come to a negative answer. Had there been a State of Israel and no Shoah, it would have been much easier to come to a positive answer. But the relevant data are extremely ambivalent and exceedingly ambiguous.

Q: I wonder how impressed you would be with the following point: Granted that there is evil, but there is also the response to evil. Evil may destroy an innocent person, or thousands of people, or, as in the Shoah, six million people. But what is never destroyed is the expectation and the will for justice. Where does this indestructible sense of justice come from?

KATZ: It's an interesting claim; but it could have a completely naturalistic explanation, a kind of will for survival. A biologist once said that human reproduction is only a clever way the genes have come up with to reproduce themselves. So I'm not very persuaded by that. The form of the argument you have suggested is reminiscent of Eliezer Berkovits's point that the Shoah was not completely negative because it gave people an opportunity for heroism. But, given the existence of an omniscient and omnipotent divine providence, it would, I think, be better not to have evil in the first place, that is to say, it would be better if people weren't hungry so that someone didn't have to come and feed them. Moreover, though there certainly were saints, men and women of immense courage and heroism, the fact is that people died because they were hungry. People died because they didn't have sufficient medical care. People died in gas chambers. So, in the end, I find this particular line of argument more apologetic than valid.

Q: We would probably agree that it is not only the better part of wisdom, but perhaps the only wisdom, concerning the Shoah, to say "I don't know."

KATZ: That's a large part of the true wisdom we have to come to at a certain point. But that is different from what I might call the agnosticism that is bought very cheaply, i.e., someone mentions Auschwitz and right away people throw up their hands.

Alternatively, there's the agnosticism that comes at the end of a very difficult, very complicated, struggle, the silence, for example, that comes at the end of the Book of Job. There's a famous work by an English mystic called *The Cloud of Unknowing* and though he meant something different, there is an unknowing, a special kind of ignorance, that becomes appropriate at the end of one's deliberations. But it is only appropriate at the end of one's very deep, very honest, reflection.

Q: Of course the greatness of Job is that he is willing to say, I don't know, but he's adding, "yet I believe." He persists in faith despite his inability to explain his suffering rationally. In the light of the Shoah, a very basic Jewish belief that has become problematic is the idea of the chosen people. Does it still make sense to you?

KATZ: Yes, it does make sense. There's a peculiarity in the Tanakh. The Bible begins with a universal principle, not a narrow one. In the beginning God creates everything and everyone. And then the Bible does a very odd thing, it narrows down, generation by generation, first to the patriarch, Avraham, and then to Yitzhak, i.e., to one side of Avraham's family, and so on as if to teach us that particularity, singularity, is essential to the unfolding of God's purpose in Creation. Moreover, there has been something remarkable about Jewish existence, in particular a peculiarly intense struggle for redemption and for holiness, for the hallowing of our world, as well as a unique fidelity to its own self-understanding of Israel's role in history despite immense oppression generation after generation, sometimes by pogroms, and sometimes by seduction, "Come over and be something else."

Q: Are you then looking for the evidence in the arena of history?

KATZ: No, the historical evidence is corroboration not confirmation. I cannot imagine, or account for, the survival of the Jewish people apart from some kind of special history, *Heilsgeschichte* [salvation history], but I don't claim that there is sufficient hard evidence of the existence of such a special history to persuade someone else of its reality. At the same time, however, I am fully prepared to argue that the history of the Jewish people is anomalous and continually challenges, if it does not actually disconfirm, all so-called historical laws or rules. You have a rule about how history operates; Jewish history is always the exception. The Shoah comes, and out of it emerges the State of Israel. The Jews of Russia (and America) were, according to historical prognosticators, supposed to disappear; they didn't disappear. Modernity was meant to assimilate the Jews; it didn't. The church came and was to conquer, and, in turn, was succeeded by a militant Islam and crusading Marxism, yet the Jews survived two thousand years of Christendom, Islam, and Marxism. Jewish history is quite extraordinary in its continuity and its inexplicability.

Q: For you, Jewish history is evidence of a historical management which assigns to the Jewish people a special role. Would you call it a supernatural selection?

KATZ: There is something very special about Jewish history. Ben Gurion said he did not know about the chosen people, but we were a choosing people. We had chosen to follow this distinctive and difficult way. The fidelity of the Jews in the face of over-whelming pressure is something to be amazed at. It was always easier to leave; it was always possible to leave until the Shoah; it would have made empirical, pragmatic, and utilitarian sense to leave. Yet, the Jewish people did not give up. Even after the Shoah they did not give up. For me, this is very suggestive, though obviously not conclusive, evidence for a kind of transcendental selection.

Q: Probably the most questionable article of faith today is the Messiah idea which, until not too long ago, was Judaism's most passionately held hope. Today, except for a relatively small number of *Gush Emunim* [settlers in Israel] and the Lubavitch Hasidic movement, Jews prefer to keep a discreet silence on the Messiah. How do you fit the Messianic tradition into your personal beliefs today?

KATZ: There is no doubt that what you say is absolutely right. The whole tradition hinges on the Messianic idea. Secondly, as you again rightly say, almost all Jews today are, in some sense, embarrassed by it and don't discuss it. That is true even of the modern Orthodox and certainly of all the varieties of Judaism to the left of modern Orthodoxy. It's only on the far right that one finds authentic and overt Messianic enthusiasm.

Q: Might this Messianic fervor just be a mask for political expansion?

KATZ: No doubt it is a very important tool for political aggrandizement. However, one has to be careful not to throw the baby out with the bath water. To quote the Gemara, "On the day the *beit ha-mikdash* [temple] was destroyed, the Messiah was born."

Jewish life, its continuity, would be almost unimaginable without some Messianic concept, without some meaningful Messianic hopefulness. By that I mean not the eschatology you find today in Lubavitch or in Gush Emunim, though in some sense it is admirable that to them the Messiah idea is so incarnate, that they believe that we can directly influence the imminent realization of the Messianic era here and now. Whereas, all of us say *l'shanah haba biYerushalayim* [next year in Jerusalem] at the end of our seders and at the end of Rosh Hashanah or Yom Kippur, we don't believe it, they do.

Q: I've seen a bumper sticker that says, "we want *Moshiach* now."

KATZ: Indeed. Lubavitch is typical of this kind of eschatological enthusiasm, and its pitfalls. However, alternatively, I believe that the Messianic hope, though real, must be muted. The Gemara says, "If someone is planting a tree and he hears the shofar blow and they say, 'the Messiah is coming,' first finish planting the tree and then go out to meet the Messiah."

The paradox of Jewish life is that, on the one hand, we cannot survive without Messianism. On the other hand, any time we get too close to Messianism, it's such a fire that it consumes us: Shabbatai Zvi,* Jacob Frank,† Christianity, Marxism as a secular manifestation, perhaps Gush Emunim, aspects of contemporary Lubavitch and the like. But I'm convinced that without the Messianic hope there is no meaning to Jewish life. Jewish life looks forward to the providential reordering of Creation promised by Messianism. Here, I would add, the tradition is more pluralistic than one usually thinks. You have what one might call the minimalist view of the *Rambam*, that the Messianic fulfillment is essentially a worldly revolution with a reconstituted Jewish state, as over against the maximalist view(s) of those like the *Ramban*.‡ However you interpret it, though, some intelligible conception of Messianism is required to sustain the Jewish tradition. There must be some sense of an ultimate resolution of all that has gone on, some final refuge from despair. So Messianism is important.

---

* Shabbatai Zvi, seventeenth-century Messianic pretender.
† Jacob Frank, scandalous founder of a kabbalistic sect in the eighteenth century.
‡ Acronym for Rabbi Moshe ben Nachman (Nachmanides, 1194–1270).

Q: I hear you say that, at the very least, Messianism means that God remains involved in the world and in human destiny some way or other. But you might even go a step further. You spoke of a "resolution." How do you mean that? How would God bring about this "resolution"? Would it be through a personal Messiah or a Messianic Age?

KATZ: The question of Messiah/Messianic Age is in a sense immaterial. Half of the prophets, roughly, talk about a personal, individual Messiah; all of them point to a Messianic Age. In Kabbalah, it is essentially the Messianic Age that's important. Therefore, the doctrine of an individual Messianic person, of whether there is to be an individual Messiah, I leave aside. When I, or rather the Jewish tradition, talk about "resolution," it means this. We know all too well that history, as Hegel said, is a slaughter bench. It is fraught with evil, fraught with the terrible things we've been talking about—the Shoah, the victims of the Gulag, the persecutions of the ages. And all these things make a mockery of what we have been discussing. It is the counterevidence. The notion that Messianism is a "resolution" is to say that, at some point, all of this suffering will find some redemption. Human history, for all of the very real counterevidences, will finally be set right and there will be a just government, a caring government, a government for the people. People will receive what they deserve. That is what is meant by a "resolution," that at some future time Creation will be taken up in God's hands and remade with the kind of perfection that all of us would wish it to have.

Q: What does immortality and the hereafter mean to you?

KATZ: I don't know with any describable specificity. The *Rambam* said that of the thirteen principles of faith he could, more or less, find arguments or reasons for twelve of them. But *t'chiat ha-metim*, resurrection of the dead, was so unlike anything in our experience that we could not understand it by any form of reasoning. This is truly an article of faith in Kierkegaard's sense, i.e., it can be affirmed only by a leap of faith. One takes it as a fundamental belief, literally in contradiction to all the available evidence.

Q: Is it important to you personally?

KATZ: Sometimes it is and sometimes it's not. Not so much when I reflect on my own life, but especially when I reflect on the life of my parents. When I went to the funeral of my parents and thought about these two *tzadikim* [righteous ones], I wondered, is this all? Also, my grandmother who was a *tzedeikah*—I think, is this all there was to their goodness that they should be interred in the ground and become food for worms and in that moment, one hopes, one yearns, one longs for something more, that there be an eternity. And even with regard to one's own life, the notion that one is just, as Bertrand Russell said, a fetid drop of semen, to be eventually devoured by the creatures of the ground, is a rather unsavory notion. One doesn't dwell on it, but it's comforting, even in the absence of evidence, to think that death is not the end.

Q: There is sufficient vagueness in the doctrine of immortality that almost anything could be accommodated by it, but that's not true of resurrection. That is and remains a scandal to our reason. Can you, personally, make an affirmative statement on resurrection?

KATZ: *Ani ma-amin* [I believe], I'm willing to believe it, but I cannot make any sense of it other than as a faith statement. As such, it is the most uncorroborated faith statement that one could make.

Norman Lamm

B orn in Williamsburg, Brooklyn, into a religious family of rabbis and scholars going back several generations, Rabbi Norman Lamm was reared in the old tradition but also encouraged to study secular subjects. He received his general as well as Jewish education at Yeshiva University and the Rabbi Isaac Elchanan Theological Seminary, both of which institutions he now heads as president, and is today the leading spokesman of moderate Orthodoxy in America. His years of experience as a congregational rabbi and pulpit preacher are reflected in his ability to focus upon the relevance of Jewish law and Jewish beliefs to contemporary problems. He has published in Hebrew and English. His most recent books include: *Faith and Doubt: Studies in Traditional Jewish Thought* (1986), *Torah Lishmah: Torah for Torah's Sake* (1989), and *Torah Umadda: The Encounter of Religious Learning and Worldly Knowledge in the Jewish Tradition* (1990). The Mosad Harav Kook in Jerusalem, an important center of Jewish scholarship in Israel, recently awarded him the Maimon prize.

Norman Lamm represents a felicitous blend of modern culture and Orthodox Judaism at its best. Without making a violent break with his thoroughly traditional roots, he enriched his mind with a wide range of secular knowledge, literature and psychology. Secular learning was thus for him not an obstacle but another step on the ladder of intellectual development, climaxed by a final leap of faith.

I found Lamm's comments on the personal and impersonal aspects of God especially illuminating. Likewise impressive is his avoidance of simplistic notions of revelation associated with the Orthodox doctrine of the "giving" of the Torah.

Like other partners in these dialogues, he too is baffled by the Holocaust. When faced with the problem of evil—"How can a good God abide such cruelty and suffering of an apparently innocent people?"—he is humble enough to say, "I don't know. I don't have an answer any more than Job did." We spoke in Lamm's office at Yeshiva University in New York, September 12, 1991.

Q: What religious or Jewish upbringing did you have? Did you come from a very traditional home?

LAMM: Yes, I grew up in a community that once was famous, some might say infamous, and that is Williamsburg, Brooklyn, which later became the center of Satmarer Hasidim. But when I was growing up, Williamsburg was a lower-middle-class Jewish neighborhood; middle, middle-class, very fine, not at all wealthy, but we didn't know it as children. We thought we were just normal people and had no sense of disappointment in our lot. It was a very rich Jewish life. My father comes from observant Jews in Lemberg [Lvov], Poland. His father, as my father often said, made a living out of not making a living. My mother comes from a rabbinical family that traces itself way, way back up to Rashi. My maternal grandfather, I recognize as one of my two major *rebbey-im* [rabbis]. He passed away when I was twenty-one, but from the time I started Gemara [Talmud] when I was about nine years old or so, he was my teacher.

Q: Where did your family come from?

LAMM: In Europe, my mother's family was from a small town, because there were rabbis in a small town, places like Shavniz, Kroczienko, etc.

Q: Anywhere near Lemberg?

LAMM: Well, my father was from Lemberg.

Q: My mother came from Rava Ruska and my father from Sambor.

LAMM: Galitzianer! Most of the Viennese Jews were Galitzianer. I grew up in what to me was a normal Jewish way. I went to Yeshivah Torah vDaas, which then was far less extreme than it is today. My grandfather impressed upon me the need to continue learning before going to college. He wanted me to go to college. He was a *Rav* [rabbi]. He was a big *Talmid Chacham* [scholar]. There are *teshuvot* [responsa] of his that were world famous, collected in his two-volume Emek Halakhah.

Q: Was he a follower of Torah im Derekh Eretz [combination of Torah and secular education]?

LAMM: Oh, no; he was a *heimisher* [warmly familiar] Rav.

Q: He just wanted you to have a good education.

LAMM: Right. He wanted me to go to Yeshiva University and study under Rabbi Soloveitchik. So for one year, I took off from high school to spend half a day in Torah vDaas and the other half a day "learning" with him and his brother. At night, after it was all done, I did a little bit of autodidactic work. I read through a good deal of philosophy and all of Freud, Jung, and Adler. It was a great year, my greatest year so far as study is concerned.

Q: So you ventured into psychological and philosophical studies?

LAMM: Yes, early on and that was my Jewish background. From there I went on to Yeshiva University and got my Semichah [ordination] and my doctorate.

Q: Did you ever experience what some people call a major turning point, religiously or theologically, in your life, or has it been an ongoing, steady development?

LAMM: Yes, it was an ongoing development and maturation. There were points, of course, at which I probably regressed and then progressed.

Q: The normal crises of doubt?

LAMM: Precisely. And I experienced that, as I suppose every intelligent or sensitive person always does. You have your feelings of distance and feelings of closeness and probably it accounts for the fact that I've been thinking about these issues all my life.

Q: If you were to trace your way to God, your faith in God, which sources would play the major role? Books, or people, or events, or ideas?

LAMM: I think all of that. I'm not particularly linked to any one of these. Personalities, of course, had a profound influence on me. Intellectually, my grandfather, and *l'havdil beyn chayim L'chayim* [let us distinguish the living from the dead], Rabbi Soloveitchik had a very strong influence. I'm just finishing my first year of mourning for both my parents, people of no great intellectual attainments, yet they had a tremendous effect on me. They set an example by way of elemental human decency. I was very fortunate to have come from a home where love was never talked about, but always practiced; very little demonstrative, but ever-present. It predisposed me to think that the kind of life they were leading helped in the development of this kind of supportive, happy atmosphere between parents and children. Also, that may account for the fact that I'm so traditionally inclined. I'm not ready to overturn tradition at mere whim. I prefer to examine things very carefully because tradition has a *chazakah* [a prior claim or hold] in my own intellectual life, and it requires a lot to overturn a chazakah. It can be done, but it requires very strong proof.

Q: Is there some kind of mystical or intuitional side to your faith in God?

LAMM: Oh sure, I find it very difficult to see how one can separate cleanly between the purely intellectual, rational approach and an intuitive, and if you will, a somewhat mystical approach, too.

Q: To what extent would you say your faith in God was shaped by one side or the other?

LAMM: It's hard to say. We think rationally. But what I think is very much akin to what Judah Halevi says about prophecy. He agrees with the *Rambam* [Maimonides], whom he didn't know, that you have to prepare yourself intellectually for it, but then the last spark is an intuitive one. God had to choose you, but you can prepare yourself intellectually. I would apply that not only to prophecy, but even to my own religious development. I strongly believe that one must spell it out intellectually to be able to handle it with a certain degree of discrimination, but the ultimate acceptance, the ultimate commitment, requires that final, but very decisive, leap of faith that we call "intuition."

Q: Do words like "encounter" or "dialogue" with God mean anything to you?

LAMM: Yes, they do. I think, of course, the words become buzz words and after a while they become emptied of all content. I think it is always necessary for every generation, maybe for every thinking person, to develop his own neologisms, because the old words sometimes carry baggage which no longer is real. Now when Buber started to talk about it, he used the special terms of "encounter" and "dialogue." I think they were fresh, they meant something, even if not exactly defined. But it meant something. But after a while, it becomes so overused that if I say "Hello" to you, we're "dialoguing." If I meet you in the street, it's an "encounter." The word loses its special quality.

Q: Can we define a little more clearly what is meant by an "encounter" with God?

LAMM: I try to encounter God three times a day. To me, *t'fillah* [prayer] if done with *kavanah* [devotion], is an encounter. Is it a dialogue? I don't know. Dialogue means that the other side answers, and while I'm always sure that God is a *shomea t'fillah* [one who hears prayer], I'm not always sure that He is an *oneh t'fillah* [one who answers prayer], the way I'd like it. Of course as someone once said, No is also an answer. But I do feel that He's listening.

Q: You incline toward a concept of God that is personal?

LAMM: Oh, sure.

Q: You favor a personal divine being as against an impersonal force or power?

LAMM: Yes, but let me define that a little better. I believe both are true. I don't believe we can *onchappen dem Ribbon-shel-olam beim bord* [grab God by His beard]. I don't think we can pigeonhole Him quite that well. Perhaps the best way to express it is a kabalistic way, that there is a core aspect of God which is *ein sof* [infinity], and then there is the revelational aspect of the *esser sefirot* [ten aspects of divinity]. I believe that it may be contrary to the way we think of divinity. We think that the personal is a higher degree than the impersonal. It may be that with God, looking down *mim'eon kodsho* [from His holy abode], it is the reverse, i.e., the highest level is the impersonal one, but then He relates to us through His personal aspect. So, it is a personal God I believe in, but the personal God is more than personal. Personality is an aspect of God. If the *chitzoni* [external aspect of God] is represented, as it were, by the esser sefirot, then the essence of God is far beyond personality. As a human being I cannot relate to it. But I can aver it.

Q: One of the most troubling articles of faith has to do with the element of revelation in the Bible. In what way do you sense the Bible to be God's word?

LAMM: The word "word" is wisely chosen, because that's the term the Chumash [Pentateuch] uses and the *nevi'im* [prophets] use: *ne'um ha-Shem, d'var ha-Shem* [utterance of God, word of God] from which the term "logos" is derived. I do believe that there was revelation, that the revelations are authentic, that God speaks in one voice, but it is heard in many ways. We can say that with regard to the *aseret ha-dibrot* [ten commandments]: *shamor v'zachor bedibbur echad*. ["Keep" and "remember" in one expression, i.e., the two versions of the Sabbath Commandment in the Decalogue, Exodus ch. 20 and Deuteronomy ch. 5, were simultaneously uttered.] It comes in one expression, as if it were, not a physical voice, of course, but as one message, and each person hears it in his own way. Each man or woman, to whomever the *nevuah* [prophecy] comes to. *Ein shnei neviim mitnab'im b'signon echad* [no two prophets prophesy in the same manner] is also a reference to the ways they perceive it. One symphony is heard in many ways by many listeners. I believe that there was a period in human history when God's revelation was direct.

Q: As an external event or as something felt from within?

LAMM: Oh, I think it was felt within, but objective nonetheless.

Q: Historical?

LAMM: Yes, I believe that, let's say that when Moses says *vayomer ha-Shem el mosheh l'emor* [and God spoke to Moses, saying] or when one prophet says *vayehi d'var ha-Shem elai* [and the word of God came to me], I don't think that an acoustically sensitive instrument could have measured the decibels in which God spoke. That would be far too literal. It is simply the only way one can express it. I believe that revelation occupied a major, very significant part of human history until that part of religious history faded away to be replaced by the intellectual and behavioral medium and God, as it were, left the Torah in the hands of man and said "I've given you *my* speech, now go ahead. Maybe someday I'll speak to you again"; but right now that more direct form of revelation is done and we remain with the fruits of that revelation. Now, God reveals Himself in events as well as in words. Events, therefore, have the same importance today that direct revelation had at one time.

I think what is happening to us has meaning and in the same way as with the earlier revelation. In the period of the *tekufat ha-nevuah* [era of prophecy] from Moses until the *anshei haknesset hagedolah* [men of the Great Assembly], God spoke and the prophets heard Him. It was essentially the same message, but with certain nuances that were different; some people refused to hear Him. There is a *hakovesh nevuato* [the prophet who willfully suppresses his prophecy]. There is *nevuat sheker* or *navi sheker* [false prophecy or a false prophet]. Once prophecy is real, then other forms of *avodat ha-Shem* [worship of God] expressions, including the most spurious forms, cluster around it, which becomes a question of which is authentic, and which is unauthentic, which the Torah itself discusses. Now the same thing is true of revelation, not through word but through event: the *Shoah*, the *gerush sefarad* [the Holocaust, the expulsion from Spain], a pogrom, *medinat Yisrael* [State of Israel]. Now these are events which are the contemporary form of the divine word. And they, too, can be understood differently by different people and they, too, can be misunderstood, even as was the original word.

Q: Are you suggesting that divine *hashgakhah* [providence] is in some way fulfilled through events? That God participates in events?

LAMM: Yes, he does participate especially in the great historical events and it is His way of addressing us in a contemporary form, but it all depends on how we're going to understand, perceive, and react. And I think we've fluffed many of them in the course of our history.

Q: I hear you say that you do believe in the historicity of revelation. That God reaches us through a message, whether it is in writing or whether it is oral; but you are struggling, as all of us must, with the limitations of speech to understand and describe what ultimately is a mystery.

LAMM: Of course!

Q: Those messages which guide us, which are perceived as mitzvot, commands, how do you relate those to morality? Is morality the outgrowth of the mitzvot or are they the outgrowth of morality?

LAMM: I do not have a definitive answer for that. I'm struggling with it, I'm still struggling with it and have not come to a conclusion. I know that they must be tied into each other. I do not accept that the mitzvot are a pure form of *avodat ha-Shem* [service of God] that has nothing to do with morality. This kind of thing is popularized by Yeshayahu Leibowitz.

Q: Then you obviously do not favor Kierkegaard's interpretation of the *akeda* [binding of Isaac]?*

---

*In fierce opposition to what Kierkegaard considered a shallow moralizing rationalism fashionable in the mid-nineteenth century liberal Protestantism, the Danish existentialist

LAMM: No, I don't accept it. To me there is a relation. Does it mean, therefore, that mitzvot are all subservient to a moral test? Since morality or conceptions of morality change in every generation, do I believe that the mitzvot rise or fall? No, because then my performance of a mitzvah is no longer obedience to God but to my own fallible sense of what is moral, and that I don't think I can trust. The history of mankind does not inspire much confidence in man's moral judgment in and of itself. I would say, likewise, that we have no right to be so terribly confident in man's religious judgment in and of itself. Incidentally, in the classical sources there is *yesh dorshim l'khan v'yesh dorshim l'khan* [one can interpret either way], one can look both ways. On the one hand, for instance, the famous statement that *mah li shechita min ha-tzavar mah li shechita min ha-oref—lo nitnu mitzvot l'Yisrael ela lizrof bahen et ha-briot* [whether you slaughter the animal this way or that, the commandments were given to Israel only for their refinement].

So the mitzvot are there for a moral purpose, to purify man's character. At the same time the mitzvot are beyond morality. I do not believe they conflict with morality in essence. In certain special cases they can. I refer now especially to (this may be irrelevant to a theological discussion, but to me it is not irrelevant because Halakhah has a great deal to say about it) the Halakhic discussion mainly in the *tekufat ha-geonim*, e.g., Rav Hai Gaon asks why you make the benediction "*asher kidd'shanu b'mitzvotav, v'tzivanu*" [who has sanctified us by His commandments and commanded us] only for certain mitzvot and not for others? For instance, why not for *tzedakah* [charitable deeds]? Why not for *leket shikhekha, u'peah* [the sheaf or corner of field left for the poor]? He says that any mitzvah that is morally rational, does not require the *berakhah* [benediction]. Only mitzvot which do not have any obvious rational or moral basis and which are neutral and which otherwise I would not do, require the berakhah. Why? Because total obedience, submission of man with his whole being including his intellect to God, leads to *kedushah* [holiness]. So,

philosopher cited the story of Abraham's test (Genesis 22) in which the patriarch proved willing to sacrifice his son Isaac at God's command. Kierkegaard, pointing to the immorality of God's command and Abraham's obedience, underscored the rationally incomprehensible, even demonic aspects of God's ways. In Kierkegaard's view, religion and morality represent separate concerns.

therefore, in a mitzvah like Shabbat or *t'fillin* [phylacteries], etc. which has no moral dimension or no obvious moral dimension, I achieve kedushah, because I am going beyond myself, beyond my own concern. Whereas a mitzvah like *tzedakah* [charity], which even without the Torah I would understand, is something very important, but not because God told me.

Q: So in other words, obeying the mitzvot, you feel you are rising to a higher level?

LAMM: A higher level *than* morality.

Q: But your moral tenets or principles are not all exclusively derived from the mitzvot?

LAMM: No!

Q: And what would be the other source?

LAMM: The other source, I believe, with all apologies to Judge Clarence Thomas's critics, I do believe is a form of natural law and I think the Torah itself alludes to it. Why was Cain punished?

Q: Because he offended.

LAMM: Of course; he offended natural law.

Q: Can you conceive of God caring one way or the other how you and I behave?

LAMM: I would be dismayed with the kind of God who didn't give a damn about how we behaved. All He could do would be to create a physical world, then, let all of man's spiritual achievements be just unforeseen accidents of the creation of the physical universe. I don't believe that.

Q: What would you answer a person who has studied a little astronomy, knows a little physics, knows a little chemistry and tells you, Professor Lamm, do you realize what you are saying? In this vast cosmos, I, as a human being, am a speck of dust; my time in life is so short as not to count measured against astronomical time. There are millions and billions of creatures like myself; could God really be concerned about my being?

LAMM: I would tell this astronomer, astrophysicist, chemist, biologist or what you will, it all depends on how big a God you believe in. Somehow a small computer has only a certain number of bytes but a very big computer can process a great deal more information. I believe in a very big God who can be concerned with everything, even a speck as apparently insignificant as my own life in this vast universe.

Q: Turning to the Holocaust and the immense amount of suffering which afflicts the innocent, even the just, can we still uphold belief in retribution for evil, reward for good, or must we fall in with the despairing judgment of Kohelet [Book of Ecclesiastes] that there is no evidence that the good is favored or rewarded as against the evil doer?

LAMM: Well, that problem is as old as religion itself. It probably is the oldest and the most excruciating problem with which any religion, particularly a monotheistic religion must deal. The problem was stated long ago as *tzaddik v'ra lo, rasha, v'tov lo* [righteous, yet badly off; evil, yet prosperous]. The whole Shoah experience is different only because it is so different in number, when quantity alters quality.

Q: We can raise the question about innocent suffering, even in the case of a single child who is run over by a drunken driver.

LAMM: You see, the fundamental question remains. It becomes a somewhat different question on a national, universal basis. But the fundamental question is there. How can a good God abide such cruelty and such suffering of apparently innocent people. I don't have an answer any more than Job did. All I know is that when God appeared out of the whirlwind to Job, Job retracted not his questions, but the poignancy of his questions. I think that what Job retracted was his expectation of an answer, because the problem remains a problem. But when he demands of God an answer, that part is blunted at the very end. To ask the question not only is permissible, I think it is inevitable. Any moral human being, any moral religious person, must ask the question. But there comes a point when you bow your head and you say, *af al pi chen*, nevertheless, I accept. I don't know why. All I know is that I am mortal and my mortality not only makes me vulnerable to pain in suffering, but it makes me vulnerable to not understanding why I am suffering.

Q: In the light of history, the Shoah as well as the establishment of the State of Israel, can you believe that the people Israel is the chosen people?

LAMM: Oh, if I ever have any doubts, I believe it now. What a small country Israel is, a tiny state, a small, tiny country! Consider that the Jews of that country are one-tenth of one percent of mankind and whatever happens in that tiny little country, called Israel, is trumpeted throughout the world. I think there are more people of the world press in Tel Aviv and Jerusalem than there are in Moscow or Washington or anyplace else. Why, what's going on? Is it all because of "Real-Politik"? Not so. There is a mystery there that is so evident that you overlook it. We seem to have been the subject of fascination by mankind ever since Sinai. Yes, of course, I believe we are a chosen people. I don't believe "chosen" in a sense of "superior." I believe we are just a different kind of people and it goes back to belief in revelation. I believe we were meant to do something and be something in the world. Have we succeeded? No we have not. Not yet. Do we seem to be succeeding right now? No, I don't think so. But it doesn't mean we don't have that mission. History goes on, it goes on beyond our lifetime. I think the obligation of every Jew is to see to it that the Jewish people, Israel, does fulfill its mission as we were charged at Sinai.

Q: You base the idea of election on the *brit*, the covenant?

LAMM: Yes.

Q: Why would God need a special people to fulfill His will or His plan?

LAMM: He tried twice without it and the alternatives failed. This is Buber's way of reading and I agree with him there. He tried it universally, without anyone special, and that was the end of it. A flood came. He tried it with Noah and again the experiment failed and the knowledge, the awareness, and the service of the one God simply did not take hold. So God decided to make a nation, the people of Abraham, and we are still around and now some of us are trying hard to convince ourselves that we are "unchosen." What other people has expended so much effort to prove that it is not special?

Q: With regard to the idea of a mission, a special role, are we not promised help in the form of the Messiah? What do you think of the expectation of a redeemer? Do you think there is a need for the Messiah?

LAMM: Yes I do. That the concept, or the belief in the coming of the Messiah has caused us grief such as in the days of Shabbatai Zvi, or, for that matter Christianity itself, I have no doubt. But two things have to be said. First, you have to make a cost-benefit analysis, to use crass managerial terms, of the whole belief in Messiah. It has cost us. And what has it given us? It has given us a sense of hope to know that despite two thousand years in *galut* [diaspora] we are going to make it, and if I won't, my great, great grandchildren will. Only because of a belief that there will be a *geulah* [redemption], there will be a Messiah. As much as it has cost us, it has given us much more. I think in purely empirical terms what the concept of Messiah has meant for the people of Israel. Second, I believe that any great concept has negative features and the greater the concept, the more negative the features. The Zohar teaches that God, the *ein sof* [the Infinite], revealed Himself in the *esser sefirot*, and these were the *esser sefirot d'kedushah* [ten aspects of holiness]. But, simultaneously there were also revealed or emanated what the Zohar calls the ten aspects of contamination, of evil. Every idea has an equal and opposite coordinate that is negative. You show me an idea that has no possibility of negative results and I will show you an idea that is insignificant. You take any idea—love, peace, any of the great ideas that inspire mankind—they all can be corrupted, and the more inspiring they are, the more potentially positive they are, the more potentially negative they are too.

Q: The *Rambam* (Maimonides) was leery about specifying a Messianic concept. Did he not try to distance himself from it?

LAMM: I don't think he tried to keep a distance; after all, he did write about the Messiah extensively in his *iggeret teman* [letter to

Yemen]. But he took a much more rational view which, I think, fits in with his whole outlook and probably is much closer to us and what is going to happen some day. But without the poetry behind it, people would not have been inspired by it. If Isaiah, the prophet, had said there will come a day when we Jews are not going to be bothered by the rest of mankind, when we're going to have time to sit and study Torah and philosophize about the nature of God, how would that have affected his contemporaries as compared to his vision of "the wolf shall dwell with the lamb and the leopard shall lie down with the kid" (Is. 11.6)? There is no comparison. Poetry has the ability to ignite a fire in the soul. Ideas can make it go up only very slowly.

Q: Is the Messiah as a person merely symbolic? Would you say that we are to hope for a development of mankind, of history, toward the kind of reconciliation and peace that is expressed by Isaiah and other visionaries? Should we speak of a Messianic Age rather than a Messiah (as a person)?

LAMM: I take the more naive view, perhaps more primitive view, in the eyes of some, which I think ultimately may be more sophisticated psychologically. Yes, there is a tendency that we have to sort of depersonify the Messiah and read him as a concept, an age, a feeling—but that is part of the whole tendency to depersonalize religion, isn't it? God is an idea within; He's a concept; Messiah is an age; the next thing you'll know is that man is a concept too so that you can go around killing individual men because only man as a concept matters.

I'm rather personalistic in my approach, keeping in mind what I said originally, that there is "something beyond personality" as I referred originally to the nature of God. The same thing holds true of the Messiah. If you read what *chazal* [the sages] said, you see there is a pre-Messianic age which has nothing to do with individuals, but is the gathering storm which cleanses, as it were, the world for a different kind of era or epoch. The preparation for Messiah and the era itself which is ushered in or symbolized by a personality is far more than a personality. Don't forget that the Messiah in classical Jewish sources was never looked upon as a magician, as a miracle maker, or as someone who could rival the prophets, let's say Moses. He was always a human being. As *Ram-*

bam, believing in a Messianic King, said, he will rise and die after he has accomplished his mission. If the concept is altogether woven into the personality of Messiah, into the glorification of a personality, it becomes the cult of a personality, and all else is forgotten. When that person dies or leaves the people disappointed, the sense of frustration is crushing. Jesus came and some of his Jewish followers saw him as Messiah. Then, he died or was killed, and the promises that Messiah should have brought to the world never were fulfilled. But they were so convinced of the importance of a personality that they followed the Guru and ignored the realities. Now look at all the other false Messiahs.

Q: Bar Kokhba?

LAMM: Bar Kokhba was not a false Messiah. Rabbi Akiba thought he was the Messiah, but most of the sages never accepted him, nor am I acquainted with anything in the historical record which speaks of a personality cult. I think that Rabbi Akiba came to regard him as the Messiah, because Rabbi Akiba saw the beginnings of Jewish liberation and redemption and since Bar Kokhba was the general leading it, he said, "You are the Messiah." Akiba's designation of Bar Kokhba as the Messiah was proof that it is not a personality cult.

Q: Do you see in the readiness today of hundreds of thousands, if not millions of Jews, to once again follow a cult figure, a Messianic undercurrent that could erupt anytime? Does that trouble you?

LAMM: It troubles me very much. But it points to a psychological fact which I may not like but which is very real, and that is something in which all modernist forms of Judaism sin, including what I stand for. We always underestimate the power of personality. We are so inebriated with the power of ideas, we fail to realize that people respond more to people than they do to concepts.

And that is why I said that my belief in the Messiah, and in a personal Messiah, may sound more primitive, but ultimately is more sophisticated because it recognizes the power of personal relationship. If you have a charismatic figure or a figure that is attractive, magnetic, and has influence, his ideas will win. The best ideas can flounder if there is no one to symbolize them or personify them.

Q: The two are logically inseparable because there will never be a Messianic age unless there are fitting personalities for it.

LAMM: And there will never be a Messiah without an age which will reflect his influence.

Q: Let me get to the last point, one vastly underrated or neglected in current Jewish thought and particularly in contemporary rabbinic teaching and preaching. It has to do with the life of the soul, the hereafter, and the resurrection of the dead. We say too little, and tradition perhaps too much, for us to accept this idea today. How do you see this? Does that cluster of ideas play a role in your own religious, spiritual life?

LAMM: In my intellectual religious life, no. In my personal, spiritual religious life, yes. Judaism tells us about the resurrection, but it tells us so remarkably little, that it should be easy to accept. Consider what Judaism tells us about the "other world" and about the resurrection of the dead: It is far less than what we get in Islam, for instance, which is also a monotheistic religion. The Sages deemphasized the "other world," simply asserting its existence, but being mostly concerned with this world. Sometimes I sit back and wonder at it. Look at our entire literature. How much of this is devoted to the hereafter, to the resurrection of the dead? It's a tiny portion, a drop in the ocean. It's nothing compared to the overwhelming amount that Torah tells you about your diet, about your sex life, about your cycle of leisure and work, or your clothing. It's a fantastic emphasis on how to live in this world, as if to say, listen, we can't know very much about that other world. We believe it exists because the spiritual is simply beyond the physical.

To get back to what I originally said, I think there is a pattern there, the physical is the underside of the spiritual, and therefore there is a kind of movement between one and the other. But we don't know very much about the total, extracorporeal or noncorporeal existence. So, all we can do is say it's there and it's the scene of the rectification of the ills of this world in an ultimate sense. But it is no longer a place of active participation. This is the world—what did someone call it?—the vale of soul making. This is the realm where we make and recreate ourselves.

Q: Can you conceive of continued identity as a soul in a here-after?

LAMM: I just don't know. I should like to think that there is. Why shouldn't there be? Why is it so easy to believe about separate identity here and not separate identities in another realm? Once you accept that there is another realm, you are over your major hurdle.

Q: But you do not become obsessed with it?

LAMM: No, I'm not obsessed with it at all. Because I do believe that transcendent realm, beyond the physical universe, is the realm of the HolyOne, blessed be He. And listen, if I won't have a separate identity, I'll be identified with Him.

Q: A final question. What do you see ahead for the Jewish people or for Israel?

LAMM: I'll tell you a story about the two Israelis who were talking and one said to the other, "Are you an optimist or a pessimist? He said, "I'm an optimist". He says, "If you're such an optimist, why do you look so terrible?" The other answers, "You think it's so easy to be an optimist today?"

Philip Leder

One of the world's leading scientists in molecular genetics, Philip Leder completed his undergraduate and graduate studies in medicine at Harvard University where he now teaches and pursues research as Professor and Chairman of the Department of Genetics. He is a native of Washington, D.C., who was reared in a traditionally oriented home which imbued him with a strong sense of Jewish identity. However, his formal Jewish education at a conservative synagogue in northern Virginia was minimal. His wife, an Israeli, as he put it, "tends to be more observant" and "more spiritual."

Searching for a person who, while far removed from the faith and practice of Judaism as a religion, identifies positively as a Jew, my choice fell on Professor Leder. This brilliant scientist represents a very large number of secular Jews who may be described as near-agnostics or agnostics. The people I refer to are neither atheists nor religious in any conventional sense, yet keep an open mind on matters of Jewish belief albeit without any great urge to develop them.

Leder would not reject the idea of God. "God is certainly not just a word," he said. What kind of God, then, does he believe in? His answer: "The abiding notion which remains with me as a great mystery is the nature of the universe." Further on, he speaks of God as the ultimate explanation of the universe, "More a series of questions. How did we get there? Where are we going?"

Acknowledging the wide gap between his Jewish and general knowledge, Leder confesses: "One of the sad things, in a way, is that my Jewish education is probably on a second- or third-grade level . . . I frankly regret that I've never had an opportunity to encounter Judaism intellectually at the level that would be satisfying to me." When he added ruefully, "Judaism hasn't been an area in which I have read much recently and maybe I'll come back to it," I wondered how much longer the organized Jewish community will neglect the opportunity to engage such minds as his in study programs on a sufficiently sophisticated level. We spoke in Leder's office at the National Academy of Science in Washington, D.C., October 15, 1991.

Q: What can you tell me about your own Jewish background? How do you identify yourself as a Jew?

LEDER: My childhood Jewish education and orientation took place in Arlington, Virginia, where I grew up, in the Arlington Jewish Center Congregation. I'm a Conservative Jew.

Q: Was this the religious posture of your parents?

LEDER: Yes.

Q: Was your father also a professional?

LEDER: No, my father was a merchant. He had a children's wear business in Arlington and Falls Church, Virginia.

Q: Your mother?

LEDER: She was a nurse until she married, and then a housewife and mother.

Q: Who was the religiously more vocal of your parents?

LEDER: I would have to say that my father was.

Q: To what extent was he observant? Did he get up in the morning and put on *t'fillin* [phylacteries] every day?

LEDER: No, no. As a youngster I would go to Hebrew School in the afternoons, after school, and Saturday we would go to services. There were very few Jews in Arlington during the Second World War and, often, there was not enough participation to have a minyan [quorum for worship] and to take the Torah out on Shabbat.

Q: Did you come to the "rescue" on occasions?

LEDER: Well, as a child, before bar mitzvah, I guess, I couldn't. We went on the High Holy Days to services and observed Passover at home.

Q: Did you have a kosher home?

LEDER: No.

Q: Do you keep a kosher home now?

LEDER: No.

Q: Is your wife also traditionally oriented?

LEDER: No, my wife is an Israeli. She comes from a socialist background. Politically, the orientation of her parents was that of the *halutzim* [pioneers] who settled on the kibbutz. However, if anything, she tends to be more observant. As for observances, I guess we are both about the same, but she's more spiritual than I.

Q: You would define your wife and yourself as positive Jews?

LEDER: I am as much a Jew as anyone and very affirmatively Jewish.

Q: Are you aware of any kind of development in your own religious beliefs? Are you a believer?

LEDER: Well, one of the sad things, in a way, is that my Jewish education is probably on a second- or third-grade level. The sophistication of my Jewish training can't in any way be compared to other areas of educational contact that I've had, and that's the sad thing.

Q: This is the most frequent Jewish self-definition I've heard: "I have done a good deal in many fields, but my Jewish knowledge is about at the second- or third-grade level."

LEDER: I would say this applies particularly to my Jewish knowledge with respect to theology, systems of belief, philosophy. I'm familiar with observance and I have a notion of what that can mean in the Orthodox and the Reform sense, but deeper questions of a religious nature seldom occur to me or do not even trouble me. Maybe that's not a good thing.

Q: Have you ever encountered any Jewish thinker, rabbi or teacher who challenged you, who aroused your interest in a deeper understanding of Judaism?

LEDER: As a child, with a child's faith and a child's belief, I didn't need a justification for observance. But as a college student, when I associated myself with the practices and symbols of faith, I was really never challenged or inspired. I don't know what one should expect out of the worship service or the prayers or the melodies in terms of religious experience, or what one may expect in terms of inspirational thought or spirituality from the pulpit, but rarely have I encountered that.

Q: Is there anything that you recall, either from your youth or later years, as a personal response to God? Have you had experiences that expanded or raised your consciousness in this respect? Is God for you a mere word?

LEDER: No, God is certainly not just a word. Even if I were only a sociologist, it would be of too great importance to suggest that God was merely a word. After childhood and adolescence and a period of contemplation in college, the abiding notion which remains with me as a great mystery is the nature of the universe. If I had to define God, I would define God in terms of that mystery.

Q: The wonder of the world?

LEDER: As the basis and as explanation, in the last analysis, of the universe, God is for me more a series of questions. How did we get here? Where are we going? How can we look forward to understanding the rules that have designed this universe for us?

Q: Whether we are Jewish or Christian or Buddhist, the great question that challenges us all is why there is something instead of nothing. It is the question that has inspired Jewish mystic thought more than any other question. Why is there something instead of nothing?

LEDER: Right. That formulation is very good, though I've never used it myself. We have ended up the way we are sitting here and talking through a series of incredible accidents that could have gone in any direction and this event would have never occurred, and this is not necessarily a part of God's or nature's plan that we are here. But the question that you touch on, why something instead of nothing, is the essential one for me and that's a great mystery.

Q: Would you relate that to God in any way?

LEDER: The whole notion of God incorporates this question as a possible explanation and answer to it. What matters to me, at least, is the question itself, rather than the answer to the question.

Q: Are you satisfied with merely being alive and conscious of this wonder, or do you feel a need to explore it and to link what exists with the ground of all being, call it God?

LEDER: Not exactly. As a scientist I work towards an answer to this question, but very remotely, at its most distant edges, in terms of biology. If there is an answer to such a mysterious question as our existence, I think that it will come through science. You asked me if I have need to answer this question. It's my profession, as it's yours.

Q: So you would try to find answers in science rather than assumptions of faith?

LEDER: That is correct. Suppositions of faith assume that we have the answer and, frankly, I'm not convinced that that's so. I'm not that presumptuous of man's ability to have an answer to such a profound question revealed to him. I doubt that even God would want us to know that answer without a lot more work.

Q: My faith not only tells me what to lean on, but it also tells me, the mind is not big enough to grasp it. How would you relate God, if at all, to this mystery of being?

LEDER: Some people's notion of God is an attempt to answer that very fundamental and basic question. It may be very presumptuous of me to say so, but maybe we will understand. After all, many religions feel that answers, in fact, have been revealed.

Q: Indeed, we claim that through revelation we were given an understanding of the origin of all being. But this is not a position that you would take?

LEDER: That's right.

Q: Do you sense any kind of personal relatedness to God, whatever God is?

LEDER: As I said before, it's not an issue that I think about very much. I labor at a great remove directed towards this understanding. I work at biology and genetics and trying to understand them which will never lead me to the answer to this question that we've posed. But I'm satisfied to work on it at that level, frankly, and not think too much about God and faith. Maybe that is the task that God has given me, and an uncluttered mind allows me to work more effectively, perhaps.

Q: How do you react to words like these from the Nineteenth Psalm: "The heavens declared the glory of God and the firmament showeth forth His handiwork"?

LEDER: My question would be, what do we really mean by God? Would I be satisfied if someone said, let's substitute nature for God, if you don't mind?

Q: Would you mind making this substitution?

LEDER: Yes, I would. I would equate the two in terms of that mystery that I don't understand. It's a wonderful thing, it's an amazing thing, this universe, but I don't understand it.

Q: Have you ever had experiences, intimations, mystic states?

LEDER: No, I never had. I mean I could be moved in a way during a synagogue service, but this may be related to being with my own family and to my knowledge of the history of the Jewish people and so on. However, I have not been moved in a spiritual way.

Q: Have you had what William James might call those luminous moments that partake of an ecstatic mood in which there seems to be a wider vision?

LEDER: I've had moments like that, but not related to religiosity, rather to my own work, insights, observations, experiments that get me extremely excited.

Q: A frequently quoted statement of Albert Einstein testifies to his reverence for what he calls "supreme intelligence." Does that mean anything to you?

LEDER: I would have to invest those words with my own meaning. I suppose "supreme intelligence" refers to the answer to the ultimate questions.

Q: Would you equate "supreme intelligence" with some extraordinary genetic code?

LEDER: It is the answer to existence and I don't think we are at this answer. Would I equate this with God who revealed himself to Abraham and established the law as basis for moral behavior?

Q: And gave revelation to Moses and the people of Israel at Sinai. Is that credible in your own judgment?

LEDER: It is credible, but, in my view, it is the work of man. You can say as the faithful do, that it is the work of God *through* man, but that I don't know.

Q: In other words, you don't take these claims as fraudulent, but as the honest convictions of people who, as a result of experiences attributed to God, let their minds function, in a way, as an extension of divine speech.

LEDER: Right.

Q: You look upon the human being in all of your work as an organism. Does the term "soul" or "spirit," as something other than physical substance, mean anything to you?

LEDER: Maybe it's very unfair for me to respond to that, having given such matters so little thought over a lifetime, but I would say, no. And I'm sad to say no, but I would have, nevertheless, to say that. Do I make distinctions between human beings and other forms of life? Yes, I certainly do. Is that difference, soul? I don't think so.

Q: Do you think it conceivable that there may be other dimensions of reality, not subject to physical investigations, dimensions such as spirituality?

LEDER: No. I think spirituality as we experience it will eventually be explicable in the molecular chemical terms.

Q: Would you call spirituality inseparable from its organic seat in the brain?

LEDER: That is correct. Emotion, memory, altruism, spirituality if you will, insanity in all aspects of behavior, while very difficult to understand, will be explained in physical terms.

Q: Do you think it conceivable that the human mind, comparable let us say to a radio receiver, might be receptive to messages from some cosmic source?

LEDER: Well I would say that the human mind is constantly receptive to messages delivered in the form of stimulation which can be experience, conversation, and so on. I don't want to rule out anything. Is there a cosmic source? We *are* the recipient of some form of stimulation from outer space. I mean, we see the stars and, therefore, we are seeing light waves that are stimulating the retina in the back of our eyes, sending images into our brain. That's very easy to understand. What other sources of stimulation we will receive will depend upon our senses and our ability to react to them. Do we receive such stimulation from the cosmos on a spiritual, mysterious level, of some sort? I think, no. These are things that, eventually, we'll understand.

Q: You do not, in other words, believe that there can be what we call inspiration or revelation from another source?

LEDER: Inspiration, definitely, yes, as a reaction to a stimulus coming from wherever in the universe or from the earth itself. But a supernatural being transmitting something into our brains fully formed that we have no code book ever explaining, no.

Q: Can you think of any kind of life after death?

LEDER: Our posterity is that which we pass on to our children. Your children have fifty percent of your genes and they will pass those on, entering and reentering the pool. As long as human existence occurs and this earth lasts, which is surely not eternal, you will continue to live in that posterity. But eventually that, too, will disappear. We know that that will happen.

Q: What do you mean it will disappear?

LEDER: Well, this earth and this solar system, of course, is about five billion years old and our sun will probably last another five billion years. It's a long time, so we don't have to worry about it very much. But then it will come. The star upon which our whole life depends will end unless we figure some way of leaving this planet and entering another solar system, associated with another star. But in answer to your question about an afterlife, I'm not very confident of that.

Q: At the outset you spoke of yourself as a Jew. What connects you with the Jewish people?

LEDER: I feel a part of Jewish peoplehood. I share with our people a common moral tradition, a common history, a common burden which must be overcome; even a task, yes. And I value that highly.

Q: When we talk about the Jewish march through history and the role that Jews have played, does it lead to something? Can you make a case for the Messianic hope or the idea that whatever is wrong with the world will somehow be rectified, and that there might be some intervention from a higher source to perfect the human being?

LEDER: I think the Messianic idea is one that addresses the human condition and seeks to improve it; that sees human problems and reaches out to solve them. I like that idea; I think it's a very attractive idea and it's quite consistent with my own view that, as we know more, as we learn more, as our understanding grows, given whatever light we have to expand that understanding, we affect in a positive way the human condition. The idea of the Messiah, as a divine intervention, is one that I don't require. We are placed on earth as humans by whatever set of laws or whatever forces, or by God, and it's our obligation to address this condition. The condition of our fellow man, the whole issue of peace, that is our work.

Q: Do you look upon the Messianic hope as wishful thinking? Or do you see it as an evolution, perhaps expressed in theological terminology, but as something that is taking place organically or physically?

LEDER: Yes. I don't have the Messianic concept that there will be simple solutions to complicated human problems in a single stroke. On the other hand, I do have faith that, as we come to understand ourselves more as beings, as individuals, as genetically programmed organisms, this knowledge will contribute to bettering the human condition. It's a little hard to equate that with a Messianic faith, but that's my Messianic faith in a way.

Q: What do you call better? What makes a thing better?

LEDER: That's a very difficult question.

Q: What's your standard of judgment?

LEDER: Peace not war. Hunger, not starvation. Health in useful years and not disease. Happiness and not grief.

Q: Another code of ethics could be rationally defended, which favors the destruction of the inferior so that the superior would have more chance for proliferation. If that means hunger and pain and suffering for inferior species or people, so what?

LEDER: This is a sort of distorted Darwinian sociology.

Q: What's wrong with that? Why should the strongest not survive at the expense of the weaker? Is this not nature's law?

LEDER: Nature's law does not necessarily serve the strong over the weak as you conventionally think of it, but really serves the most readily reproduced and sustainable life. That's what Darwin is really talking about in a way. In biological terms that sometimes means extinction; it sometimes means an overrunning of the universe with locusts and a diminution of competition for scarce resources. My Messianic vision is one that reaches out for an equitable human equilibrium.

Q: You mentioned a set of moral values. Are they derived from your study of science?

LEDER: I don't think genetics establishes a set of moral values, nor does Darwin. These are my body of received wisdom and yours.

Q: Received from where?

LEDER: You might say, divinely inspired, but I would rather say they are the consequence of human experience. The Ten Commandments are self-evident based on human experience. These are good ideas. Anybody could have had them. Moses had them.

Q: Would we not then expect some form of universal religion? How come the vast majority of mankind came to different conclusions?

LEDER: Because people are experientially different. However, even in cultures and civilizations that readily accept the Ten Commandments as divinely inspired, they are very frequently observed in the breach.

Q: You are strongly committed to a certain code of morals. Can you trace its source? Where does it come from?

LEDER: I can trace my morality to what has been taught to me by my parents, by the synagogue, by my experience with religion, and by my participation in American society. Had I, as a Jew, lived in a completely different context, I am sure that I would not have come out with the same strain of moral values, despite the commonality of my Judaism. For example, I might not have developed an allegiance to the democratic tradition, to the Bill of Rights, and to liberty. Even my notions about the best way to organize a society economically might have been different. So, I'm a product of this mosaic of experiences, not a small part of which has been my Jewish experience.

Q: You would not credit any discipline of science for the origin of these moral principles, but feel that they come from a certain social and cultural environment?

LEDER: Yes, which, I would argue, could be explained in more scientific terms than are now available to the examiner.

Q: How would you explain this moral development and growth, scientifically, genetically?

LEDER: Given the opportunity, I could train a fellow human being to be a brute, to be a warrior, to be a murderer, to be an executioner, to be a torturer. It's not the set of values that *I've* embraced or with which I have been inculcated. But I could have become a terrible Nazi under different circumstances.

Q: So you would not point to your particular genetic makeup but rather to your social background and the cultural and ethical traditions you imbibed.

LEDER: Genetics provides a basis and a framework to which your environment, including education and what people refer to as nurture, contributes enormously. It is that interaction between your nature, which is established genetically, and your interaction with the environment that produces the outcome which we call a human being. A very interesting experiment was done by two neurobiologists at Harvard about twenty-five to thirty years ago. They took a newborn kitten whose eyes were closed and kept the eyes of the newborn kitten closed until it grew up to be a cat. Then they noticed that the connections that were made between the nerve cells in the back of the eye and the centers in the back of the brain, where these are interpreted, never were made. That means that establishing that connection required the input of light. The kitten was no different, genetically, than any other kitten, but simply couldn't develop properly and make the right connection unless there was that stimulation of light.

Q: What happened to the kitten?

LEDER: The kitten was, of course, blind, permanently blind. It didn't have the connections. It never made the connections. What I'm saying by that is that we are in a way a vessel. The vessel is formed by our genetic program. But the vessel is incomplete and may never fully develop, and certainly will differently develop depending upon the environmental cues, the training, the inculcation.

Q: So it is nature plus nurture.

LEDER: Absolutely, of course.

Q: Do you feel any urge to study the Bible, the classics of Judaism and the wide range of Jewish thought and philosophy which you have missed in your Jewish education?

LEDER: I frankly regret that I've never had an opportunity to encounter Judaism intellectually at a level that would now be satisfying to me.

Q: Is that regret strong enough to move you to a systematic study of these fields?

LEDER: At the moment probably not, but I have a way of moving along parallel paths, that is, my own professional endeavors in science and some other interest outside of science in which I like to read. Judaism hasn't been an area in which I have read very much recently, and maybe I'll come back to it. Why not? It's as attractive and perhaps more so than many other fields.

Yeshayahu Leibowitz

Yeshayahu Leibowitz, professor of organic and biochemistry and neurophysiology, and a man of letters with Jewish scholarly credentials, is one of Israel's most controversial figures, admired by some groups and loathed by others. His admirers see him as a prophet, his detractors call him Israel's worst demagogue, a charlatan and a fraud. He is as combative at the age of ninety as he was at sixty when he called for the separation of state and religion in Israel, declaring the state devoid of any religious significance. He is a passionate debater, unyielding and at times, explosive. In a recent public television appearance, he called a member of the Israeli Knesset (parliament) a "worthless rag." He turned down the Israel Prize, the nation's most prestigious award, when Prime Minister Yitzhak Rabin announced that he would boycott the award ceremony.

Strictly Orthodox, he recognizes only voluntary submission to God and acceptance of the "yoke of command" as valid religious attitudes. He denies religious significance to human history since such an assertion would bestow upon humanity an importance which properly belongs only to God.

Professor Leibowitz occupies a modest apartment in Jerusalem with his spouse of sixty years, also a scientist. A conversation with him will quickly explode the notion that Orthodoxy is a monolithic form of Jewish traditionalism. He is the most extreme individualist in thought even while scrupulously conforming to Orthodoxy in practice. This nonagenarian curmudgeon is so much the challenger that, even before I could ask my questions, he let go with a barrage of questions of his own, and without waiting for my reply, shouted out his answers.

Leibowitz's religious Orthodoxy, as he never tires of repeating, is a free act of his will to accept the "yoke of the commandments." So also, his morality is a decision of will. For him, faith is not a body of beliefs but an obligation. As far as he is concerned, the revelation at Mount Sinai never happened. The people who witnessed it didn't believe it. It was a total failure. The only communication between God and man occurs in the fulfillment of the mitzvot. I strenuously tried to get his view on how the mitzvah relates to God. "Who defines the mitzvah?" I asked. His answer: "The Halakhah." And who defines the Halakhah? "The Halakhah defines itself," was his reply. He refuses to say that Halakhah is conveyed by God's revelation. What he is saying, it seems, is that the authority of the Halakhah rests upon the Jewish people's will to obey it.

It is impossible to tell how many Jews are represented by Leibowitz. He may well be the only one of his kind. But it is significant that a person of such a unique religious outlook can be accommodated within the ranks of Orthodoxy today.

A collection of his essays recently appeared in English, *Judaism, Human Values and the Jewish State*. We spoke in Professor Leibowitz's apartment in Jerusalem, Sunday and Monday, June 21–22, 1992.

Q: I would like to tell you what I am looking for. What I am looking for are the personal views, the personal beliefs of some very interesting Jewish artists, thinkers, writers, rabbis, and scholars. Also, I am looking for signs and trends pointing to a new condition of Jewish beliefs.

LEIBOWITZ: What is the meaning of the term "new condition?"

Q: We live in an age of tremendous transition, an age in which former beliefs have been shaken, in which old ideologies have crumbled and collapsed. How do Jews today respond to the realities of their life and, particularly, to the events of the last century, specifically, the Holocaust, the establishment of the State of Israel, and the meaning of Jewish peoplehood? I think that the Jewish public is interested in knowing what believing Jews really believe.

LEIBOWITZ: Here is my question: "These twelve or fourteen million human beings who are today conscious of their Jewishness, what do they have in common?"

Q: It is a difficult question. I think that a popular answer would be that Judaism is a shared destiny more than a shared belief.

LEIBOWITZ: Jews never had it so good as today everywhere in the world. They enjoy peace and security. There is only one place where we exist in a state of permanent danger and that is *Medinat Yisrael* [the State of Israel].

Q: Ironic, since the State was meant to be a refuge and a strong center of the Jewish people.

LEIBOWITZ: It never was established as a refuge.

Q: But it was so understood in the diaspora.

LEIBOWITZ: No, never. The refuge was the U.S.A.

Q: Numerically, that is what it turned out to be.

LEIBOWITZ: The meaning of the U.S.A. for Eastern European Jewry was as a land of refuge, not *Eretz Yisrael* [the Land of Israel].

Q: But was Eretz Yisrael not also meant to bring about self-realization?

LEIBOWITZ: That has no connection with security. The meaning of Zionism was the reestablishment of the political-national independence of the Jewish people.

Q: Why did you choose to come to Israel? You were in Germany in 1933–34 and you were in the academic life. You went to Basel and got your doctorate there. Did you have choices? Could you have stayed in Switzerland or come to America?

LEIBOWITZ: I never dreamed about remaining in Europe.

Q: You were a pre-Hitler Zionist.

LEIBOWITZ: Certainly.

Q: What was your vision of Israel?

LEIBOWITZ: I had no vision. My dream was the political and national independence of the Jewish people. But, the problem today is, what is the contemporary Jewish people? I can't answer this question.

Q: One must answer it on several levels because there are several kinds of Jewish people.

LEIBOWITZ: Which means that there is no Jewish people! The historical Jewish people ceased to exist in the nineteenth century.

Q: The formal emancipation of Jews in the nineteenth century put an end to the status and the self-image of the Jews as a nation. Nevertheless, there remained a sense that Judaism is more than a religion; that it retains aspects of a national history, if not a national future.

LEIBOWITZ: It is not an answer to my question, "What do Jews today have in common?" Are there values on the level of practical life as on the level of spiritual life—values that are common for all those millions of human beings who are conscious of the fact of their Jewishness? And my answer is, "No."

Q: You are a scientist. You have a rare combination of science and grounding in traditional Jewish learning.

LEIBOWITZ: There is no combination between them.

Q: Are your own personal beliefs grounded in science or in Jewish sources, or have you absorbed them from your environment?

LEIBOWITZ: I don't understand what you mean by belief in science.

Q: I am asking about your belief in God, not in science.

LEIBOWITZ: I would use the term *kabbalat ol malchut ha-shamayim v'ol ha-mitzvot* [accepting the yoke of the heavenly kingdom and of the commandments].

Q: Why would you? What inspired you to do so?

LEIBOWITZ: That is a *decision*. I'll ask you a question. Why should you be honest and decent? You could just as well be a scoundrel. The answer is absolutely clear. You *decided* to be honest and decent.

Q: I'm not sure that is a complete answer.

LEIBOWITZ: It is a complete answer. There is no better answer. Nothing in nature and in history imposes on a person the decision to be honest and decent; he can just as well be a scoundrel.

Q: Does a moralist think of the sources of his morality?

LEIBOWITZ: He certainly thinks about his sources of morality. It is a decision of his will.

Q: But is it my own morality that I have willed to follow or is it the morality of my father, my mother, my teachers, and possibly the morality inspired by some other source?

LEIBOWITZ: You can reject everything your father and mother taught you.

Q: To what extent is this morality shaped by the Tanakh, by Halakhah?

LEIBOWITZ: It can be shaped by anything and you can reject everything. You can reject all teachings, you can reject human history. It depends on whether you decide to be honest and decent.

Q: Do I decide this myself or is there some other spiritual force that guides me in that decision, that pushes me in that direction?

LEIBOWITZ: The spiritual force is your will, that is the spiritual force.

Q: When Amos, for example, said, "God has spoken, who can but be a prophet?" (Amos 3.8), what did he mean? Did he say it was his own conscience?

LEIBOWITZ: Amos was rejected by the people of Israel. All prophets were total failures.

Q: Historically speaking, in that time, they were rejected. But how, then, have the prophets become the authoritative moralists in our tradition?

LEIBOWITZ: Because later generations of Jews decided to accept them.

Q: Do you see anything of God in the moral standards or principles of the prophets? Do you think they expressed their own personal ideas or was there some operative revelation which they experienced and expressed?

LEIBOWITZ: We accepted prophets as *kitve ha-kodesh* [Holy Scriptures]. It is also a decision.

Q: But are their words *divreh elohim* [words of God]?

LEIBOWITZ: Which means kitve ha-kodesh. It is my decision to accept it.

Q: But what is there in their words that make them divreh elohim? Is it your own personal decision? Then why do you and I and many others see it?

LEIBOWITZ: Most people don't see it. Why are people nationalists? Why are they ready to kill and die for their country and their nation?

Q: Sociologists would answer that this is part of the social force, the community.

LEIBOWITZ: Men can rebel against social forces. There always were rebels and there are rebels today.

Q: In most cases, people follow the crowd; they follow their community; they follow tradition without thinking too much about it. Also, they sense a kind of shared interest or a shared security which they are eager to strengthen for each other, selfishly and also unselfishly.

LEIBOWITZ: As I mentioned, there are people who are ready to *die* for their country and their nation.

Q: Does that trouble you?

LEIBOWITZ: No, that doesn't trouble me at all. I know that all human values are decisions of human will and have no objectivity. No human value has any objectivity.

Q: That is a Nietzschean position.

LEIBOWITZ: I think it is an intelligent position. Objectivity exists only in scientific thinking and science is valueless.

Q: Valueless as far as guiding us in morality is concerned?

LEIBOWITZ: Science is no guide for anything.

Q: Tell me, what do we need God for if what we are doing or think we should be doing is a matter of personal decision?

LEIBOWITZ: There are some people for whom the highest value, even the one and only value, is *avodat ha-Shem* [service or worship of God].

Q: Is avodat ha-Shem directed toward a specific being? Or, is avodat ha-Shem directed toward an idea? Or, is avodat ha-Shem merely a symbol of reverence for life, as Schweitzer said?

LEIBOWITZ: No; it is part of *kabbalat ol ha-torah v'ol hamitzvot* [acceptance of the yoke of the Torah and the commandments].

Q: It is submission, is it not?

LEIBOWITZ: It is acceptance. It is also a free decision.

Q: Does not a decision of the will to accept the *ol ha-mitzvot*, the yoke of commandments, in some way relate to belief in a higher being, God, to whom one submits?

LEIBOWITZ: That *is* the meaning of belief in God! Or, do you believe in some old man in heaven who pulls the strings of the world?

Q: For many people that is what their belief in God is all about, some superior power up in heaven that acts like a tyrant. No, I can not believe that.

LEIBOWITZ: It is not a religious belief at all.

Q: That is mythology, paganism.

LEIBOWITZ: Yes, that is paganism, *avodah zarah* [idolatry]. Faith is an obligation.

Q: How is it inspired?

LEIBOWITZ: There is no inspiration. Revelation at Mount Sinai was a total failure.

Q: Did it take place? Was it a historical fact? Would you agree with Judah Halevi and say it happened?

LEIBOWITZ: According to the report of the Bible, the people who were witnesses of this revelation didn't believe it. They made the Golden Calf.

Q: But that is only one side. The other side is the persistence of the idea of *matan Torah* [the revelation of the Torah].

LEIBOWITZ: But it didn't persist. For many generations they served the idols Baal, Astarte, and Moloch.

Q: Getting back to the idea of God, can you personally see a development, stages in your own perception of God?

LEIBOWITZ: I never had another perception of God than the acceptance of ol malchut ha-shamayim v'ol ha-mitzvot. I never considered God as a manager of the world. God is not an instrument for the world or for mankind. At this time, the manager of my affairs and the affairs of four million Jews is Mr. Yitzhak Shamir, our prime minister. That is his function and there is nothing divine in it. God doesn't have a function. God doesn't have an office.

Q: What does God do, if anything? That is the problem of believing Jews today who are on the verge of not believing.

LEIBOWITZ: Always there were believers and nonbelievers. Nothing has changed.

Q: Does revelation, *hitgalut*, have any meaning for you?

LEIBOWITZ: It proved to be a total failure.

Q: Do you believe there is any communication between God and man?

LEIBOWITZ: Certainly.

Q: In what form?

LEIBOWITZ: In the fulfillment of mitzvot.

Q: Only in the mitzvot?

LEIBOWITZ: That's communication with God.

Q: How about the communication from man to God in the form of prayer?

LEIBOWITZ: Prayer is a mitzvah. Do you think I'm here to molest God with my wishes?

Q: But you would pray to him? Don't you?

LEIBOWITZ: Because it is a mitzvah.

Q: But it is a mitzvah which tries to influence God.

LEIBOWITZ: No. To influence God is a pagan notion.

Q: If prayer, to you, is not designed to influence God, is it strictly humanistic, a way of purging the mind?

LEIBOWITZ: No. It is fulfillment of a mitzvah. It is avodat ha-Shem.

Q: Is avodat ha-Shem a kind of submission?

LEIBOWITZ: No, not submission; I decided to accept it. It is my autonomous decision.

Q: It is a paradox, is it not? I decide, in freedom, to do what I think God commands me to do.

LEIBOWITZ: A moral man accepts the categorical imperative.

Q: Is the categorical imperative to you the essence of morality?

LEIBOWITZ: For a moral man, yes.

Q: Are you drawing that from the philosophy of Kant?

LEIBOWITZ: No.

Q: Do you think Kant expressed what Jews have always felt?

LEIBOWITZ: My knowledge of Judaism was imparted to me twenty years before I knew about Kant.

Q: You started out by asking me, "What unites the Jewish people?"

LEIBOWITZ: Since the nineteenth century.

Q: I have a more troublesome question for you. Can we still speak of a *bechirah* [election]? Is there a chosen people?

LEIBOWITZ: In the traditional sense. We are chosen to be a people responsible for the mitzvot.

Q: Who chose us?

LEIBOWITZ: We accepted this task.

Q: You mean all of a sudden the Jewish people said, "God wants us to do something."

LEIBOWITZ: Many generations, the great bulk of the Jewish people, accepted it.

Q: And do you think this is still true?

LEIBOWITZ: No. It ceased in the nineteenth century.

Q: The Jews rejected it?

LEIBOWITZ: Yes.

Q: The chief pillar of Jewish theology has been belief in God.

LEIBOWITZ: What is the meaning of belief in God? Is it believing in an old man in heaven who pulls the strings of the world?

Q: Principally, it means belief in God as a redeemer and helper.

Q: Does that have meaning for you?

LEIBOWITZ: No. It is a Christian notion.

Q: What about the Messiah? Is the Messiah a Christian notion? Or can you do without the Messiah?

LEIBOWITZ: If you believe in God, why do you need a Messiah? The Messiah is a substitute for faith. The Jewish people, for two thousand years, lived without the Messiah.

Q: What do you think of the human being? You are a scientist and you are a Jew with deep roots in our whole tradition. Is a human being to you anything more than a body? Do you see in the human being the indefinable, spiritual essence, shall we call it the *neshamah*, the *nefesh* [soul].

LEIBOWITZ: I don't know anything about the neshamah or nefesh, but I know something about man. Man doesn't belong to nature, because man has consciousness and will. In nature there is never consciousness nor will. From the nucleus of the atom to the galaxies in a distance of fifteen billion light years, there is no consciousness and no will. But in you and in me, there are consciousness and will.

Q: Man, you are saying, belongs to a realm other than nature through his consciousness and will. Why are you leaving *emunah* [faith] out? Should you not include faith also as a uniquely human capacity?

LEIBOWITZ: I told you what my faith is. My faith is to accept the yoke of mitzvot. That man has consciousness and will is not an element of faith; it is a statement of a fact.

Q: But man also has the capacity for faith, does he not?

LEIBOWITZ: What do you mean he has a capacity for faith?

Q: The potential to organize his life, to direct his life with trust, with reliance upon a higher being or power, with hope. Is man other than nature, or more than nature?

LEIBOWITZ: I don't believe man is more than nature, but he can raise himself above nature by accepting the Yoke of the Torah.

Q: Is man different from the animal world?

LEIBOWITZ: Different not only from the animal world, but different from the cosmos—from the sun and the moon and the galaxies.

Q: Is there something in man that is immortal? Does *t'chiat ha-metim* [resurrection] mean anything to you? Do you believe in the survival of something human at the end of our so-called earthly life?

LEIBOWITZ: I know man only as a living being.

Q: You would rather not make a statement about immortality?

LEIBOWITZ: I do not even understand the meaning of it. In the order of Yom Kippur, there is no mention of the immortality of the soul. Moreover, on Yom Kippur there is no mention of the soul at all. Nefesh or neshamah do not exist in our Yom Kippur tradition.

Q: It is the total human being that stands before God.

LEIBOWITZ: Only the living human being. Even in the *sh'moneh esre* [eighteen daily benedictions], which is our service of God everyday, there is no mention of neshamah and no mention of *olam habah* [hereafter]. All problems of man exist in human life.

Q: But there is mention in the sh'monah esre of the *goel* [redeemer].

LEIBOWITZ: Sure.

Q: How do you understand the word "redeem"?

LEIBOWITZ: To liberate us from peril. It is a political notion. It is not a religious notion.

Q: You do not see it in a transcendent sense?

LEIBOWITZ: No, not at all.

Q: Do you see in religion anything other than a social phenomenon?

LEIBOWITZ: What do you mean by "social phenomenon"?

Q: A creation of society for the preservation of order among human beings. What is religion to you?

LEIBOWITZ: Religion is not a public utility.

Q: Then what is religion to you, private?

LEIBOWITZ: It is not private. I accept the Jewish religion as my religion.

Q: Which Jewish religious thinkers have had the most influence upon you? To whom do you feel closest?

LEIBOWITZ: That is a good question, very difficult to answer. It is probably impossible for a human being to analyze himself.

Q: Who was the first Jewish thinker who made a deep impression on you?

LEIBOWITZ: It is very difficult to answer.

Q: Were you influenced by any of the medieval theologians such as Saadia Gaon, *Rambam*, Judah Halevi?

LEIBOWITZ: Certainly. I know them very well.

Q: Do you identify with any of their thinking?

LEIBOWITZ: In the acceptance of the ol ha-mitzvot, yes.

Q: How about the modern Jewish thinkers?

LEIBOWITZ: Whom do you mean?

Q: To start with, Moses Mendelssohn?

LEIBOWITZ: Mendelssohn was a traditional Orthodox Jew.

Q: How about Abraham Geiger, Samuel Hirsch, S. L. Steinheim, Hermann Cohen, Martin Buber, Franz Rosenzweig, Abraham Heschel. Do any of them speak to you?

LEIBOWITZ: No, none of them.

Q: How about the modern philosophers? You mentioned Kant.

LEIBOWITZ: It's impossible to think philosophically without a relation to Kant, whether we accept him or don't accept him.

Q: Any thinker after Kant? Were you influenced by Hegel or Kierkegaard, the two opposites?

LEIBOWITZ: Hegel was an intellectual charlatan. He believed in the meaning of human history. The realization of the Absolute "Geist," spirit. For me history is just what Edward Gibbon called it, the chronicle of the crimes, follies, and misfortunes of mankind. That is human history.

Q: You will not say anything positive.

LEIBOWITZ: Yes. Because Edward Gibbon told only one-half of the truth. History is a chronicle of the crimes, follies, and misfortunes of mankind. But history is also the chronicle of man's struggle against crimes, against follies, against misfortunes.

Q: I am glad you said that.

LEIBOWITZ: And these two things together make human history. But this struggle is eternal.

Q: Do you believe that Hegel ignored the realities of history, imposing his scheme upon it?

LEIBOWITZ: Absolutely. He saw in history direction, the realization of spirit. I see in history only the struggle between crimes, follies, and misfortune given by nature and the struggle against the crimes, against the follies, and against the misfortune. The struggle derives from the will of some people of all generations and of all races in all civilizations to fight the crimes and to fight the follies and to fight the misfortune.

Q: Hegel's severest critic was Kierkegaard. Do you have interest in Kierkegaard?

LEIBOWITZ: No, not at all. He was a Christian.

Q: Have the two most important or popular Jewish thinkers of modern times, Buber and Rosenzweig, impressed you in any way?

LEIBOWITZ: As to Buber, Buber was a Jewish theologian for *goyim* [non-Jews] and a philosopher for "ladies." I didn't say philosopher for "women," because women are just as capable as men in philosophical thinking. But there is a kind of philosopher for "ladies". . .

Q: A matinee thinker?

LEIBOWITZ: That is Buber for me. Rosenzweig's personality is a phenomenon, but not his thought. As a Jewish person, he is a great figure.

Q: The example of his life?

LEIBOWITZ: Exactly, and his decision to cleave to Judaism. As a person, he is a great Jewish phenomenon, but his thought is utterly unimportant for us.

Q: Is it because in his major work *The Star of Redemption*, he tried to systematize what can not be systematized?

LEIBOWITZ: Well, you may characterize it thus. In any case, he doesn't represent for me deep Jewish thought.

Q: How do you react to Soloveitchik?

LEIBOWITZ: That is a very interesting question. I had the *zechut* [privilege] to know him personally. Some twenty years ago I met him in Boston and fifteen years ago in New York at the Yeshiva University. We had many talks. He is certainly a deep religious thinker. But he is not a leader. He is not a spiritual leader.

Q: Do you see anybody in Israel today or in the last century who has reached that level of influence? For example, Harav Kook?

LEIBOWITZ: His influence was disastrous.

Q: Are you referring only to his Messianic expectations and the excitement of political renewal here?

LEIBOWITZ: I mean his idea of holiness, *kedushah*.

Q: Why was it disastrous?

LEIBOWITZ: Seeing kedushah in reality is the source of the greatest disasters in the human mind and even in human existence. I told him once, "You don't understand the meaning of *ha-mavdil bein kodesh l'chol* [distinguishing between holy and profane].

Q: Was it with reference to his hopes for the restoration of the *mikdash* [temple]?

LEIBOWITZ: That is not the decisive thing.

Q: Did you object to the identification of peoplehood with holiness?

LEIBOWITZ: Not of peoplehood, but of reality!

Q: Is holiness to you transcendent?

LEIBOWITZ: Holiness is a divine attribute. It doesn't pertain to anything, not to the cosmos, not to history, not to humanity, not to the Jewish people or to anything. There is no kedushah in the world. It is not an original idea of mine. *Ein shum davar kadosh ba-olam* [there is nothing holy in the world], only God is Holy.

Q: That may be a tragic fact, but is it what it *ought* to be or *could* be? What do you make of the Biblical command *kedoshim tiheyu* ["Ye shall be holy"—Lev. 19.2]?

LEIBOWITZ: *Tiheyu* ["ye *shall* be"] means you are not *now*.

Q: But does it not imply you *could* be?

LEIBOWITZ: That is not so sure. You see, here we must make a decisive point about values: faith, justice, freedom, beauty—each of these values isn't what is, and not even so certain that it will be, but what *ought* to be. That is the meaning of values.

Q: Can you see two separate dimensions of the human mind which operates in the world that is, but at the same time pulls us toward the world that ought to be?

LEIBOWITZ: It doesn't pull us. I decide. The "human" in man is ready to fight, to die, and to kill for justice. There is no justice in the world. It may be there never will be. Nevertheless, man can consecrate his life, to fight for justice.

Q: You are critical of the Lubavitch Hasidic movement. Do you have the same negative opinion about all Hasidic groups? Do you think that Hasidism, as an offshoot of Jewish mysticism, is the way of error and paganism?

LEIBOWITZ: Since Hasidism didn't delete Torah or mitzvot, they belong to traditional Judaism. It was a great error of the Gaon of Vilna to condemn Hasidism as a heresy. After all, they accepted Torah and mitzvot.

Q: You do not consider yourself a Hasid?

LEIBOWITZ: No. Not at all. I never had sympathy nor even understanding for their bloody nonsense.

Q: Do you have any appreciation for Jewish mysticism, of any kind?

LEIBOWITZ: You mean Kabbalah?

Q: Yes.

LEIBOWITZ: Why is it necessary?

Q: It is theology, is it not?

LEIBOWITZ: Yes. It is theology.

Q: Is it the mainstream of Jewish theology?

LEIBOWITZ: No. It started in the thirteenth century.

Q: But has it not, in the last five or six centuries been the mainstream of Jewish thinking?

LEIBOWITZ: Not the mainstream, but one of its powerful streams—and a disastrous one at that!

Q: How do you relate to the *Rambam* (Maimonides) in your understanding of Judaism as a religion? Are you a Maimonidean?

LEIBOWITZ: Certainly our world view is not the world view of Maimonides. But I think that he represents the highest expression of the Jewish traditional faith. In my book *The Faith of Maimonides*, I point out the difference between Maimonides and most of the great figures of the Jewish faith. They all were believers. But what is special about Maimonides is that he didn't believe in anything but God. He didn't believe in anything else, not in humanity, not in human values, not in history. That was his faith. Religion and God.

Q: And religion meant the acceptance of mitzvot, the ol hamitzvot?

LEIBOWITZ: Of course. Beyond the service of God nothing is of value. That's a deep truth.

Q: Do you personally hold that view also? Do you take the same stance toward your own life?

LEIBOWITZ: Certainly, as we are told in Pirke Avot (IV.29): "Regardless of your will, you are formed. Regardless of your will, you are born, regardless of your will you live and regardless of your will you die." It doesn't make any sense. But if during the sixty or seventy or eighty years given to you, you serve God, then your life has meaning. Let me quote Maimonides: "We must bear in mind that all practices of worship such as reading the Torah, prayer, and the performance of the other *mitzvot*, serve only the end of training you to occupy yourself with the precepts of God." This sentence seems to be paradoxical. From its first words it appears that the practical commandments are a means to a certain intellectual purpose. But, the very purpose to which this means leads us is revealed to be nothing but the idea of the performance of these commandments. Maimonides continues, "to occupy and fill our minds with the precepts of God and free us from worldly business." But worldly business is, after all, the emendation of the body. Worldly business is necessary, but it is not the final aim. Here Maimonides reaches the pinnacle of pure faith, "you should act as if you were occupied with God and not with any other thing." If I say *hamotzi** before eating, I occupy myself with God. There is no other meaning of the program of life according to the Halakhah.

Q: Is this to you *kedushah* [sanctification]?

LEIBOWITZ: This is kedushah, the performance of the mitzvot.

Q: Is the performance of the mitzvah a reaching out to God?

LEIBOWITZ: Not reaching out. I occupy myself with God. I deal in God.

Q: You connect, you deal in God; that is a good answer.

---

*Literally, "who brings forth," referring to the standard blessing before the meal praising God for bringing forth bread from the earth.

LEIBOWITZ: Is there any reason, a philosophical reason, a moral reason, a social reason, or a national reason for *kashrut* [dietary observance]?

Q: None is specified in the Torah.

LEIBOWITZ: I occupy myself with God by observing the *diney kashrut* [dietary laws]. Think about sexual life and the observance of the *niddah* and *tevilah* [laws of impurity and ritual bathing]. I deal in God. There is no human interest in the observance of these rules.

Q: Are you suggesting that kedushah, or dealing in God, or performing mitzvot, is a way of transcending our humanity?

LEIBOWITZ: Not transcending our humanity.

Q: Is it fulfilling our humanity?

LEIBOWITZ: It is fulfilling our humanity. Humanity as such has no sense whatever. If you try to understand the world as seen by science, you get the deep impression, that the world of nature doesn't have any sense.

Q: It is certainly impossible for the human mind to see a purpose or sense in the world. As difficult as it is to understand the world, even more difficult is it to understand why there is a world in the first place?

LEIBOWITZ: That is the fundamental question of metaphysics. Existence doesn't make sense. Scientific knowledge is the one and only universal human good, but it implicates no value.

Q: Except that it enhances human power, it extends our power to control. To understand scientifically, means to control.

LEIBOWITZ: If I have the wish to apply scientific knowledge, that is my decision. Some fifteen years ago, at an International Congress for Philosophy of Science in New York, I had an opportunity to talk with Isidor Rabi, one of the central figures of modern physics and a Nobel Prize laureate. He told me that when he was scientific adviser to President Truman, during a visit to the White House, President Truman told him, "I beg you to do me a service. Please talk with your colleague, Robert Oppenheimer, and make him cease importuning me with his problems and his conscience. He feels himself to be responsible for the calamities of the atomic age. Please try to explain to him that he isn't responsible for anything. What did he do? He made the atomic bomb. By making the atomic bomb, he didn't harm a louse. I gave the order to use it."

Q: Are you saying that science is good but the uses of science can be disastrous?

LEIBOWITZ: No, no. Science is knowledge, without moral implication. But that is the highest human faculty.

Q: Would you not give to kedushah, the achievement, or the quest for kedushah, a higher rating?

LEIBOWITZ: But that is not a universal quest of human beings.

Q: Is it particularly Jewish?

LEIBOWITZ: No, not at all. The highest expression of humanity is the power to know something and that is universal. You may know Chinese grammar, or the structure of the atom or the Talmud. Knowing, that is the highest human faculty.

Q: And where do the values come from?

LEIBOWITZ: From the will.

Q: Then the will is really the most mysterious of all human qualities?

LEIBOWITZ: Why mysterious? It is absolutely clear. For example, I have at this moment the will to answer your question. That is absolutely clear; clearer than the fact that I, as a human being really exist. Maybe I am dreaming and don't exist at all. But I can not doubt the fact that I have the will at this moment to answer your questions. I am absolutely sure and certain about that.

Q: So it seems then that you are grounding religion in the human will.

LEIBOWITZ: But it is not the universal human will.

Q: You are saying now that it is purely a matter of my will or your will to accept the ol ha-mitzvot.

LEIBOWITZ: Yes. And there may be another person, human exactly as you and me, and his strongest will is to have maximum sexual satisfaction, to keep as many women as possible, because for him this is the highest goal.

Q: How do we know which is better?

LEIBOWITZ: I don't understand the meaning of the term "better"?

Q: Do we have an absolute standard of right and wrong?

LEIBOWITZ: Certainly, I have my standard, my absolute standard, for me and you don't have to accept it. You see, Adolf Hitler was a highly moral person; he was deeply convinced in his soul that the highest value for human existence is the domination of the world by the Germanic race. And for this purpose, he was ready not only to kill, but to die. Adolf Hitler was a highly moral person.

Q: But only to the limited extent that he was trying to live up to an ideal that he had in his mind. This makes morality synonymous with "consistency" and it applies equally to the good man and the criminal who makes great efforts and sacrifices to carry out his will.

LEIBOWITZ: Yes, but it is highly important to understand it. You can't argue about values, but only fight for them.

Q: But we Jews do believe that certain values are absolute. You say, I believe because *I* want to believe.

LEIBOWITZ: "Believe" means I have this will. That is the meaning of believing.

Q: And yet, as Jews, we do not accept a strictly subjective, relativistic morality. We believe that our moral standards have universal significance, for us as Jews, at least. For example, the *aseret ha-dibrot* [ten commandments] are not just a matter of your personal will to observe; they have an absolute validity.

LEIBOWITZ: But they are not accepted by the majority of humanity. They are not universal values. There are no universal values.

Can you name any value that is a universal human value?

Q: No, not in terms of present reality, not in terms of what *is*, but in terms of what *ought* to be.

LEIBOWITZ: What *I* think ought to be may be just the contrary of what *you* think ought to be.

Q: I was impressed by the point you made that the essence of Judaism is the will of the Jew to accept the *ol malchut ha-shamayim* [the yoke of the heavenly kingdom], that is to say, to accept and observe the mitzvot. The essence of Judaism, you say, is the will of the Jew to do so.

LEIBOWITZ: Historical Judaism, yes.

Q: That raises a very serious question. Who defines the mitzvot [commandments]? Do I myself choose what is a mitzvah and what is not? That is the position of reform Judaism, a Judaism of choice. Where is the *metzaveh* [commander]? Am I the metzaveh? Or, is God the metzaveh?

LEIBOWITZ: It is the Halakhah.

Q: Who defines the Halakhah?

LEIBOWITZ: The Halakhah defines itself. It is a decisive point whether you recognize the authority of the Halakhah or you don't. The great break came in the nineteenth century.

Q: But that raises the very question which you have not answered. Who is the metzaveh? Is the Halakhah self-validating? Or, is there a higher source of the Halakhah?

LEIBOWITZ: The Halakhah *is* the source. The Halakhah is the objectification of the Torah.

Q: But then you are saying the Halakhah as part of Torah, is a book without an author.

LEIBOWITZ: It is not a book.

Q: It is a library without an author.

LEIBOWITZ: It's not a library. It is a program of life.

Q: What gives it authority?

LEIBOWITZ: *Itself* is the authority. That is the basis of historical Judaism for about two thousand and two hundred years. That is a matter of fact, the essence of Judaism.

Q: Are you not sacralizing a literary text? *You* are making it sacred. You are saying it is the authority. What is your proof?

LEIBOWITZ: That is my decision. What is your authority for you to be honest and decent instead of the contrary?

Q: But that is precisely the problem. Suppose I say, the Halakhah has no authority?

LEIBOWITZ: You may say so.

Q: Then, it is my decision?

LEIBOWITZ: The majority of Jews now say it. But that is the make-up of historical Judaism.

Q: But once more I want to pinpoint the question. When I think of mitzvot, I imply a metzaveh. Who is the metzaveh? Is it Moses, Hillel, Shammai, Akiba?

LEIBOWITZ: No, it is the Torah itself. Who is the authority for you to be honest and decent and not a scoundrel? Honesty and decency are the authority.

Q: And suppose I don't believe in honesty and decency. Suppose I say honesty and decency is the standard of fools.

LEIBOWITZ: Then you won't be an honest and decent person.

Q: That leaves us precisely where you started out.

LEIBOWITZ: If you don't accept the authority of the Halakhah, you cease to be a follower of historical Judaism. That is the crisis of historical Judaism today.

Q: What do you think of liberal or Reform Jews who say, the Halakhah is good for guidance but not for governance. I want to make my own choice. "Governance" means dictating, imposing upon me a way of life. "Guidance" suggests giving instruction, a model.

LEIBOWITZ: Why do we accept the authority of the state? It is your decision to accept it.

Q: And do you have any problem with Reform Jews who make a different decision from Orthodox Jews?

LEIBOWITZ: Certainly, it is a total break between us. We can't eat at the same table; we can't intermarry; we can't work at the same working place; we can not educate our children together and we won't even be buried together.

Q: But the Reform Jew makes a conscientious choice.

LEIBOWITZ: Certainly, I don't deny it.

Q: So his conscience tells him that, e.g., *shatnez* [Biblical prohibition of mixing certain fibers] is a folkloristic idea, and not a divine commandment.

LEIBOWITZ: I know. But that is a total break between us.

Q: Why would you say that the conscience, the decision of the Reform Jew to set aside much of the Halakhah is less valid than your conscience which tells you that Halakhah is the authoritative written and oral tradition as formulated by the Orthodox rabbinate and binding as such?

LEIBOWITZ: That is my decision, I accept it as valid.

Q: I think that is your final word.

LEIBOWITZ: It is my final word. The same goes for decency and honesty. Exactly the same thing.

Q: Let me turn to another matter. We discussed briefly Martin Buber. You made your opinion very clear. Buber and others speak of the "encounter with God." Does "encounter" or the experience of God by man make any sense to you?

LEIBOWITZ: Certainly, encounter with God is the fulfillment of the mitzvot.

Q: Is that the only kind of encounter?

LEIBOWITZ: If I washed today, at half past six in the morning, and went to the *bet ha-knesset* [synagogue] to fulfill the *mitzvot t'fillah* [prayer duty], that was my encounter with God.

Q: And suppose you have a different encounter, suppose like Elijah you hear a *kol d'mamah dakkah* [still, small voice]?

LEIBOWITZ: I don't hear any voice.

Q: Would you, then, credit the experiences of others who say that God told them, or in some way inspired them, or guided them, to do or say this or that?

LEIBOWITZ: Why should the psychology of other people bother me?

Q: Then, you do not recognize encounters other than the performance of mitzvah, which is the meeting place between the Jew and the metzaveh?

LEIBOWITZ: Any other encounter is paganism.

Q: Would you say it's a fake?

LEIBOWITZ: It is a service of *elohim acherim* [other gods].

Q: I have one more question which we left out of our discussion. It has to do with the meaning of *brit*, of covenant. You asked me beforehand when we started, what holds the Jewish people together.

LEIBOWITZ: Today—nothing.

Q: Nothing?

LEIBOWITZ: Certainly. Some element of consciousness.

Q: How about memory?

LEIBOWITZ: I don't know whether it is memory.

Q: What about those of us who believe in a covenant, in a brit?

LEIBOWITZ: Certainly, brit means obligation.

Q: Do you think that such a covenant actually exists between God and the Jewish people?

LEIBOWITZ: Which means the obligation of the Jewish people to accept the ol malchut ha-shamayim. Certainly it exists. But, it is not now observed by the majority of Jews.

Q: Then what does God do about it?

LEIBOWITZ: *Ha-tachat elohim ani*? [Am I in the place of God?] How can I tell you what God will do?

Q: What about the Biblical blessings and curses, the promises that God will reward the people for the fulfillment and punish them for the violation of the brit?*

LEIBOWITZ: I know the history of 3,500 years of the Jewish people and this history doesn't reflect the intervention of God in human affairs. It reflects the relationship that sixty or eighty generations of Jews had with God.

---

*See Deut. 28.

Cynthia Ozick

C ynthia Ozick defines herself as a "traditional" but not strictly
observant Jew. Her husband is president of an Orthodox
synagogue. Her uncle on her mother's side was the Hebrew poet
Abraham Regelson. Lively in conversation, she keeps a sharp and
slightly mischievous eye open, ready to exploit a comical situation. She is very much the wife and mother despite her absorbing
commitment to art. Her novels including *The Cannibal Galaxy, The
Messiah of Stockholm, The Shawl*, as well as her volumes of short stories, notably *The Pagan Rabbi and Other Stories*, have made her a
major figure in American letters. *What Henry James Knew and Other
Essays on Writers* and her first play, *Angel*, are soon to be published.

As a young adult, Ozick began to read Jewish history and philosophy seriously, and she credits her learned father for her
Litvish misnagdish rationalism in opposition to the emotionalism of
the Hasidim. Her daughter received a Hebrew day school education and spent time in Israel on an archeological dig. For Cynthia
Ozick the support and defense of Israel is a moral imperative.

Ozick scintillates in conversation. Not only her ideas but her

153

whole personality come across with charm and humor. After categorically rejecting the belief in the hereafter, she playfully indulges fantasies about paradise such as "eating tons of fudge" or having her mother sit with her to "tell her everything."

She speaks of her prayer experience of exultation and boredom and the books that have influenced her most. She describes herself as an absolute monotheist. No attribute can do justice to God. Any description would deflect from the true God and lead to that which is not God, a step to paganism. She respects the Orthodox practice of avoiding even the word "God" by referring to "the Name." She would go a step further and speak of the One "without name." Her personal credo, in which she tells of the joy of being Jewish, should hearten every Jew throughout the world. We spoke at the Lotus Club, 5 East 66th Street, in Manhattan, Sunday, February 2, 1992.

Q: When asking you about your religious beliefs, be assured I am not looking for textbook theology. I take it for granted that—

OZICK: That I don't know any.

Q: No, I take it for granted that there is a considerable amount of skepticism, as well as half-hearted beliefs and half-baked religious ideas among contemporary Jews, including rabbis. Do you see yourself as an ethnic Jew or as a religious Jew?

OZICK: Well, the first adjective, "ethnic," I repudiate one hundred percent. If you look it up in a dictionary, an old dictionary before sociology has taken hold, you discover that the definition of ethnic is "neither Christian nor Jew"; it derives from the Greek word for pagan. Neither Christian nor Jew is precisely what its first meaning is. And then the sociologists come along and give the word the resonance of nationality or primary identity; but I reject that totally.

Q: It doesn't apply to you?

OZICK: It doesn't apply to Jews because in this society it suggests a marginality, away from the mainstream, and I regard being a Jew, whether religious or not, as part of the mainstream. I can't call myself a religious Jew either, because, again, I have a problem with the word "religious." It lacks a Jewish sensibility.

Q: A "believing" Jew, is that a better word?

OZICK: That's even more difficult. I feel with Geoffrey Hartman that there are three pillars of Western civilization: Classicism, Christianity, and Judaism. And since "ethnic" is so marginalizing, I wonder how you can possibly apply it to one of the main-stream's pillars.

Q: What would you apply to the over one million Jews who, according to the latest 1990 Jewish population survey, identify themselves as Jews without religion?

OZICK: They are Jews.

Q: You insist that they're Jews though not religious. Would you agree that they are religiously uninformed or uncommitted?

OZICK: Are they uncommitted?

Q: They declare no religion.

OZICK: Still, they might be committed to something. They might have, at the least, a kind of instinctive feeling for the survival of Israel.

Q: Would you consider yourself a Jew in the broad cultural sense, which would include identification with the religious experience of our people?

OZICK: Yes, I believe there is something to the covenant. I feel myself to be a covenanted Jew. But I worry about words like "religious" or "believing" because all these terms lead us to some kind of substantive declaration about the Godhead. I admire the practice of traditional Jews when they put a hyphen between the G and the D in the spelling of God because they want to avoid all attributes whatsoever. If I say I am religious, then somebody is going to ask, "Does that mean you believe in God?" And then if I say, if I even utter, "God," it seems to me I am ascribing some imagery to that syllable. We should take very seriously the series of fences around what we call God. When the children in our day schools refer to *ha-Shem* [the Name, i.e., God], it makes me smile;

maybe they should say *b'li Shem* [without a name]. At any rate, I'm afraid to voice the concept. I don't want to seem to imply anything descriptive.

Q: Without wanting to describe God, would you say that you live in awareness of the reality or presence of God? Is this a part of your consciousness—perhaps, at certain times, with great intensity, and at other times not at all?

OZICK: Yom Kippur does it. That's the day when I probably can call myself a believer. Year after year this happens; it may be the result of fasting and of immersing oneself, saturating oneself, in prayer and poetry all day long. In general, I am nonmystical and I don't think about God.

Q: What kind of synagogue do you attend on Yom Kippur? Is it the same always or do you go to different synagogues?

OZICK: No, it is the same always. I am a member of an Orthodox synagogue in New Rochelle.

Q: Do you sense something of the numinous, something of the charismatic presence of the deity?

OZICK: It sometimes comes flying out of the text. It will not come out of the social context of the synagogue. Sometimes it comes out of the liturgy, although at times I have the sense of a prayer wheel, e.g., during the Mussaf* year after year.

Q: It stirs you?

OZICK: The opposite; it stirs me to intense tedium.

Q: That is one of the fascinations of religion. It can switch from tedium to inspiration and back to tedium again.

OZICK: Certain aspects never become tedious. The Alenu† prayer never turns into a prayer wheel. The Alenu prayer always has the

---

*Literally, "addition," referring to special prayers added for the Sabbath and festivals to the standard liturgy.
†A visionary prayer in conclusion of every Jewish worship service which reaffirms the covenant and envisages the perfection of the world and the unification of all humanity under the one and only God.

capacity to kind of kick me into an awareness and excitement, week after week.

Q: Does religion function otherwise in your personal life?

OZICK: Oh yes, on Shabbat.

Q: To what extent? Lighting candles?

OZICK: Lighting candles, Kiddush [sanctification of the day], *challah* [twisted bread], and chicken for dinner . . .

Q: Family togetherness?

OZICK: Our family is tiny—my husband, myself, and my daughter. She is usually away from home, but just now she happens to be with us for a few months, and so Shabbat sort of increases. Last Friday night, after the Kiddush and after the meal, we sat and read aloud from the new issue of *Commentary*, Robert Alter's piece on the Dead Sea Scrolls which wasn't exactly *zemirot* [songs].

Q: But it focused on something Jewish. Do you generally try to structure Shabbat as a day different from other days?

OZICK: Yes. We go to *shul* [synagogue].

Q: Regularly? Does your husband also have a traditional Orthodox background?

OZICK: He is the president of our shul. Right now he is getting an *Eruv* [extension of area in which it is permitted to carry things on the Sabbath] for our shul. That's a big project.

Q: Then he is a real activist.

OZICK: He had to be persuaded! He said: "If nominated, I will not accept, if elected I will not serve." But he has now begun his second term. That doesn't make either one of us models of full observance. Yet we have *kashrut* and we have shabbat.

Q: So you keep a kosher home?

OZICK: I feel that *kashrut* is one of the great gifts of and to the Jewish people. It is a tremendous source for the idea of *havdalah* [distinction].

Q: The distinction between the forbidden and the permitted? Or do you mean havdalah in another sense?

OZICK: The separation of *milchik* and *fleishik* [dairy and meat], forks and knives, you might say, has no overt *metaphysical* importance. It certainly—superficially—suggests triviality.

Q: It doesn't make much rational sense to you?

OZICK: I wouldn't say it is irrational in terms of the rabbinic argument for not mixing meat and dairy food. But beyond this, it's a constant reminder of larger ideas. First of all, it teaches you on a simple, trivial everyday plane, that one thing is not another thing. And so, if you follow that up, you come to a huge, thundering reminder: God is not man. Is there a distinction between the Creator and the created? In other words, this quotidian, humble, knives-and-forks reminder of distinction-making becomes a daily monitor of larger distinctions—so that you will never commit intellectual blurring.

Distinction-making has an intellectual resonance which leads to the heart of monotheism. You are never going to be, you could not become a Christian, if you separate milchik from fleishik, because you will know that you cannot blur or blend the mind of the human creature with the mind of the Creator, you must *not* confuse man with God. Another reason to value *kashrut* is that wherever I go, this practice sets me aside as a Jew. It will never be forgotten by me or by anybody else. I was recently a writer-in-residence at a college. Great efforts were made to accommodate me with food. Nobody could forget that I was a Jew because of the fuss over the food, a minor fuss, it wasn't a lot, nevertheless it reminded me—and them.

Q: Would you consider yourself more observant, more religious than your parents were?

OZICK: My parents were a lot less observant than I was as a child. My father used to call me *frum vi a shtekn* [pious as a stick]. My parents were pharmacists and they had their pharmacy open seven days a week with incredibly long hours. Nevertheless they retained kashrut meticulously and were intensely conscious Jews. My father was a *talmid chacham* [scholar] and my mother's brother,

Abraham Regelson, was a Hebrew poet and a Zionist. He left in '33 for Palestine; then in '36 there were the Arab riots and he lost a child. He came back and went again, permanently, in '48.

Q: Did any personal experience, a book or an event or encounter with someone, radically change your thinking?

OZICK: At the age of twenty-five I read an essay by Leo Baeck, "Romantic Religion,"* and that, I must say, impassioned me in terms of distinction-making, Baeck's distinction between romantic and classical religion. I have not read that essay for many years and I don't know how it would impress me today, but at the time it seemed to clarify and decode a world for me, and I think I owe everything that happened in my reading afterward to the encounter with that, to me, then, very remarkable essay. It is distinguished by great insight and erudition and is not merely a polemic against Christianity, but against all essentially mystical religion. I guess you could also define it as a *mitnaggedik* [opposed to Hasidism] essay.

Q: Do you think of God in the Platonic-Aristotelian sense as an idea, the first cause, the immovable mover, or do you think of God as also a personal being with whom you can maintain some kind of relationship?

OZICK: Well, there are times when I am a primitive Jew or a primitive child, when I privately say Sh'ma [declaration of God's oneness, Deut. 6.4] with huge passion and feel the immediacy of that cry, and the urgency, and my need for it and, in a sense, the universe's need for it. But when my soul is not in danger or when Israel is not in peril, I think probably more along Aristotelian lines as you've just described it, intellectually, yet enormously contradicted by life's crises and emergencies.

Q: Have you been affected by any modern Jewish thinker—Buber, Rosenzweig, Fackenheim, Heschel?

OZICK: In my twenties I read Buber. Later I was very interested in Fackenheim's book *Encounters Between Judaism and Modern Phi-*

---

*In Leo Baeck, *Judaism and Christianity*, Jewish Publication Society, Philadelphia, 1958.

*losophy.** I was quite swept away by it. Heschel is probably, at least in part, too mystical for me. Rosenzweig's *The Star of Redemption*† is too hard for me.

Q: For that matter even Buber's *I and Thou* is virtually incomprehensible over a number of pages.

OZICK: But still we know what he is getting at.

Q: The core idea comes across.

OZICK: Yes, Buber is accessible and the *Tales of the Hasidim*‡ are, I think, a literary masterwork.

Q: Have you been able to relate to God in any personal sense, through prayer, for example?

OZICK: Well, lately I've taken to waking up in the morning, and saying: "*Modah-ani* [I thank Thee]." I think this is a function of age and gratitude.

Q: Strange that this grateful affirmation of life, the first words of prayer to be recited by the Jew each day, should come from the Book of Lamentations, which was composed in the depth of national distress.

OZICK: It testifies to having survived so much. As for our unitary credo, the Sh'ma, I may sometimes be guilty of turning it into a kind of mantra, although I have a rule concerning my "use" of the Sh'ma: It must never be trivialized; it must never be personal; it must be related to peoplehood. I certainly wouldn't recite it, or any kind of prayer, in a personal or petitional way.

Q: Do you believe the Torah was revealed or inspired by God? What do you think of the claim of the prophet, "Thus says the Lord"?

---

*See Emil L. Fackenheim, *Encounters Between Judaism and Modern Philosophy*, Basic Books, New York, 1973.
†Franz Rosenzweig, *The Star of Redemption*, transl. William W. Hallo, Holt, Rinehart and Winston, New York, 1970.
‡Martin Buber, *Tales of the Hasidim*, Vols. I and II, Schocken Books, New York, 1947–48.

OZICK: If indeed there was revelation, I would want to say that it came to an end and not make a claim for on-going revelation. On-going interpretation of text, yes, but not on-going revelation. I am a member of a seminar at the Jewish Theological Seminary which meets once a month—the Genesis Seminar. We've been meeting for three-and-a-half years and we're still in Genesis! It goes very, very slowly. It's a once-a-month ecstasy, an "invention" in the sense that it combines Christians and Jews, but much more so in the sense that it puts together two groups between whom there is a great, natural, inborn barrier: imaginative writers and Biblical scholars, who think in two very different molds. And the premise of this seminar is that the text is a purely human product, that there is no divine inspiration, that J and E and P,* are types of minds and that what we have is a kind of workaday weaving together of old myths, folklore, poems. That is the premise. Nevertheless there is one person there, a writer who keeps almost literally tearing her hair and crying out, "But remember,"—her accent is wonderfully British—"Remember we are talking here about Gawd, Gawd." She brings us back to "Gawd" all the time.

Even though this is so strictly a secular, scholarly enterprise, I wonder, why do all these people come together in a room once a month? What inspires them? Is it just an old book that has been around for a long time? There is something here which deserves this tricky word "inspiration."

Q: So you don't want to make a final statement about whether God is in the Bible or whether God inspired or revealed it?

OZICK: I would not want to make any statement about the nature of God, the works of God, or the conduct of God.

Q: You are treating the Bible as a human document?

OZICK: Well, it is; yes, it is a human document. Your question seems to go beyond that to ask, is it inspired?

Q: Underlying the whole concept of the human being may well be the assumption that the human being is never separated from

---

*For J and P see footnote on p. 68. E refers to the Elohist source according to the Documentary Theory.

God. Whatever is part of human creativity may well have a divine element in it. The difficulty is how to tell apart the human element from the divine element.

OZICK: One of the terribly troubling aspects of this train of reflection is the dread fact of mortality. My daughter is an archeologist specializing in tombs. In connection with Robert Alter's piece about the Dead Sea Scrolls, we were talking about the Egyptians and their chemistry, their efforts to preserve the human body. In a shallow burial, the corpse is reduced to bones in forty years; in another hundred years, bones are dust, literally powder. And so you wonder, what is there about the structure of our universe which, on the one hand, turns us to dust—in the most literal way, we utterly vanish—and on the other hand, gives us this spark within us which demands to know and to continue and refuses to be snuffed out?

Q: Our mental and spiritual outreach is far greater than our normal environment would call for.

OZICK: But if you think of this from the point of view of the Creator, it seems to me an abyss of cruelty that we are inspirited with this longing, this curiosity, with what seems like the divine spark, only to have it end. Of course it goes on in the plasma from generation to generation. The individual dies, the species doesn't.

Q: One theologian put it this way. We human beings seem to carry with us much more baggage than is necessary for our journey on earth.

OZICK: Or, perhaps not enough baggage because you don't want to let go.

Q: Not enough to know where we are going . . . You are very covenant conscious. You feel that there is some sort of bond between yourself and our people. Is this bond something metaphysical? Can you think of God having chosen our people?

OZICK: I think so. I do. In a post-Enlightenment world this belief is an embarrassment; it seems like dreadful exclusivity. You can find numbers of tribes here, there, and everywhere which also make this claim of chosenness: So, you can bring a great deal of anthropological skepticism to such a proposition. But then, you look at the course of human history, how the Jews have outlasted everyone, except for the Chinese, who have likewise been there immemorially. But not with a steady and single-minded idea. The Chinese have changed their metaphysics from primitive cults to Confucianism to Buddhism to state communism. We've always been and remained monotheists.

Q: Yet there have been many different cultural transformations in our history.

OZICK: Right, but aren't we essentially what we were when Father Abraham expressed his first religious insight? And our history has been as turbulent as it has been because of our stiffnecked-ness in clinging to this metaphysical singularity, which seems to be compromised in all its other forms. Christianity, though it would deny it, appears to be a compromised monotheism. Islam compromises in a different way. Though steadfastly monotheistic in principle, Islam's belief in fate, I think, casts a compromising shadow.

Q: You feel that monotheism is the golden thread tying together the millennial Jewish experience and underlying the Jewish sense of identity?

OZICK: Yes, it is that which differentiates the Jewish view of God from all other God-concepts on the planet. The idea of One Creator unifies humankind. It obviates divisions like "your God" and "my God."

Q: The concept of a chosen people plainly suggests a role for God in history. Can you believe in that?

OZICK: I don't see it rationally and intellectually. Yet, in some underground way, I feel that Jewish history has a chosen quality to it, and I don't mean chosen for victimization. Quite the opposite. I mean rather, chosen to say "no" to what the ordinary human creature wants to do; to say "no" to the evil impulse, to causeless hatred, to violence. It's no accident that the Commandments are largely negative. If unrestrained, untamed, the human being is a predator, a beast of prey.

Jacques Maritain, a truly Catholic philosopher, once remarked that evil is really *someone*; I think that is very striking. He said it from a Catholic point of view, given that he's got Satan in his theology. Yet we know that there are beings in the form of humans who actually *are* vessels of evil. We've lived to see the hatred of Jews overcome a whole people, a whole continent. I'm reminded of Ruth Wisse's interpretation of a story by Mendele* called *The Mayor*; there is a vision at the end where a would-be medical student is carried aloft by the devil to look over all of Europe, and all of Europe is one big bloody pogrom.

Q:That's a visionary isn't it? Prophetic!

OZICK: As a pre-Holocaust story, it *was* prophetic. But perhaps not so prophetic after all, because if you consider the history of Europe relating to the Jews since the eleventh century, from the time of the first Crusade, you may see it as a kind of vertical Holocaust—not horizontal, all at once, but in sporadic outbursts through the centuries. As I view it, Jews are not exempt from the temptations to violence of the ordinary human article. But, our heritage urges "no." Torah teaches restraint.

Q: Can you imagine divine intercession in the affairs of humanity and, ultimately, in personal life?

OZICK: Rationally, no. But I like what Maurice Samuel said about the salvational outcome of the Six Day War, something like: the miracle of it is that it wasn't a miracle.

Q: The Messiah is the personification of our belief that God will intercede, intervene, and play a role in our life. What do you think of the Messiah?

OZICK: I am drawn to Maimonides' definition of Messianism. I guess it was the *Rambam* [Maimonides] my father was referring to when in 1948 he said we live in *Moshiach Zeiten* [Messianic times]. The *Rambam* defined the Messianic Age as the time when the Jewish people would be restored to political autonomy.

Q: Shaking off bondage and oppression?

---

*Mendele Mocher Sforim, pseudonym of Shalom Jacob Abramovitsch (d. 1917), very popular Yiddish writer.

OZICK: Yes. And even though we've achieved that, we know the Messiah still hasn't come. A free and independent Israel is an absolute requirement, but then there is more work to do after that.

Q: What I hear you saying is that the Messiah is a *symbol* of development in human affairs or in history. What about the Messiah as a person?

OZICK: Unacceptable. Whenever we have held such a belief, it has engendered devastation afterward: Bar Kochba, and Shabbatai Zvi whose movement degenerated in the Frankist sect, even as much earlier a Messiah cult led to Christianity. And haven't we seen the Messiah idea, personified and concretized, reflected in the Soviet Union?

Q: Are you referring to political utopianism?

OZICK: Yes. Messianism, when it departs from the yoke of Torah, goes wild. There is peril in Messianism without Torah. But even if Messianism doesn't cancel out Torah, I believe that once you have the Messiah personified in an individual or in a state or in a system of any kind, you have already broken with monotheism.

Q: Can you imagine any significant improvement in human affairs without a human agent producing it?

OZICK: We are all agents for the extension of justice. We have been given the means, the instrument, which is Torah. Our task then is to saturate ourselves in Torah and to begin to apply it. No individual is going to come wrapped in the mantle of the Messiah and do it for us. We've got to do it ourselves.

Q: Looking now into the farthest future, namely the other world—what do you think?

OZICK: The afterlife? *Gan eden* [paradise]?

Q: With regard to the hereafter, the soul, the spirit and the belief in resurrection which is still, at least, formally maintained by Orthodox Judaism—what do you personally believe?

OZICK: These beliefs came in very late, from Persian sources, I think.

Q: Correct. You find the first important Biblical reference to the hereafter in the rather late Book of Daniel, chapter 12, which speaks of the righteous of this earth rising from the dust to eternal life.

OZICK: A coincidence! I was just reading the Book of Daniel last night.

Q: You will find it in the last chapter. Now, is this in any way meaningful to you?

OZICK: No, I utterly reject any notion of afterlife.

Q: Immortality, in any sense, is not an important idea in your own vocabulary of faith?

OZICK: No, in fact I think it an illusion or delusion. I think it a superstition. The tradition was wiser at an earlier time. *Olam haba* [the world-to-come] is a pleasant fairy tale. No, it is not a reality for me. It's something to talk about in a mythical and fictional way. For instance, I know exactly what I want to do in the afterlife, and I've already written it in a story. I want to sit under a tree and eat tons of fudge without ever getting tooth decay; and read piles of books that I am never going to get to in this life, such as *Kristin Lavransdatter*, by Sigrid Undset, and countless others, all huge and, so far, unread.

Q: You are probably looking at your library and feel accused by hundreds of books that charge you with neglect.

OZICK: They are for the afterlife. And I have another program for the afterlife. Literary history offers minds that would have been wonderful candidates for Judaism but never had the opportunity to acquire this learning while alive. For instance, Samuel Johnson. If I gave you, Rabbi Haberman, Samuel Johnson for half an hour, he is so on the verge and such a *mitnagged** that you could convert him in no time at all. But this won't happen in the absence of *olam haba* because you have to have a meeting place. That is the function of the afterlife for me, just fun.

_____

*Specifically "anti-Hasidic," but here meant in the broader sense of "skeptical."

Q: Is it a metaphor? A dream?

OZICK: A fantasy of paradise.

Q: Of beautiful things that may have been denied to you in this life?

OZICK: And I would also like so much to have my mother catch up on things. I would like in gan eden to sit with my mother and tell her everything.

Q: Well, isn't this something that all of us feel? If only we could renew the relationship with our parents or grandparents who have predeceased us. Such a relationship is never severed, not even by death. The survivor continues to build and rebuild the relationship.

OZICK: It is an eternal dialogue.

Q: What appeals to you the most in your Jewish heritage? What makes you feel good about being Jewish? Do you have moments of alienation and anxiety when you are embarrassed by your people and by your faith?

OZICK: No, I am never embarrassed as a Jew. As a Jew I am free. I feel enormously grateful to be a Jew. I despise the phrase "proud to be a Jew." It is usually spoken, obtusely, by half-illiterates; the person who says it is, in his heart, vulnerable and ashamed. But I feel free, facing the whole wide world in my Jewishness. I may not be able to say what God is, who God is, how God is; I can make no definitive statement, no attributive statement about the Source of Being. But I can say what the Source is not. I'm free of idols, I'm not going to fall for false gods, false ideas. I'm buoyed up, I'm shaped by ethical monotheism, by Torah. And I'm not going to be tempted, nor will I ever be fooled, by an idol. You can see through such a device, you know an idol from miles away because you have been taught Torah. You know how to make a distinction between reality and illusion, between the actual and the fraudulent. Judaism is a training toward intellectual freedom and expansiveness and insight. That is what Jewishness does for me today. It has helped me come through. I had a very difficult childhood. I was stoned, I was called a Christ killer.

Q: Where was that?

OZICK: In the Northeast Bronx, an entirely gentile neighborhood. My parents had a drugstore there. I was the only Jewish
kid in my class, practically in the whole school. The teachers were
mainly Irish-Catholic. I encountered a great deal of anti-Semitism in my childhood and knew very few Jews outside of my own
family. A psychiatrist once drew me aside and said a canny thing:
"You have a rather ideal view of the Jewish people because you
didn't grow up with Jews." There might be some truth in that.

Q: Your antagonists in early life were not Jews but gentiles?

OZICK: That's right. And for a long, long time I had no sense of
Jewish sociology. I didn't know the difference between the Jewish
intellectual and the Jewish worker. Even in my twenties, I didn't
understand a thing about class or locality. I didn't know what
Jewish deprivation was because, even though my eyes would see
Jews living in poor tenements, these to me were aristocrats, ideal-
ists. This is the childhood lesson I got from my mother who, as a
buffer against all the neighborhood anti-Semitism, told me that I
was, after all, the offspring of Queen Esther—royalty, a blue-
blood, an aristocrat. And so I absolutely grew up with the idea of
the Jews as an aristocratic people. And in terms of a heritage of
high civilization, we *are* an aristocratic people. Nevertheless, I
have since encountered *amcha* [our ordinary people] and have
learned a little more.

Q: You are a writer to whom books are very important. On what
scale would you put the Bible in terms of influencing your thinking as an author and as a Jew?

OZICK: As a writer in English, I have been influenced by the literary tradition of England and the U.S. The Bible in English has
not been an influence on me in any literary way at all, essentially
because in my formative years I did not encounter it in English.
In fact, my earliest experience of it was through the *Tsena U'rena*
["Come out and see"—title of an immensely popular Yiddish
Bible commentary]. My *bubba* [grandmother] read it aloud to
me, and I was enchanted. Now there is art, the "Dickens" of the
Jewish people; and the loveliness of the retellings and the closeness of God and Yiddish! These things formed me as a Jew with

their "heimishkeit" (familiarity), the sense of the closeness of God. The exclamation *Gottenyu!* [our God] is not a cry of frustration but a cherishing diminutive, expressing love, coziness, closeness . . .

Q: It expresses a whole faith, doesn't it?

OZICK: Yes.

Q: Have you read further in the Bible, in English or Hebrew, beyond Genesis and Exodus?

OZICK: Of course I have read Tanakh [Bible] again and again. You can hardly be a *shul*-goer without an annual exposure to Chumash [Pentateuch]! Only as an adult did I bring together the experience of the Jewish child and the broader literary temper. I began to read extensively in Jewish history and Jewish philosophy. In my middle twenties, after encountering Baeck, I fell into a huge, mad undertaking. I was reading in those years sixteen hours a day, insatiably. This went on for five, six or seven years, reading not only but preponderantly Jewish things. An autodidact has huge gaps—what is the phrase—if you teach yourself, you have a fool for a teacher. It was all done in English, an obvious limitation.

Q: Which Jewish book, either in the Bible or outside the Bible, would you credit with the most direct influence upon you?

OZICK: It is probably the least "Jewish" book of all and that is Koheleth [Book of Ecclesiastes].

Q: You found it intriguing?

OZICK: For its truth and the gravity of its realism. Also, the Psalms and the Joseph story. When you get to the Joseph story in the round of Torah reading in shul and you read it with absorption and concentration, you are made to weep anew every year.

Q: You mentioned Leo Baeck—did any of the Jewish poets, medieval or modern, or other Jewish writers or thinkers play a particular role in your reading or in your thinking?

OZICK: Among the poets, Judah Halevi, sweet singer of Israel of the Spanish period. In *Haskalah* [Enlightenment] literature, I remember reading in college, when I began to study modern Hebrew, a novel which thrilled me, Mordecai Zeeb Feirberg's *Le'an*. That was an arresting novel, even though it was so negative about the boy sitting in the dusty synagogue with his studies and waiting to escape.

Q: How often have you been to Israel?

OZICK: Nine times.

Q: Do you share any of the misgivings voiced by a number of American Jews about Israel's political course?

OZICK: I want them to rationalize their electoral system. I want them to privatize their economy and not be the last socialist entity on the face of the earth.

Q: Where do you usually stay in Israel?

OZICK: Mostly Jerusalem.

Q: Does Jerusalem affect you in any particular way?

OZICK: Oh God, yes, absolutely. There is such a sense of coming home. Sometimes I am suspicious of how happy I am in Israel. How can such a thing be? Miracles do happen in Jerusalem. I remember how one Friday the telephones were out of order in the hotel where we were staying and no one could reach us. The next day my husband and I were walking along the street, trying to decide what *shul* to go to on that Shabbat morning, and I saw a woman coming toward us, an utter stranger. She was carrying a siddur [prayerbook] and, just on an impulse, I went up to her and said, "We are looking for a service to go to." She answered me, "I am going to Penina Pelli's women's minyan [quorum for a public worship service]." So I abandoned my husband and went with her. When I got there Penina Pelli said, "You know I was trying to reach you by telephone to invite you to this minyan."

Q: When you look over the panorama of Jewish life, does anything impress you particularly? For example, what do you think of the Lubavitch movement, going after Jews in all corners of the world, trying to bring them back?

OZICK: Pragmatically speaking, if a Jewish kid is wearing a saffron robe, better he should be with Lubavitch. Hasidim lived as Jews and they certainly died as Jews in great numbers in the Holocaust. Yet, I confess I think certain aspects of the Hasidic movement are Christological and, in some way, heretical. The adoration, even the veneration, of the rebbe, for instance. I have a college friend who is now a member of a Hasidic community, one unlike the Lubavitch, not given to outreach. She is a rational person, a businesswoman of great intelligence and huge worldly ability. She believes that the rebbe can see the future. I am immediately put off by such magical beliefs.

Q: Are they heretical?

OZICK: They are cultic. And yet Hasidism is a part of Jewish history. Maybe this touch of occultism should be overlooked because Hasidim are, after all, Jews, and have suffered as Jews.

Q: There are in Israel today groups, not very strong ones or powerful groups, but there are groups who believe in the imminence of the Messiah. They are waiting for a personal Messiah—not a symbol, not an age, but a real Messiah. Is this a viable possibility? I personally cannot bring myself to believe that a Messiah, as a single person, will make an appearance, but I have some second thoughts. After all, the great changes in human history have come about through great individuals who tremendously influenced their own and future generations.

OZICK: This is a hope for great leadership. But that is different from the hope for a supernatural Messiah.

Q: Now just a few weeks ago, I read an interesting article by the late Rabbi Steven Schwarzschild who was professor at Washington University in St. Louis, in which he argued for the rehabilitation of the Messianic person, feeling that it is not contrary to reason. To believe in the Messiah as a person is no more unreasonable than to believe in the Messianic Age.

OZICK: There is an article in the current *New Yorker* about Jesse Jackson, who adheres to just this point of view. It isn't a stupid article about a stupid person by any means. But there is a difference between wanting significant leadership and wanting a leader. The craving for a hero is very dangerous, both for the putative hero and for his followers.

Q: I wonder, could such a world-redeeming leader be just an ordinary person? Could he do the job all by himself? Could this happen without some major change in human nature?

OZICK: It's Utopia!

Q: Such a leader could only come about when the rest of mankind has also risen to a very high level, not yet foreseeable.
OZICK: Is this what the Hasidim mean when they say that the Messiah will come on the day that all Jews observe the Sabbath together?

Q: When they observe two successive Sabbaths to perfection. In other words, there would have to be a correspondence between the superiority of the Messiah and the superiority of the generation in which he can become effective. Each generation gets the leader it deserves.

OZICK: You know, rabbi, the democratic nature of the Jewish people is brought home to me in shul whenever, during the *duchanen* [priestly blessing] the *Kohanim* [priests] appear veiled by their prayer shawls and I know exactly which members of our congregation they are. They are not all very elevated human beings. I steal looks at them (though we're not supposed to glance at them because folklore says we'll go blind), and their great dignity with the *Shekhinah* [divine presence] over their *taleitim* [prayer shawls] is always subverted by my sense of who this or that Mister Cohen really is.

Q: It is almost humorous, isn't it?

OZICK: Right. I'm glad that we are a democratic people and have leaders that are funny. Herzl, our great Zionist, was after all a frivolous playwright, a boulevardier.

Q: We have more or less successfully avoided deifying our leaders. Herzl has turned out, on closer examination, to have been a rather defective person and certainly a very inadequate Jew.

OZICK: His son converted.

Q: His whole family life was abominable and his own character leaves much to be desired. However, isn't it amazing how persons lacking so much can do so much more than we would expect.

OZICK: That is the other side of the story.

Arno Penzias

A 1978 Nobel laureate in physics, Arno Penzias spent his early childhood in Munich. In 1939, at the age of six, he escaped with his family to England, and arrived in New York a year later. He studied chemistry at the City College of New York and chose physics as a profession in order to escape the poverty his family encountered in the United States. After obtaining his Ph.D. from Columbia, he joined the staff of AT&T Bell Laboratories where his research on cosmic radio emissions led to the so-called Big Bang theory of the origin of the universe.

Raised in a traditionally observant home—his mother had converted to Judaism—Arno Penzias is an active member of a Conservative synagogue in New Brunswick, New Jersey. A fiercely loyal Jew with a strong attachment to Israel, he helped Russian Jewish Refuseniks in their struggle for the right to emigrate. Immediately after he received the Nobel Prize he went from Stockholm to Moscow to deliver his Nobel Lecture at the home of Viktor Brailovsky, the Soviet Jewish dissident who was later imprisoned for eight years and released in 1988. Penzias's daughter, Shifra, is studying to be a rabbi at the Hebrew Union College-Jewish Institute of Religion.

If anyone still thinks that science is in conflict with religion, a dialogue with Arno Penzias should lay that notion to rest. Science and religion are not conflicting but complementary competencies, according to Penzias, who thinks science is best when descriptive but is on shaky ground when it tries to explain things. Religion is mankind's attempt at explaining the world. Explanations cannot be proven. His definition of religion: "Religion is that which we know beyond what we can prove."

The God he believes in is not one he has come to know through personal experience. It is a God derived from the evidence of order in the universe. Order implies purpose and purpose points to someone who creates it. God is for Penzias the "owner" of the world's purpose. But his faith is by no means certain: "The thing I wrestle with at all times is the reality of God."

Belief in the chosenness of the Jewish people is among his strongest affirmations. The divine blueprint for the world must have reserved a special place for the Jewish people even if we grant that "chosenness is a two-way street," which is to say, "God chose the Jews but the Jews also chose God." We spoke in Jerusalem on November 11, 1991.

Q: Would you say that you are Conservative, Orthodox, Reform, or "none of the above"?

PENZIAS: I call myself Conservative. We chose a very, very observant Conservative synagogue in our area. You may be surprised to hear that at Sukkot [Feast of Tabernacles], for example, on a weekday, the majority of the congregation will be in *shul* [synagogue]. Maybe 500 people in shul on a weekday Sukkot. They will sell 200 or 300 *etrogim* [citrus fruit]. There are some 150 sukkot built in town. It's unique in the Conservative movement.

Q: Do you attribute that to the rabbi?

PENZIAS: Partly to the rabbi, Yaacov Hilsenrath. He is a remarkable man. He has turned people who lived in other towns Orthodox so that they moved to his town. The only problem is that he loses the kids, that is, the kids become Orthodox. Then, some of the people he has actually converted, made their homes kosher, and, after a while, stopped *davenning* [praying] in his Conservative shul.

Q: That is ironic, isn't it?

PENZIAS: Yes, it is. He himself is a Conservative rabbi but his own private observances go quite far. His lifestyle is that of an Orthodox person.

Q: What was your own religious upbringing?

PENZIAS: It was what we would call New York Conservative. I was born in Germany, in Munich. My father's family were Polish Jews and, as such, not terribly well accepted by the local Jews in Munich. The synagogue they belonged to was a Polish synagogue. The only synagogue that survived the war is the Polish because it was built between two apartment houses and the Nazis couldn't burn it down on *Kristallnacht*. I actually went back to the synagogue and gave a little talk once. There were ten children in my grandfather's family. One died in a concentration camp, but most of them survived and went to England. They had four sons and six daughters; one son married a Jewish woman in England; the other three sons married gentiles, including my father. My mother was the only one of these spouses that converted to Judaism.

Q: Did they came over to the U.S.A.?

PENZIAS: No. One actually remained in Germany where he was able to hide during the war. His son still lives there as a Christian. Another one went to England where he died. His children were raised in England, also as Christians. The youngest son married in England and has Jewish children. He has one son in America who became a Hasid, of all things. He also married a non-Jewish woman who converted, and both became Hasidim.

Q: You have a fascinating family.

PENZIAS: To be Jewish is to have a fascinating family. There are very few dull Jewish histories.

Q: So your mother was not born Jewish, she converted?

PENZIAS: Yes. She passed away earlier this year, after she was felled by a stroke in 1974 and progressively deteriorated, and was housebound for the last eight or ten years.

Q: Was your father observant?

PENZIAS: My father is very religious but not observant.

Q: Religious in a spiritual sense?

PENZIAS: Very much so. He has a very deep and emotional connection to Judaism. When he came to America, he had a complete set of personal prayer books. Even though we were quite poor as immigrants, we always were affiliated with the synagogue. We went to Hebrew School and, always, as a family, went to High Holy Day services where my parents were very proud of the fact that they, during all their lives, paid for seats. So, they weren't just "Yiskor-Jews" [Jews attending synagogue only at memorial services]. The house was not kosher.

Q: Were there Sabbath candles?

PENZIAS: Yes, there were candles lit. A big effort was made at Passover time to make the house kosher and use special Passover dishes. But we were not *shomer Shabbat* [strict Sabbath law observers]. Before I married my wife, a rabbi's daughter, I did actually put on *t'fillin* [phylacteries], partly as a way of identifying. I wanted some kind of personal observance. But when I became serious with Anne and I realized I was going to marry her, I stopped putting on t'fillin, because I now had another way of identifying with Judaism. Out of that came a much deeper level of observance, because my wife was shomer Shabbat. We keep a kosher home and only eat kosher foods in restaurants, even to this day. In fact, AT&T gets me kosher meals, so that at the vast majority of my functions, I eat only kosher food. When the food is questionable, I follow the Conservative standard of eating only fish or salads. I don't eat shellfish and I won't eat nonkosher meat.

Q: You evidently had a basically traditional upbringing and a positive orientation toward Judaism.

PENZIAS: There was also a negative factor, that is, I was negative toward Hitler. The one thing that Jews agree on, after the Holocaust, is that we must deny Hitler a posthumous victory. But that is really a negative.

Q: Emil Fackenheim is the originator of this rule which he calls the eleventh commandment, to deny Hitler a posthumous victory.

PENZIAS: It may not be the purpose of Jewish existence, but it certainly is a motive for Jewish activism, a driving force.

Q: As a student, did you have any inclinations toward religion or the humanities, or were you single-minded in your study of science?

PENZIAS: I was single-minded, economically driven. I didn't want to be poor any more. At first, I went to a technical high school and began an engineering course. Then I switched to physics, basically, with the notion that people who went to college lived better.

Q: Was your father college educated?

PENZIAS: Oh no. I was the first person in my family to attend university.

Q: When you pursued the study of physics, how intense was your feeling of conflict between science and religion?

PENZIAS: I've never felt a conflict between the two.

Q: Why not?

PENZIAS: To the extent that I ever thought about it, I always felt that they cover very different areas of human knowledge. I see science as describing the world. Science has no way of *explaining* the world. Religion attempts to explain it. When religion tries to get in the description business, it gets into trouble. On the other hand, when scientists are trying to explain things, *they* get in trouble.

Q: So you have made a separation between the areas of competence between religion and science.

PENZIAS: I think that science and religion are complementary competences. The underlying notions of science describe a physical world in unprovable but emotionally attractive terms. There is no way of proving that one scientific theory is correct and another one is not; there is no such thing. No one has ever proven a scientific theory. All one has ever done is accept one. I can take any scientific theory to make it fit the data simply by making it complicated enough. For example, we cannot prove that Newton's Laws are governing the motion of the universe. It may all be an accident or illusion. But the chances of that happening to us sound so silly that we reject it. We reject it simply because it is silly. I mean, suppose somebody said, "Oh no, it is a bunch of angels doing it and they made it look as if Newton's law wasn't working."

Q: Philosophers would say that you can not prove metaphysical assertions.

PENZIAS: True. What we are saying is that we have a body of knowledge, scientific knowledge, which describes the world in a very economical and very powerful way. It doesn't really say why anything happens. If I were to drop a fork right now, I would be able to say, "It falls because of gravity." All I'm really saying is that gravity is nothing more than a description of the force field between two bodies which have a property called "mass," which is itself described by other properties. But I don't know why the fork falls. I'm merely telling you how it falls.

Q: So your approach to science is really phenomenological, descriptive.

PENZIAS: That is all science does. When it prepares to do something else, it goes beyond its competence. There are people who, in the name of science, want to use science as a bludgeon with which to settle old scores, but I have little patience with such people. On the other hand, if someone were to announce miracles, I wouldn't believe in them. Human gullibility isn't what I see as religion. What I see as religion is that which we know beyond what we can prove. I don't see a conflict.

Q: Do you personally feel a need for religion?

PENZIAS: That is what I am wrestling with right now. I'm aware of my need for religion. I see so much pain in the world and I find a meaningless world almost unendurable. So now I ask myself, is what I call religion really religion? I'm having some doubts at this point. I wonder, do I accept religion just because I need religion? Is this religion a reflection of some higher truth or wish-fulfillment? That's the question I'm wrestling with right now.

Q: Where are you at this point in your life?

PENZIAS: I have an awareness of meaning in the world beyond what I am able to articulate and, certainly, beyond what I am able to prove. I have studied proof a great deal in connection with computers. Computers must seem "logical" and have to proceed from arbitrarily imposed inputs. This mechanical implementation of logic is something that the Greeks started and invented. You make some kind of assumption and then you work from it. The hollowness, or the shakiness—the almost illusionary nature—of the computer's understanding, in some sense, mirrors human existence. Most of the certainties of life, when exposed to detailed, logical attack, turn out to be grounded in unprovables. So science, despite its great triumphs, is based, at heart, on things which we can't prove. Scientists have no right to be more smug than theologians, because their findings are also based on a series of unprovable assumptions. So, where am I out of all this? I give a higher value to intuition and feeling than I might have some years ago when I thought that science or the experiences of the senses, somehow, have a greater, or almost absolute, validity. I have moved away from that and have come to think that my feelings hold a higher position in the hierarchy than I believed some years ago.

Q: Would you say that you have moved from a cerebral, strictly intellectual, rational view to a deeper appreciation of feeling?

PENZIAS: Well, I'm not sure it's cerebral. It is rather that I have focused my intellectual awareness equally. You learn something in Hebrew School when you're six or eight years old, something that is taught to you badly and imperfectly, and because you learn about the Bible or whatever when you are very young, you somehow equate religion with naivete. When, as an adult, one uses intellect to examine what we call rationality and what we call feelings, we find that we come up with rather interesting results. We cannot say that one is all a matter of the intellect and the other a matter of the spirit. Rather, I think that the part we intellectualize is a kind of an abstraction of our own making. When we use our intellect to really probe our intellect and see how we really behave, I think the distinction disappears. It appears that the senses are more primitive, or, at least, are acquired earlier than the tools of logic, but I don't think one is necessarily higher than the other.

Q: Would you say that in maturity you have gained a new respect for the metaphysical realm?

PENZIAS: Yes, I certainly would say that. I despair of the fact that people are exploited by things like horoscopes. I think that the Bible is correct in its condemnation of soothsayers, diviners and witches. But at the same time, the struggle for some kind of objectivity and the grip on reality that we all need shouldn't blind us to the fact that the metaphysical also plays a role in human experience. Metaphysics is probably too important to be left to the church; it should also not be left to Hare Krishna or somebody of that sort, to people who use it as a tool for their own ends. But it is something which thinking, rational people ought to take into account and not merely with reference to the opinions of someone else, but in terms of their own feelings as well. Rational, educated people don't normally talk about their feelings. Those who do are somehow thought of as underemployed California hippies. That's pejorative and causes us to underutilize information that we as thinking human beings have access to.

Q: Are you concerned about metaphysical frauds?

PENZIAS: Well, some of them are metaphysical frauds. Others may be excessive rather than fraudulent. Some are self-deluding. On the other hand, people who come up with very tightly reasoned approaches to God, also are a little fraudulent. Somebody like Descartes, brilliant as he was, engaged in a little bit of cover-up. When Descartes got up at 2:00 A.M. and thought a little bit more about some of the things he was writing in the daytime, he was probably covering up some holes.

Q: You referred to changes in your own life and outlook. Can you point to any experience which brought you to a closer awareness of God?

PENZIAS: Certainly one of the things is parenthood. Nothing makes you confront the meaning of life as much as bringing another life into the world. To love anyone is to risk danger, but in the case of bringing someone up Jewish, you risk even more. A family in France, a very famous Jewish family, during World War II, became Protestants simply to spare their children. I had to confront that question about my children, whether to bring them up as Jews in a world where the Jewish experience has been painful at best and where the Jewish future is unanswered.

Q: Have you found, in raising children, a connection with the source of life?

PENZIAS: In watching children grow, one can see evidence for the biological doctrine of "recapitulation" according to which the birth of the human being, to some extent, recapitulates evolution. There is something to that. It is almost as if, in creating a child, one re-creates the world. It is very hard to look at a child and not see Creation right in front of you.

Q: Have you sensed somehow, a personal relationship or connection with God?

PENZIAS: No. My wife, and other people I know, feel a personal relationship with God. I don't feel that way, no.

Q: What is God to you? Is God a concept, a mathematical formula?

PENZIAS: Oh no, definitely not a mathematical formula by any means.

Q: Do you think that the word "God" is meaningful?

PENZIAS: I think the word "God" is certainly meaningful, that is, I would like to believe in a purposeful world. Purpose implies an "owner" of that purpose and I think that God is the owner of the purpose of the world.

Q: Is such a purpose intelligible to the human mind?

PENZIAS: By looking at the Creation one can infer purpose. Nature, blind nature, is driven by chance, by the laws of probability which revolve around what one would call "the second law of thermodynamics." For example, if you were to put a pinch of salt in one part of a boiling kettle of soup, sooner or later that salt would end up dispersed throughout. In other words, it would reach the most disordered possible state. Nature, through random chance, seeks disorder. Life, on the other hand, somehow works against that; it organizes, makes things orderly. If we go out and we see a forest of trees and all of a sudden the trees are planted in a row of equal spaces, we would see purpose. Order implies purpose. Once we look at the purpose, we can, then, go one step further, and say something about the engine of that purpose and the owner of that purpose. If there are a bunch of fruit trees, one can say that whoever created these fruit trees wanted some apples. In other words, by looking at the order in the world, we can infer purpose and from purpose we begin to get some knowledge of the Creator, the Planner of all this. This is, then, how I look at God. I look at God through the works of God's hands and from those works imply intentions. From these intentions, I receive an impression of the Almighty.

Q: Are you responding to the world in the spirit of the Nineteenth Psalm: "The Heavens declare the glory of God and the firmament shows forth His handiwork"?

PENZIAS: The second part, not the first. As for the first part, it depends on what one means by glory. I have a question about lavish praise. I would say, and it is not good poetry, "The heavens lead us towards the attributes of God by showing us his handiwork."

Q: That's a good statement.

PENZIAS: But that isn't poetry. I am thinking of the so-called thirteen attributes of God: "The Lord, the Lord, God, merciful and gracious, long-suffering, etc." (Ex. 34.6). How did we get those?

We surmised them from God's actions. In other words, we learn about the Almighty through, what we assume, are results of His work. In that particular case, some of them presumably involve God's interventions in history which I have a hard time with, but that's another story.

Q: You say you are wrestling with God. Can you be more specific?

PENZIAS: My concept of a purposeful Creator doesn't give me a problem. But I have some doubts. Is this a valid conclusion? Is it a substitute or security blanket, for, otherwise, how can I face the world? The thing I wrestle with at all times is the reality of God.

Q: Bertrand Russell was asked what he would say if, contrary to his expectations as an agnostic, he found out that God really existed and was face to face with Him? Russell replied, "Dear God, you should have given me more evidence of your existence." Is that what you are looking for, more evidence?

PENZIAS: No, the evidence is there. The problem is with me. There is evidence everywhere; the question is how to sift through it.

Q: A few minutes ago, you referred to a very important Biblical passage ("The Lord, the Lord, God, merciful . . .") which is frequently used in our prayer book. How do you feel when you pray? Is prayer for you an act of identification or is it something deeper?

PENZIAS: Most of the time, it remains on the level of personal identification, but sometimes it moves higher. I can almost believe that a teddy bear is something more than rags after a child has loved it for decades. It is not that the item itself has any significance. It is the use to which it is put. So, in the same way, the significance of the prayers are in the use to which they have been put. The people who recited those prayers give them significance. And this is why I have so much trouble with people creating new prayers.

I remember going to a "modern" Mass once and I wanted to go up and shake the priest afterwards. I was so furious at this man because what was done at that service was what the Reform Jews did years ago. This business of turning out your own prayers is ill-advised. I mean, my God, they have something which has been sanctified by two thousand years of love and faith and they are throwing it away because somebody sat down and decided to write something else. It is like redoing the Psalms. In the '60s, they put out prayers in loose-leaf books with pictures of Robert Kennedy standing, looking out at the seashore. Compare that with the timelessness of the King James version!

The "sanctification" we use is very important to me, even though an Orthodox morning service turns me off beyond belief. Standing there, mumbling for an hour really bothers me. But, on the other hand, when the congregation says the Sh'ma together, or when people are putting on t'fillin in the same way as has been done for centuries, the "sanctification" we recite later in this connection does more than just identify me with our people and our history. It brings me closer to something which has sanctity so that, sometimes, I am able to feel that sanctity.

Q: Do you have a sense of the Jewish people being radically, absolutely different from any other, in terms of their destiny, their relationship to God, their history? How do you regard the concept of the chosenness of the Jewish people?

PENZIAS: I believe in it. It is certainly easy to put arguments in place. One just has to look out the window here, to see the mosque and the church built on the spiritual foundations of our people who lived in this corner of the Eastern Mediterranean. The unique role that the Jews have played in that history, is evidence of a very special role. The Midrash includes one about Israel as a self-selecting people. I think that, to some extent, chosenness is a two-way street. That is, that somehow through our own actions and through history, we continue to occupy a very special place in the evolution of mankind.

Q: Why invoke God as the One who chose Israel when chosenness is interpreted as uniqueness, borne out simply by the facts of history?

PENZIAS: It is not simply a historical fact. It is a belief, but if you look for evidence in history, you may see it there. Take, for example, the accounts of the politicking surrounding King David's death. It may sound ridiculous to others, but I can see it as one of the manifestations of a divine plan.

Q: Do you believe in a divine plan that calls for a chosen people?

PENZIAS: I don't include the details. For example, I can't imagine that the composition of next Thursday's bus from here to Rehovot is already in God's mind. But I think that there is a purpose for human history and in it there seems to be room for a chosen people even if we did some choosing ourselves.

There really is a chosen people in history and it seems to be us. Whether we chose ourselves or God somehow decided it early on is irrelevant to me because, if God created the universe, surely He did it elegantly. "Elegantly" means He doesn't have to monkey with it as time goes on. The most elegant job is to set things in motion at the beginning, getting everything working right, so you don't have to go back to fix things up. It's the difference between a Mercedes and a cheap car. The Mercedes comes out of the factory and it works the first day and the next five hundred thousand miles, while the other car has to go back to the shop every two weeks for repairs. The "elegance" of the Mercedes is in the workmanship which anticipates possible problems of its use. Similarly, "elegance" of God's plan in history would imply unique roles or contributions by individuals or peoples. The unique thing about the Jews, I suppose, is that they continue to play a role at critical junctions throughout history.

Q: As interpreters of justice and advocates of a pure idea of God?

PENZIAS: I won't say that the development of civilization in so many different ways revolves or springs from a mere handful of people who share a Jewish identity. All of human existence has something which reflects, to use the phrase of the Psalm 19, "the glory of God" and, so, I think that the Jewish role in history, whether it has to do with theology or with anything else, is still part of the evolution of humanity and therefore part of what you might call God's plan or the human consequences of God's plan.

Q: Would you define the Jewish role as the realization of sanctity in life?

PENZIAS: I wouldn't say "realize" sanctity. Life *is* sacred, life has sanctity in it.

Q: You referred before to Sinai. This brings up one of the most complex problems—revelation. Do you think that God revealed Himself at Sinai?

PENZIAS: Or, maybe God always reveals Himself? Again I think as Psalm 19, "the heavens proclaim the glory of God," that is, God reveals Himself in all there is. All reality, to a greater or lesser extent, reveals the purpose of God. There is some connection to the purpose and order of the world in all aspects of human experience.

Q: When you read or hear the Torah, is it to you the word of Moses or the word of God?

PENZIAS: Well, to me it is the word of Moses and the word of God through Moses.

Q: Then why did Sinai happen?

PENZIAS: I don't have a good answer, except that Sinai was important for Judaism and important for the future of the world. It was a place where God chose the Jews, but the Jews also chose God. It was a historical moment in which a spiritual connection was made.

Q: If I were to say that the human and divine elements are inseparable, how would you respond?

PENZIAS: Some people might quibble slightly with that, but there is an inseparability of the human and the divine. Since I see the human and the divine together, I think that the event at Sinai was a reflection of divinity which resides in human life or spirit.

Q: What happens when death comes? Would you be completely finished, annihilated? Do you believe there is some kind of continuation of the God-given soul or spirit? Or is this a thought that doesn't really bother you one way or the other?

PENZIAS: The interesting thing is it doesn't bother me a lot. The best I can come up with is what Mordecai said to Esther, "Perhaps God put you in this place to do the thing you are supposed to do." That is probably as close as one comes to immortality, that is, playing a role in continuing life. Whether you, as an individual, die afterwards, is almost irrelevant because the life process of which you are a part continues either through your offspring or through the actions you take. Your human existence, the impact you make, remains part of life and in dying you don't leave it. I don't have to believe I'm going to feast on meat, fish, and delicacies every day somewhere in paradise after this life, in order to make me feel that I shall achieve immortality.

Q: Suppose a baby dies on the sixth or seventh day of life. This baby has had no chance of making any impact on society, the family, anybody. Would the death of such an infant be total extinction?

PENZIAS: That is not completely true. All you may say is that its impact is very small. The death of an infant certainly affects the family and, in that sense, the rest of the world. It may not have had a conscious impact on the world, that is, the child never went out and planted a tree, or taught a course, or helped build a house; I don't think the connection with the larger life is limited to such overt actions. Just by being born, the infant becomes part of the life process and partakes of immortality.

Q: So any life, short or long, has some measurable impact upon the environment?

PENZIAS: "Measurable" is the wrong word. It may not be possible to measure it, but it has an impact.

Q: Would you say, it is like the ripple of a pebble thrown into a quiet lake?

PENZIAS: It has the effect of carrying some of the sand from Jerusalem on my shoes back to New Jersey. There is a connection; some is large, some is small. We cannot quantify it. There is a cartoon about an Italian Renaissance prince who is looking at a painting which he commissioned for his death. The picture shows the patron saint of his city introducing him to an enthroned deity. There is this prince a few inches high in the picture and the patron saint six inches high and God maybe a foot high. The prince may be only a quarter the size of God in the painting and what I remember about it is that he tells the artist, "Put in more angels and make them glad to see me."

We are trying to confront the scale of existence. On that scale, we must say how few are our days and how little is the space we occupy, but we are here. The Talmud says, "To save a single life is like saving the entire world." Each derives importance from the much larger totality of Life. If you measure everything by its own quantity, you are bound to end up in futility. I might think, what a difference there is between myself and the infant. I have published many papers and all the infant ever did was dirty two diapers. It is arrogant of us to make such comparisons. The point is, both of us are part of this large humanity. Some of us are luckier than others in that we can feel more fulfilled in ourselves. Others have their life-force extinguished before they are able to see the things they would have liked to see, but that is all part of life. I just don't care to compensate for the loss or shortness of life by fantasies about the hereafter.

Q: You prefer to see the meaning of personal existence in its continuity within the totality of life?

PENZIAS: The story of the flood in the Bible has animals and humans drowning together. It illustrates the connection between all forms of life. If one part is corrupt, all must suffer. It's the inseparability of life in the universe.

Q: So you maintain that the meaning of the individual part is derived from the whole?

PENZIAS: Yes.

Q: Jewish speculations about the hereafter involve the Messiah. Do you believe in such a redeemer or final redemption from all evil here on earth?

PENZIAS: Yes. I believe the world has a purpose, hopefully a good purpose. So I think that a Messiah is necessary to help achieve a purposeful world. I assume the world, as created, is a good world, otherwise the whole thing would be a cruel joke.

Q: Are you thinking of a Messianic Era, something like the culmination of a historic process? Or do you assign the major role to a person, some genius, perhaps even a semidivine being, who would bring about that final perfection or purpose that God wants to have fulfilled?

PENZIAS: We are talking about the fullness of time. I'm not sure that one has to get there in one single leap. I don't think it has got to be a Messiah who fixes up the whole world, all at once— either that or nothing. Just as the whole Creation is reflected in every birth, so, I think, the Messianic Era is intimated by the good which is done by each individual. We create the Messiah among ourselves. Just as we say, if you save one life, you save the whole world, so we might say, if you perfect one little part of the world, you perfect the whole.

Q: Would you say that the Messianic work is done every day by everybody?

PENZIAS: No, I don't think that is true. I don't think everybody is doing it every day. I certainly don't think, for example, that the Nazis were helping to bring on the Messianic Era by creating conditions which indirectly, led to the building of the State of Israel. I don't believe that. I do, however, think that saintly people make a difference. In that sense, Andrei Sakharov was part of the Messiah.

Q: In other words, it is given to some, if not all, to play a redemptive role?

PENZIAS: No, not given, no. I don't mean given; only in the sense that all life is given to everyone. It depends on the will, the decision of people, as the Jews said at Sinai, "We shall do" which signalled their acceptance of the Torah. The Torah wasn't just given, it was deliberately accepted. What are the Hebrew words?

Q: *Naa-se v'nishma*, "We shall do and we shall listen." (Ex. 24.7)

PENZIAS: Right, it involves a personal decision.

Q: Do you believe that, in our collective or personal effort to improve the world, we play a preparatory role for the Messianic Era?

PENZIAS: No, no. I don't believe in the steady, continued progress of mankind. If that were the case, the world would be continuously and steadily improving, and that is not the case. Rather, throughout history, there have been opportunities for people to improve the world and those opportunities will continue. At various times in history, people will be able to make greater or smaller improvements in the world. At the same time, there will be evil and backsliding; so it's two steps forward, three steps back, four steps forward, three steps back, and so on. The world is not getting better everywhere, every day. There are opportunities, though, for individuals to create and do things which are consistent with the divine purpose. But what we call the Messianic Era is far out in the future.

Q: It was good to hear you, as a scientist, distance yourself from a concept of automatic, evolutionary progress that would simply go on and on and on as a continuous process of perfection. You reject that?

PENZIAS: The scientific abstraction of linear progression is for some people a reality. But linear progression is an abstraction which we sometimes try to apply to history. Scientists often model behavior by fitting straight lines and, if that doesn't work, they fit them in cyclically. Reality goes on chugging along in more complicated ways. History is neither steady progress nor cycles. It is a series of lurches, if you will. Things don't get steadily better, they also don't get better or worse in a neat cycle. Things happen which change the world irreversibly—inventions, events in nature or in space, or the discovery of the causes of infectious diseases. These different things are not chaotic, but if we try to model history in a simple linear way, I think we are being naive.

Q: Let me now pinpoint the question of Messianism. Do you believe that the Messiah could be one person?

PENZIAS: I can't deny the possibility. Could I have anticipated that Sakharov would be doing all he did for Russia? I would have said no. I was surprised.

Q: Do you want to leave the question about the personal Messiah open?

PENZIAS: Things can get better and things can get worse, but I think the world becomes more connected. So as the world gets to be more integrated through greater communication, as the world becomes smaller through technology, the opportunity to do things on a larger scale increases. But that may be for both good and evil. Either an enormous benefactor or a creator of evil may someday come along. Certainly the world has, over the years, become a smaller place. I don't have a lot of faith in the Messianic idea nor do I need to believe in the idea, but I don't disprove it or scoff at it. A Messiah figure, I would think, might appear mostly on a small scale, but maybe, someday, on a worldwide scale. I just don't know.

Norman Podhoretz

B orn in New York, Norman Podhoretz is editor-in-chief of
Commentary magazine and the author of six books, including
the autiobiographical *Breaking Ranks* and *Making It*. A syndicated
columnist, he has been published in most of the leading American periodicals. He appears often on radio and television and on
the university lecture platform. Former left-wing friends and col-
leagues have never forgiven his switch to neoconservatism for
which he has become a leading spokesman.

A Fulbright scholar and Kellet Fellow in England, he earned
his Bachelor's and Master's degrees in English at Cambridge University and a Bachelor's degree in Hebrew literature from the
Jewish Theological Seminary in New York.

Norman Podhoretz drew my attention as a major intellectual
pacesetter and influential opinion molder in the general as well
as Jewish community. But an even more important reason for
interviewing him was the need to better understand that group of
highly sophisticated men and women represented by him which
in any religious survey are likely to be classified as secular or even
nonreligious Jews. As our dialogue shows, intellectuals such as

Podhoretz, though by their own admission nonpracticing Jews, ardently affirm their Jewish belonging and are far from indifferent to Jewish beliefs.

Podhoretz deeply believes in God as the source of physical and moral law. He makes a moving statement about the "care" of God. The account of his mystical experience—a blazing experience of illumination—is startling. Why then, is he not a regular worshipper at home and in the synagogue? He blames himself for "spiritual laziness or even arrogance." He has not lived up to the implications of his mystical experience because he is, as he puts it, "spiritually slothful, perhaps even afraid."

Another possible reason for the religious inactivity of people like Podhoretz is suggested by his comment, "I've never found a synagogue that is fully satisfactory to me." Is this a mere excuse? Or does it point to a real lack of intellectual and spiritual stimulation in many synagogues? There is, to be sure, a latent religious sentiment of imponderable depth which is felt by nonpracticing and unaffiliated Jews—waiting to be released and activated. We spoke on October 7, 1991, at Georgetown University, Washington, D.C.

Q: How do you identify yourself as a Jew?

PODHORETZ: I belong to a Conservative synagogue which I attend only on the High Holy Days. I grew up in an Orthodox environment. Then I spent five years in the liberal-arts division of the Jewish Theological Seminary, the Seminary College of Jewish Studies. I'm not sure how I would identify myself today. I'm a bit of a Karaite.* I believe in the essential truth of Biblical religion, of Judaism, as I understand it. I have some difficulty with the rabbinic tradition. When I say "difficulty," I am talking about theological difficulty. I'm well aware of the fact that Judaism today is rabbinic in origin, more so than Biblical. But my own attachment is to the Judaism of the Bible.

---

*The Karaite sect arose in the eighth century in opposition to the so-called "oral tradition" of rabbinic Judaism including the Talmud. Karaites, now reduced to a very small remnant, mostly in Israel, recognize only the written Biblical text as authoritative law.

Q: Does that mean that you have your problems with Halakhah, with the derivation and expansion of Biblical law by interpretation?

PODHORETZ: Let me put it this way. I believe in some sense, not literally, although I'm not even sure about that, *Moshe kibbel torah missinai* [Moses received Torah at Sinai], but I'm not so sure that he transmitted it to the *anshe knesset haggedolah* [men of the great assembly].

Q: Are you suggesting that centuries of rabbinic Bible interpretation read a meaning into the text that was, originally, unintended?

PODHORETZ: The Judaism of the Bible, as I read it, for example, does not include a concept of the afterlife. Rabbinic Judaism does. Also, rabbinic Judaism puts strong emphasis on the Messiah. I don't see any such concept, not in terms that we would conceive of it today, in the Bible.

Q: You mean it's a late development?

PODHORETZ: Yes, it's a late development in Jewish history. But the basic structure of Judaism, which I find particularly in Genesis, is something that I would say is true. I find it to be a true account of the nature of things and of the nature of God and of God's relation to the world and to the Jewish people.

Q: What is most meaningful to you is Biblical metaphysics in Genesis, isn't it? Transcendence, the origin of the world by some creative act?

PODHORETZ: Yes. More concretely, what appeals to me is the idea of law governing the universe and human life; and the idea of a life lived in accordance with the law as the best life there is, as the *most* life there is—without an afterlife. I think this is one of the crucial differences between Judaism and Christianity. Judaism conceives of God as either law or the lawgiver. It is a law which, we are specifically told, we are capable of understanding. It's not beyond the powers of human beings to observe. It is the key to what today we would call the richest and fullest possible life: *etz chayyim hee la-machazikim ba* ["a tree of life to those who lay hold of it," Prov. 3.18]. The life of the law promises not an escape from death—there is no escape from death—but all the life there is to live. Of course, questions had to be raised about this concept, because the righteous suffer and die and therefore you have the questions raised by some of the prophets, and preeminently by the Book of Job.

Q: The problem of evil?

PODHORETZ: The problem of evil has to do with God's omnipotence. That's a different issue. The key to the difference between Judaism and Christianity and what made Christianity split off from Judaism even though it was founded by Jews—and pious, observant Jews as we know—was the refusal, particularly by Paul, to accept this limitation, that is, the limitation involved in mortality. He identified the law, both the Torah and the natural law, with death, and rightly so because that's a fundamental premise of the Jewish conception; he said, no, death had to be abolished. But you can't abolish death within the framework of Biblical Judaism. Some new principle had to be brought in, and that was the principle of grace which exempts you from death by giving you eternal life. I think this is an idea that is alien to Biblical Judaism, although it is an idea that, in different forms, crept into rabbinic Judaism.

Q: What do you think of God? Is God merely a symbol? A synonym for something else? Or do you believe in God as a being?

PODHORETZ: I believe in God, not as a symbol and not exactly as a being, but I believe that the picture you get of God in the Bible is about as close as one can come to apprehending this mystery. I've thought different things about the question in the course of my life, but I guess I think that one knows God, and it seems to me very Jewish, what I am about to say, through the law and through His book. I someday hope to write about this, but it's very difficult. I myself once had a mystical religious experience of the kind that William James describes in *The Varieties of Religious Experience*, and it had a great effect on my mind and soul.

Q: Could you enlarge on the situation? Was it in connection with illness?

PODHORETZ: It was in connection with a crisis, a spiritual crisis; it had to do with writing. But it wasn't an illness, well, perhaps a spiritual illness, and what I had was a blazing experience of illumination.

Q: A sense of release?

PODHORETZ: No, a sense of understanding. And what I understood, as I came to think about it, was what the Bible tells us about God and about the nature of the world and about law.

Q: Is God to you a source of ideas or the transcendent creator?

PODHORETZ: God is the creator of a meaningful universe, of a world, as I keep saying, that is governed by law, just as the devil represents the opposite principle. I don't know if I believe literally in the devil, but I've always found it useful to try to understand positives through their negations. I see the devil as the principle of nihilism and negation.

Q: Something like the black hole in the universe?

PODHORETZ: Well, yes, it's the inversion of everything. God says, "I have set before you, life and death," *u'vacharta b'chayyim* [choose life! Deut. 30.19]. Life is defined here as the life of the law which is accompanied by the promises I mentioned earlier. The devil is the principle of temptation not to live by the law. Man is free to choose, but the devil is the principle that tempts you to believe that the life outside the law is a better life or a richer life or that you are being cheated by submitting to the limitations of the law. The devil is behind such utopianism.

Q: False promises?

PODHORETZ: Yes, these are all the devil, that is, the opposite of the godly principle. I believe many people are godly without knowing that they are and some people who think they are, are not. There are people who don't believe in God, or think they don't believe in God, who live the kind of life that I would call godly, conforming to the law. And there are people who, as we know, observe mitzvot, or if they are Christians, are pious, who in fact are not godly. I don't just mean they sin. I'm talking about the spiritual condition they are in.

Q: Are you conscious of a personal connection with God?

PODHORETZ: Yes, I am. But it is a very difficult thing because the minute I say it, I think it's not true. Some of my most vivid experiences of connection with the divine have come from listening to the music of Bach. Sometimes I jokingly tell Christian friends of mine that Bach was really Jewish in the sense that his music was a demonstration of the infinite riches to be found within the strict confines of the law. He did not try to break the law of music as people who came after him did, as Beethoven did. He showed us that to obey the law does not limit you, as the devil keeps saying; it does not deprive you of the richness of experience or of life, but, in fact, makes it possible to reach the Infinite, which Bach did. So, when I listen to the *St. Matthew Passion*, which I think is the greatest single work of music ever written, I sense the Infinite.

Q: Is Bach's music for you a sort of prayer, then?

PODHORETZ: So can literature be, so can poetry be. But Bach, in particular, has given me this experience.

Q: Orderliness?

PODHORETZ: Within the pattern are the infinite riches which the devil says cannot possibly be found there.

Q: Do you find any satisfaction at all in prayer, whether formal or informal? Do you occasionally go to the synagogue?

PODHORETZ: Well, not very much. I grew up in an Orthodox synagogue where you raced through the prayers and I was quite good at racing through them when I was a kid. Now, when I go, it is a kind of hodgepodge of English and Hebrew and a lot of the prayers are inferior. Still, there are moments in the Machzor [High Holy Day prayerbook] which have given me a sense of connection with God.

Q: Which prayers?

PODHORETZ: The *U'netane tokef*,* particularly, and that whole series, starting with the U'netane tokef. These are wonderful

---

*Stirring High Holy Day prayer affirming the heavenly judgment which decrees "how many shall pass away and how many shall be brought into existence," yet is swayed by human repentance, prayer and charity, as well as God's mercy.

prayers. I don't have much of a taste for the medieval *piyyutim* [liturgical poems] that are scattered throughout that liturgy.

This may just be my own spiritual laziness or even arrogance. I believe that people do need to be members of a congregation, that is, to be reminded constantly of what is so easy to forget. I don't live by this, but in theory, I accept it. For example, the injunction in the Sh'ma to think about the law when you get up in the morning, when you go out, when you walk, etc., is psychologically profound because the easiest thing in the world is to forget those truths. There is a constant process of deterioration.

Q: Ritual is a system of memory, isn't it?

PODHORETZ: Judaism explicitly says so. You are to think about the law day and night. And, you are to repeat it to yourself.

Q: Do you feel, when you go to a synagogue, that the congregation is reconstituting our peoplehood?

PODHORETZ: To some extent. My problem is that I've never found a synagogue that is fully satisfactory to me. It is probably my own fault, but I've just never found one, not Orthodox, certainly not Reform, and not Conservative.

Q: You suggested that the fountainhead of your personal religion is the Bible and you particularly stress Genesis. Why Genesis?

PODHORETZ: Because it is all there, if you know how to read it. The first few chapters of Genesis contain practically everything you need to know about everything, about the nature of life, the awesomeness of evil, the nature of God and how one is to try to live. I have a lot of difficulty with the late Abraham Joshua Heschel who was a teacher of mine. I was even a pet of his at one time. I don't have, I'm sorry to say, a very high regard for his work. But there is one thing he stressed that was extremely important and points to the essence of the Jewish experience, and this is the sense of the blessedness of life, the fact that you are not permitted to let a moment go by without noticing it and being grateful for it.

Q: The proper response to life, he stressed, is amazement and wonder.

PODHORETZ: Or gratitude. I think he put his finger there on the key element of the Jewish experience, characteristic of a pious Jew who is in the right spiritual relation with God.

Q: Do you share the thought or the feeling that you are at the receiving end? That you are a recipient of gifts? That something is bestowed upon you?

PODHORETZ: Yes. When I castigate myself as a sinner, it's for this that I castigate myself much more than for my failure to observe some of the mitzvot, that is, for not being sufficiently alive to these gifts and sufficiently grateful for them and sufficiently joyous in receiving them. Despair is perhaps the greatest of all sins because it prevents the spirit from appreciating the gifts of God.

Q: It is our tradition to say upon awakening, *modeh ani lefanecha* [Thank you, God].

PODHORETZ: And you are supposed to "rise like a lion."

Q: You mentioned mitzvot. Of course, mitzvot [commandments] logically involve a metzaveh, a commander. How do you visualize certain commandments, whether moral or ritualistic—can you imagine God caring whether or not you eat, or share food, or keep the Sabbath?

PODHORETZ: But that is the mystery. God cares because He loves humanity and His love—and this Jewish conception of God's love is quite different from the Christian conception—expresses itself precisely in His willingness to tell you what it is you should do in order to live well. He's not keeping it a secret. He has revealed the law to you and created you with the power to observe it. The Christian idea is precisely the opposite: His love expresses itself in the willingness to exempt you from the observance of the law.

At the risk of offending a lot of people, I would say that I think both Christianity and Islam are heresies with respect to Judaism. Heresy usually results from an overemphasis on a single element in a complex whole, as e.g., mariolotry,* I would say, is a Christian heresy. Well, I think the Jewish conception, the Biblical con-

---

*Veneration of the Virgin Mary, carried to idolatrous extremes.

ception, is of a God whose two major attributes are the attribute of justice, *midat ha-din*, and the attribute of mercy, *midat ha-rachamim*. Christianity stems from an overemphasis on the attribute of mercy and Islam stems from an overemphasis on the attribute of justice. The Jewish conception embraces both equally. And it is not so much that God is just in the sense of judging you and punishing you for breaking the law. It is almost as though what you are being told is that the breaking of the law is its own punishment and the observance of the law is its own reward. I mean the rewards and punishments are built into the structure of life. That God cares is again one of the mysteries implicit in the whole idea of Creation. Why create in the first place?

Q: One of the mysteries which you acknowledge is why would God create in the first place? Why is there something instead of nothing? That question accounts for much of the development of Kabbalah mysticism. Are you at all intrigued by Kabbalah?

PODHORETZ: Yes, a little bit. I was very close to Gershom Scholem. We were friends despite the great gap in our ages. I was his editor on many occasions and learned a lot about Lurianic Kabbalah from working on his stuff. And I think that the whole idea of the contraction of God to make way for the world is very interesting. Of course, it led to terrible consequences, including the conversion of Shabbatai Zvi to Islam. Yes, I'm interested in Jewish mysticism, but less than I am in the Bible.

Q: Mysticism is not a dominant factor in your thinking?

PODHORETZ: Not in my thinking, although, as I said, I did have a kind of mystical experience.

Q: Have you come to terms with that or is it something that still calls for rethinking and reordering your life?

PODHORETZ: It happened about twenty years ago. Although it had a great effect on me, it also wore off and I have not had the power to live by it.

Q: But the strange thing about a mystical experience is that the heart always yearns for its repetition and expects it again at one time or another.

PODHORETZ: Well, I've given up expecting it. And it takes great courage, at least I found it so, to live by one of these revelations; not only courage, but enormous energy and persistence. But one is spiritually slothful, perhaps also afraid.

Q: Probably the most unreported experience is precisely this kind of personal mystic moment, an illumination that comes and passes, that you don't even want to accept as real, and yet it lingers in the mind.

PODHORETZ: William James, whose book I've read several times and again after this experience, was amazed by how similar many of the cases he reports were. I've tried to write about my own experience several times and failed. But I haven't given up yet.

Q: You speak of the Bible again and again and acknowledge its impact. One of the leading ideas in the Bible is the chosen people. Is this concept meaningful to you?

PODHORETZ: Yes, I believe in the idea of the chosen people. The irony is that it is easier to accept it as an empirical proposition than as a theological doctrine. I think it was Kierkegaard who called it the scandal of particularity.

Q: Would you say the record of history corroborates the uniqueness of the Jewish people, which is another way of calling it a "chosen people"?

PODHORETZ: It is very difficult to understand the history of the Jews without some such hypothesis. I very much believe in the idea of the chosen people.

Q: Why would God want a people?

PODHORETZ: We don't know why. One of the things we learn from the Bible is that "why" is not a question for human beings to answer. They can know what, when, how, but not why.

Q: We only have the mind to ask the question, but not answer it.

PODHORETZ: That's right. We don't know why, but what we do know is that God did choose this Beduin tribe, wandering around in the desert, to exemplify in a living history the truth of His revelation—a task, or purpose, which this people more or less voluntarily, and more or less reluctantly, accepted.

Q: What do you mean by revelation? What happened at Sinai?

PODHORETZ: What happened at Sinai was that God revealed to this tribe the nature of things: that the world had been created by a single God; that it was ruled by laws; that He made these laws knowable; that He was, in fact, telling them what they were, and that to live by these laws, or, I would say, by the principle of law, was the only way to live well. And this was to be true for all peoples who would come to learn of it through the experience of this particular people. The very survival of the Jews has been a testimony to the truth of this idea, and I even think that some of the struggles over Israel today are fundamentally about this revelation.

I see Israel as a kind of willy-nilly, inadvertent, living embodiment of the principle of choosing life and of doing what is necessary to live. I think some of the hostility and animosity that Israel has experienced in the world, which is after all not so easy to account for, has to do with the continued resistance to these Jewish truths. You asked me about mysticism. Ha-rav Kook, who was the first chief rabbi of Palestine, and a mystic, once scandalized his fellow Orthodox rabbis by saying about the Jewish pioneers in Palestine, many of whom were atheists, "I kiss the ground they walk on, it is holy ground." I brooded about that for a long time, wondering what he meant; I now think he meant that these people, unbeknownst to themselves, were fulfilling the basic commandment of Judaism to "choose life," even though they were atheists and contemptuous of the commandments.

Q: How has the Holocaust affected your beliefs?

PODHORETZ: If I think about the Holocaust in this context, it becomes the supreme example of the desire to get rid of the Jews, to wipe the Jews off the face of the earth. Why? What are the Jews? There are not that many of them despite fantasies about their power. In fact, in the 1930s and 1940s they were so powerless that they could do nothing to save themselves. A third of them were massacred very easily. Nobody did much of anything. Many people cooperated. Why? What was the Jewish offense?

You see it again in the absolute refusal, not only by the Arabs but by the world community, to accept the normal legitimacy of a sovereign Jewish State. It's still problematic. What is this all about? I think there is some very deep resentment of and resistance to the idea that the Jews were appointed to represent the revelation at Sinai.

Q: Is it a rebellion of the world against God even while it targets the Jews?

PODHORETZ: Yes, and I think that the Jewish will to live in the face of this is itself, often without conscious realization, a religious act. The defiance of the Jews against those determined to wipe them out was partly expressed in the establishment of the State of Israel; but also in the way the Jews in this country picked themselves up after World War II and tried to build something. I think that this is itself, unbeknownst as I say to many of the people participating, a religious act.

Q: Do you see a dialectic there? First, the destruction, and then, in response, an intensified will to live?

PODHORETZ: Yes, but you have to be careful not to justify the Holocaust when you talk this way. There is no justification for it. The question is what the world has against the Jews. It's a very difficult question to answer, in straight, rational terms. It makes no sense. The Nazis actually diverted necessary transports from the war effort, when they were beginning to lose the war, in order to carry Jews to Auschwitz from Hungary. Yet the Nazis who did this were not crazy people. Without saying that I understand it, it seems to me that the Jews do represent something beyond what they appear to represent by sheer numbers and their relative degree of power; I think they represent a certain principle that they were chosen to embody, against which they themselves rebelled, but it catches up with the Jews in the end.

Q: A number of theologians and also Jews, half-way believers, look upon the Holocaust as the great stumbling block in their faith. They see it as reflecting either God's nonexistence or impotence. Has the Holocaust so affected you?

PODHORETZ: No, it hasn't because I don't conceive of God as intervening in the world, either for good or evil. My understanding of free will is that God does not intervene.

Q: Your response that God does not intervene, that God has left us to act in the world as best we can, suggests already how you think about the Messiah in the Messianic Age.

PODHORETZ: True, I don't believe in the Messianic Age and I think that the Messianic impulse is very, very dangerous. In its secularized form it has created mountains of corpses and oceans of blood. I actually think that it is alien to Judaism, to the Biblical Judaism that I so value and believe in.

Q: In post-Biblical Judaism, too, we find thinkers who negated the Messiah.

PODHORETZ: Or who were very much afraid of mysticism, and I know why.

Q: What about another part of Jewish eschatology, the soul and the hereafter?

PODHORETZ: I have difficulty with that. As I understand Biblical Judaism, it does not have a conception of the hereafter. It is hardly ever mentioned, except for a phrase such as, "going down to *Sheol*,"* whatever that means.

Q: I have a final question about *Commentary*'s editorial policy on religious issues. When you took over as editor-in-chief, you wanted to establish a certain balance between general and specifically Jewish issues. Do you see a new interest in any of the Jewish issues? Is there, as some argue, a turn from ethnic to spiritual and theological topics?

PODHORETZ: To some extent. But, even in the old days, when I was on the left, I had an interest in religious questions and there was always a certain amount of preoccupation with religious and theological issues in *Commentary*. It is not for nothing that we published Emil Fackenheim and Gershom Scholem so often. So I'm

---

*Sheol refers to the netherworld, abode of the dead.

not sure there has been a real shift in this area. What is happening is that Jews nowadays, like all other Americans, are more interested in religious questions.

Q: Do you see a trend?

PODHORETZ: Yes, I think so. I don't know how permanent it is or how deep it goes, but there is something there certainly. Heine said once, *Wie es Christelt sich so Judelt's sich* (as Christians do, so do Jews). Today, too, there is probably a subtle influence from the Christian world on the Jewish world.

Q: Might it also be a fading confidence in the rationality of the world and the comprehensibility of our life?

PODHORETZ: There is no question that there has been a loss of such confidence.

Q: Disenchantment?

PODHORETZ: Oh yes, no question about that. That's true everywhere.

Chaim Potok

B orn the eldest of four children to Orthodox immigrant parents in the Bronx in 1929, Chaim Potok was educated at the high school of Yeshiva University but broke with Orthodoxy by the time he took his B.A. degree. He transferred to the Jewish Theological Seminary which allowed him to pursue advanced Jewish studies together with literature, in which he was deeply interested. He defines himself as a "non-fundamentalist, traditional Jew." Following his ordination as a Conservative rabbi he served as chaplain in the U.S. Army in Korea and earned his Ph.D. in philosophy at the University of Pennsylvania. After several years of teaching at the Jewish Theological Seminary and editing the magazine *Conservative Judaism*, he became editor-in-chief of the Jewish Publication Society.

The term "Jew by choice" denotes a convert to Judaism but, in a way, every Jew in the post-Emancipation era is a Jew by choice. Some exercise this freedom by drifting out of the Jewish community altogether; others by determining new patterns of Jewish living. Chaim Potok exemplifies the Jew who, in response to the alluring openness of American society, broke away from the particular Jewish environment in which he was reared after the faith underpinning his Orthodox fundamentalism had become untenable. Had there not been alternative modes of Jewishness, such as the theologically more liberal Conservative and Reconstructionist movements, he might well have become totally secularized and possibly lost to Judaism. As his case illustrates, religious pluralism is a point of strength for American Jewish continuity, giving the dissatisfied Jew the option to choose an intellectually and spiritually more congenial form of Judaism. The God Chaim Potok now believes in is no longer the cosmic Patriarch who governs every nook and corner of the universe, but "a God that has evolved together with the universe and with us," a God who is still struggling with his own completion. Potok no longer needs "to believe that God spoke, appeared, literally gave the Torah at Sinai, word for word." Yet, he still believes that the revelation occurred at Sinai: "The spark started from an experience that we cannot fathom."

The Jew who thinks of himself as a religious skeptic may well learn from Chaim Potok that intellectual honesty need not lead out of Judaism but rather to further reading and study and possibly to another affirmation of the Jewish faith.

Potok's first novel, The Chosen, which portrayed the clash between Orthodox faith and secular culture, met with nationwide success, and was followed by the novels, *The Promise* and *My Name Is Asher Lev*, which likewise made the best-seller lists. These were followed by *The Book of Lights*, which examines the problem of good and evil in the perspective of Kabbalah mysticism, and the lavishly illustrated one-volume Jewish history, *Wanderings*. In his entry in *Who's Who In World Jewry* (1987) Potok gallantly answered the question of what he was most proud of with the words: "having married a beautiful woman, fathered three beautiful children, and written some good books." We spoke at the Dirksen Senate Office Building in Washington, D.C., October 17, 1991.

Q: I'm curious how much of your traditional upbringing has remained with you as part of your personal outlook, values, and beliefs.

POTOK: The core elements of my upbringing which are very much a part of my life today are the value of learning, the value of reading, the commitment to the adventure of the Jewish people, to its history, to its accomplishment, its suffering, its travail, its foolishness—all these are fundamental components of my being. I have less of a commitment today to its orthodoxies than I had when I was growing up.

Q: Are you referring to Orthodox practice and observance?

POTOK: Not only to practice and observance, but also to my understanding of how the tradition developed, its beginnings, and its journey through history. So I think if I had to characterize myself, I would call myself a non-fundamentalist, traditional Jew. That is to say, an individual committed to his particular tradition, who understands that tradition as having originated in an attempt on the part of his people to understand its place and its journey and to respond out of their deepest being to what they were experiencing. Their response was an evolving one, changing as the experiences kept changing, holding on to what they felt was the core of the original response, and adding to it new responses as they continued their journey through history. The people were kept alive all through the millennia by the seminal power of the original response.

Q: You were nurtured as a Jew of destiny. Would you now call yourself a Jew of choice?

POTOK: I would call myself a Jew of destiny by choice. That's the culture fusion that has occurred. If you are inside a system and can't step out and look at it, there are no choices. What happened in the modern period is that, for the first time in our history as a species, at least on the western side of the planet and its various culture colonies, we can do both at the same time. We're part of the system and at the same time we can step outside the system and look at ourselves as part of the system and make a choice whether to remain or not, and my choice is to remain.

Q: As you review your life, can you point to certain principles or elements of faith which have gradually become inoperative, if not totally negated?

POTOK: I would say that the fundamentalism that I grew up with has become unnecessary for me. I can now live with my Jewishness in a non-fundamentalist mode. I don't need to believe that God spoke, appeared, literally gave the Torah at Sinai, word for word. I don't need that in order to live my life as a Jew. I am perfectly able to live my life as a Jew committed to things Jewish, with the understanding that the experience at Sinai—and I don't deny that an experience of some awesome kind occurred there— was not as simple and as simple-minded, I must say, as I was taught when I was a kid growing up: or not as simple as it seems from a surface reading of Exodus. If you read Exodus very carefully, you will see that it's a very complex experience.

Q: Do you see in the event at Sinai a core of revelation and a mountain of interpretation?

POTOK: That is correct. The spark started there from an experience that we cannot fathom. Just as we cannot fathom life.

Q: What does that do to the mitzvot [commandments] in your case? If they are no longer absolute mandates, do you reserve for yourself the choice to respond to some and not to others?

POTOK: Yes, but the criterion has to be an educated one. There is somebody to whom I go when there are issues concerning mitzvot that I have questions about, matters I do not understand.

Q: It should be an informed and a responsible choice.

POTOK: That is correct—a choice made not out of ignorance.

Q: Has God come to mean something else than what you imagined at an earlier stage in life?

POTOK: When I was a teenager in my very Orthodox home, God was everything that God is to an Orthodox Jew. He is Father; He is Judge: He is the one to whom you are answerable if you don't perform the commandments; He is the one to whom you pray when you want to avoid sickness, when you want something; He is the ultimate Person with a capital P. And in the final analysis, He is a being you don't think too much about introspectively. Few Orthodox Jews think deeply about God. Generally the questions about God come to you from outside Orthodoxy. Orthodox Jews can take a lot of punishment and not have their belief in God shaken. I once asked a Lubavitcher Hasid, what would it take for you to stop believing in God? What kind of philosophical proof would somebody have to muster, what kind of experience would you have to go through? He said he had never thought of the question before and he couldn't fully grasp its meaning. He just couldn't think outside the system. It took me years and years to be able to begin to think outside the system. As I was growing up, whatever it is that God meant in the Orthodox Jewish tradition, that's what God meant to me.

Q: The *ribbon shel ha-Olam* [Master of the Universe]?

POTOK: He was Master of the Universe, Father, the Being to whom you prayed, the Being to whom you cried out for help, the Being to whom you made promises when you wanted to pass your exams with good marks. That's what God was. And if, God forbid, something went wrong, then you had a sense of having been judged and punished. If you were sick, if somebody you loved died, you tried to figure out what it was that you or that individual had done that might have been wrong. You were inside a fairly straightforward, rabbinic, theological system, and that was the way you lived your life.

Q: What cracked that for you?

POTOK: Literature was the first thing that cracked it for me. Literature presented me for the first time with an alternate way of mapping the human experience. So that when I read James Joyce, Ernest Hemingway, Stephen Crane, William Faulkner, Thomas Mann, and Flaubert, for the first time in my life, I began to see the possibility of other profound readings of the human experience. Some assumed a world without God. The notion that individuals could think that way, was overwhelming to me. I remember the first time that I began to encounter the writings of Hemingway and Camus. To try to make a meaningful life for yourself without that fundamental core category of belief, called God, was for me bewildering. It took years before I could think myself into the possibility of that view of life.

So the first crack was literature and it began in my second year in college. I attended Yeshiva University. I was surrounded by

God. I was surrounded by mitzvot. I was surrounded by rabbis. Even in the English Department I was surrounded by God. My classmates in Talmud were also my classmates in English Literature and Greek Philosophy. I graduated *summa cum laude* in English literature, and I could have gone on to Harvard and done a doctorate either in American or English literature. But chance intervened. My cousin married a Jewish Theological Seminary student and they settled in the neighborhood of the Yeshiva and, in the fall of my last year in college when I was thinking of applying to Harvard and going on for a graduate degree, they invited me to have dinner with them in their apartment. I went to their apartment and there on the walls were books asking my questions and groping for answers, books that didn't exist in the Yeshiva. Not only were the books not in the Yeshiva, but the authors weren't even listed in the catalogue. They were non-people. I'm talking about individuals like, Solomon Schechter, Mordecai Kaplan, Milton Steinberg, and so on, individuals who were asking the hard questions and trying to come up with answers.

Q: Thinkers grappling with modernity?

POTOK: Right. So for about a month or two, I was reading some of the books in my cousin's library. He was then a senior in the Seminary. Pushed by him, and by something inside me that didn't want to make a total break with the tradition, I decided I would go to the Seminary instead. So I applied and was accepted. Had that not happened, I certainly would have gone on to a university like Harvard, and I would have become an altogether different kind of writer. It was a pivotal moment.

Q: How did this development finally bring you to your present state of mind? What would you say if you were to be asked point blank today, what does God mean to you?

POTOK: I would say that there are two aspects to God, one aspect that we can't talk about because words fail us; just as it's impossible for us to talk about the totality of the universe because words and mathematics fail us. We have no language for that which is beyond the human experience. I can only talk about the aspect of God that faces us, the face of God as He/She/It turns toward us. That face seems to be the sum total of the highest aspirations of each component of our species. God is the sum total of the archetypal principle, goal, direction, map of meaning of the totality of Homo sapiens. And each of us plugs into that to the extent to which we are able to.

The question immediately arises, how do you pray to that? How do you address that? I don't think that this God is just a projection of the human mind. If you're asking me whether it has ontological status, my response is that it has as much ontological status as our emotions, as our thoughts, as the universe, and I can address the universe. There are times when I talk to the universe. Do I expect the universe to respond to me? I don't know if the universe responds, but I do know that in addressing this totality of human aspirations, dreams, goals, ideals, there are resonances. One of the resonances is that it clarifies things in my head; I know what I'm still committed to. I don't ask God to heal my cold or to take care of the splinter in my hand, as I used to when I was a child. Yom Kippur to me today is not what Yom Kippur was when I was ten, eleven, twelve years old.

Q: What is it today?

POTOK: It's a time when I try to understand what I am so committed to that I am willing to go to the barricades for it; an attempt to understand where I stand vis-à-vis myself, my family, my people. Is my understanding about that day different now from what it was ten years ago? It sure is. I try on that day to assess how I've grown as a human being, how my understanding of my place in the world has altered. It's a "stop moment" for me. Yom Kippur is a stop moment. In the flux of things you need to stop and make a 360-degree turn, looking around and seeing where you're located on the navigational map, before you proceed.

Q: Are you conscious of a direct personal relationship or communication between you and God?

POTOK: I don't think that it's like communicating with an old man with a long white beard in the sky. It is a dimension of communication which is essentially inexpressible. It is a reaching out beyond the humanness in which I am trapped to see if, from whatever is beyond me, I can bring back a measure of renewed insight into what it is that I am. I am not sufficient unto myself. I don't think any human being is sufficient unto herself or himself. I think people who think that way are essentially lost or alienated individuals. No matter how much we would like to feel that we are sufficient unto ourselves, sooner or later we have to reach out beyond ourselves, and people reach out in various ways. I reach out in Jewish ways. I reach out to my people's history, I reach out to my people's way of configuring the world. I reach out to Jewish legal sources, I reach out to Midrashic sources. In very quiet moments I will reach out to whatever it is that is in me and in all of us, and outside all of us simultaneously, and try to address it, talk to it without expecting an answer, in the hope that somehow I will come back renewed.

Q: I hear you say that your outreach to God is a kind of attuning your mind and your feelings, a mental and an emotional happening, maybe even a social involvement out of which you seek God.

POTOK: That is correct.

Q: Can you reflect for a moment on anything that comes close to a God experience, or is God the focus of constant awareness?

POTOK: It is a constant feeling, with peaks and valleys.

Q: Was there ever a turning point for you, a decisive religious experience?

POTOK: No, I think it was a slow, evolving understanding, away from the naiveté of childhood and teenagehood. The more I learned about the Jewish people, its beginnings, the more my understanding of the nature of God altered.

Q: Your name, Potok, and *The Chosen*, your first novel, have become synonymous. You wrote it as a Jew who felt himself individually chosen, moved in a certain direction in his life. Is the idea of a chosen people meaningful to you at all?

POTOK: The idea of a unique people, certainly. But, chosen in a sense of superiority, no. Even the tradition doesn't like that notion, and the prophets railed against it. But the fact that Jewish destiny is unique—I don't see how anybody can argue against that. Why is it a unique destiny? There are many mysteries in the world, and this is one of them.

Q: Is "chosen," then, according to your way of understanding, merely a metaphor for a unique history, factually documented by events? Or can you see it as involving an act of God?

POTOK: I think that the people certainly saw it, theologically, as an act of God. I think if you posit the notion of a God whose fingers are constantly upon history, it becomes a simple matter to think of God choosing a people. I don't have that notion of God controlling, on a daily basis, the flow of history.

Q: It gets to be very difficult in the light of Auschwitz.

POTOK: Indeed, indeed. I think there is a quality of profound interaction between what we do as human beings and the potentiality for redemption.

Q: We obviously need a different understanding of *hashgakhah* [divine providence].

POTOK: That is correct.

Q: Have you reached a new understanding of providence?

POTOK: I think that the God whose face is turned to us is a God still struggling with the matter of Creation. He or She or It is still in the process of Creation, and we are feeling the imperfection of that process. In other words, I think that we are still in the Six Days of Creation, maybe six eons, or six eternities. I don't think Creation is over.

Q: How do you react to the idea that God gave us the tools and said, now build your own world, and ever since has kept Himself at a distance?

POTOK: Well, that's the deistic view of the seventeenth and eighteenth century rationalists.

Q: Would you go that far?

POTOK: No, I don't think so, because if that's the case, we just ought to close down the synagogues and churches. Why relate at all to such a God if He's out there somewhere and the world is just a clock. I think it's much more profound than that. There is so much around us that simply isn't complete and, yet, that seems to have a potentiality for completion. If I looked at our species and all I saw was a line going nowhere, with history the same today as it was five thousand years ago, at the beginning of writing, I would despair. But it is a very different kind of history today. Ours is a different sort of world, and we are, to no small extent, a different sort of species. Yes, with blood still on our hands, but with heightened sensitivity. And that's what gives me hope. In the past, no matter what happened, no matter what the wars, what the bloodshed, what the misery, everybody seemed to believe that there was no realistic alternative. Today we have a different reading of history, a reading we call democracy, modernism, secularism, evolution.

Q: And where do you stand with reference to that evolution?

POTOK: My feeling is that the God that I have come to learn about is a God that has evolved together with the universe and with us.

Q: God is Himself struggling?

POTOK: That is correct, and we are all participating in the struggle on different planes of being.

Q: Do you see any need for the soul? Is the human being anything more than an ephemeral, physical substance touched with spirit, but then expiring, gone forever?

POTOK: Soul is a Greek idea, it's not originally a Jewish idea.

Q: What about the Hebrew terms *nefesh* and *neshamah*?

POTOK: *Nefesh* means "the person"; *neshamah* means "the breath." Soul is a Greek concept. I am not concerned about the soul. I think we are the sum total of our aspirations, dreams, and body.

Q: As far as you are concerned, the soul would not make man more valuable or sacred?

POTOK: That's correct. Self and body, the sense that we have of ourselves, the human personality. That's an extraordinary thing. Just think, every human being has his or her own unique personality!

Q: Is this the writer or the theologian speaking?

POTOK: Both. Writers also deal in miracles. The act of writing—you put your squiggles on paper, and watch a world spring to life—is an act of Creation. Utterly miraculous!

Q: One of the most controversial issues in Jewish thought today is the Messiah. Do we really need one?

POTOK: Messianism is a consistent religious dream that at times heats up. Especially when a millennium is coming to an end. And that's what we're living through today. The notion of Messianism that makes sense to me is of a world that's trying to be healed, redeemed; the notion of a goal toward which we are constantly navigating.

Q: The Messiah is a symbol?

POTOK: The notion of Messiah as an actual individual is very dangerous, something we should be on guard against.

Q: Could you think of the Messiah as symbolic of God's intercession in a redemptive way?

POTOK: As sudden, miraculous, unexpected intercession?

Q: Yes.

POTOK: This century is not noted for such moments, except possibly the creation of the State of Israel. But that wasn't such a sudden and saving intercession. It cost about eight thousand lives.

Q: Does salvation still have any meaning?

POTOK: Salvation for me is the effort that we put into understanding our deepest selves in the most honest way that we can, so that we can look not only at our own selves, but at the selves of others around us. I think that the most important goal that confronts us now is to understand the nature of the human being. If I had my druthers and could have constructed human history, I would have done it, I think, another way. I would have had Freud born a few hundred years ago instead of Galileo, and let psychology work for a few hundred years trying to understand the nature of man, and then have Galileo born and give us all the technology. But that's not the way it went. So we've got all this technology, and we may be about to kill ourselves with it, and we still don't understand what man is all about. That's what salvation is for me—understanding our deepest selves. To that extent I am a modernist. It's not soul that preoccupies me so much as self.

Q: I had a teacher, not a great theologian, but a good rabbi, whom I served as assistant, and we were talking about the mission of the Jew; and he turned to me and said, "Josh, the mission of the Jew is to be a Jew." Would you add anything to that?

POTOK: I think the mission of the Jew is to be a Jew and a human being. I don't think you can be only a Jew and really participate in human destiny today. It is to be both your deepest self and at the same time be part of the human community.

Q: Does the Torah play any role in the mission of the Jewish people?

POTOK: Yes, yes. I don't think you can be fully a member of the Jewish people and, creatively, a member of humanity, without knowing who you yourself are. The only way you achieve a deep sense of self is to know your own beginnings. That's why Torah is important to the Jews. Torah is a Jew's sense of self, the beginning of it, the foundation stones of it. Then you can pick and choose, quarrel with it, discard this, accept that; but at least know where the shoreline is before you begin to row away from it! If you are rowing and there is no shoreline at all, then you're navigating blind, and to navigate blind is to live in dread.

Q: The Torah, then, is the chart by which we must find our way.

POTOK: That's right. Torah to me means not only the first five books of Moses.

Q: Historical experience?

POTOK: Jewish learning, Jewish history, Jewish literature, and so forth.

Q: The collective memory of our people?

POTOK: And then navigate. Then you can maneuver, if you take that chart with you. Indeed, I would encourage the maneuvering.

Q: If you had it in your power to make significant changes in American Jewish life, what would you want to see happen?

POTOK: One of the first things I'd do is somehow try to maximize both Jewish and secular education simultaneously. I would set as one of my top priorities a system of day schools whereby either education was entirely free or subsidization was of such a nature that as many as wanted could attend. And in those day schools, I would educate optimally for Jewish and for secular education, so that you would have built into the system this confrontation of cultures; choreograph it, so that kids would learn how to handle it; have them encounter it in the school system rather than outside, where they don't know how to handle it, and where they disintegrate. I would subsidize that school system at least through high school, because it's in high school and college that we lose the best of our kids. People will say that we don't have the money for it. My response is that the next generation of Jewish fund-raisers is going to suffer very seriously for the lack of committed Jews.

Q: How do you view Israel as an American Jew? You lived there for some time, didn't you?

POTOK: Four years.

Q: Are you confident about Israel's future? Are you troubled by its life and culture?

POTOK: Well, I'm very troubled. I don't think that we have to concern ourselves too much about Israel's security. Frankly, I think it's quite a strong country and can pretty much take care of itself. Nor do I think the Western world will let it disintegrate. It's not in the self-interest of the Western world to destabilize the Middle East, and the destabilization that would result from the disintegration of Israel is not to be imagined. So I'm not terribly concerned about its security in geopolitical terms. I'm very concerned about its security in political and in cultural terms.

The lack of communication in Israel between the different groups, the religious and the secular, their growing polarization, troubles me very much. Worse than that, it seems that one or the other or both sides see this polarization as desirable. Certainly, the religious see it as desirable and go out of their way to create walls of separation. What it says to me is that they are frightened of Western values. I am also troubled by the political extremists on the right. I know what Israelis have been through, all the animosities they've experienced. It's awkward for me as an American, living outside the country, to make suggestions as to how Israelis should behave. It is perfectly understandable that Israelis do not want to give anything away until they have some measure of security and sense of peace. At the same time, I must say that I've looked with great dismay upon the way that the Likud government has behaved; upon the scenarios that it put forth, the games that it played. And I wish that it weren't necessary for it to align its political life with the extremists from the religious right whose existence in the coalition makes or breaks Israeli politics. It's bitterly ironic to have individuals in power who actually question the reason for the existence of the State. They are against the State as a geopolitical entity, and yet they're the ones who control the destiny of the State.

Q: And they are driving it to an extreme position?

POTOK: Yes, and that seems to me to be the height of foolishness. So something has to be changed in Israel's political system. I don't quite know what, but they have to do something. I think it probable that the Russian aliyah will have some affect on the system of Israel. This is another cultural mix of monumental dimensions, and it cannot but bring changes.

Q: Isn't it also a great test of what Jews and Judaism are all about?

POTOK: This is where you see the Jewish tradition working. A fundamental Jewish value is to redeem and save lives. That's what they did with the Ethiopians; that's what they are now doing with the Russians.

Q: How do you react to different trends now in Judaism, some spiritual, some missionary, such as the Lubavitch, the Hasidic renewal that appears to take place in many parts of the world?

POTOK: I think they're riding the crest of the fundamentalist wave that has affected virtually the entire planet. It is a typical end-of-the-century or end-of-the-millennium phenomenon. You find it also in Islam; you find it in Catholicism. It's a response to despair. It is also a response to a felt absence in secularism, the sense of community. Whatever successes secularism has managed to achieve, the one thing it has not managed to do is create community.

Q: But you made a very important comment beforehand when you spoke of the unbearable total freedom with all the options open; of course, that is the hallmark of secularism. We need shelter within the family or within a group; we want a framework to which we may belong. The secular world, certainly the democratic West, has shattered many of these frameworks and has set a whole generation adrift. Isn't that the root of the problem?

POTOK: It has allowed virtually this entire century to be set adrift. When a young person finds himself drifting, the first thing he does is look for others who are drifting. You join a kind of drifting community, with everybody wearing the same jeans, the same style of clothes. They are all drifting together.

Q: Can you see new currents of spirituality, a yearning within the American Jew other than the normal channels of belonging and synagogue participation?

POTOK: One of the channels is the Havurah movement of the American Jewish community today. Smaller is better, smaller is more creative.

Q: And there is spontaneity.

POTOK: Yes. Smaller is more spontaneous and lends itself to greater participation on the part of its members. There seems to be a tendency away from clericalism and away from passive participation in synagogue life in search of a more active role. It's anyone's guess how synagogue life will evolve in the United States.

Natan Sharansky

In July 1978, Natan Sharansky, then a Soviet citizen, was accused of treason and sentenced by a Moscow court to thirteen years' imprisonment. His "crime" was not treason but leadership in the struggle of Russian Jews for the right to emigrate. His wife, Avital, had received her exit visa four years earlier. They were married only one day before she was permitted to leave while Sharansky was told that he would be allowed to follow her soon. Eight years had to pass before the couple were reunited in Jerusalem.

In his twelve-year struggle for emigration rights, Sharansky made the plight of the "Refuseniks" an international issue. He also underwent a spiritual transformation which is symbolized by his adoption of the Hebrew name Natan in place of his Russian name, Anatoly. At first aware only of his Jewish origin but ignorant of his cultural and religious heritage, he felt a growing thirst for Jewish knowledge, taught himself Hebrew, and became a Jew in the religious sense after undergoing a personal religious experience in prison. He is now systematically studying the Bible with commentaries, Jewish beliefs, and Jewish law in order to practice Judaism with conviction.

Our dialogue with Sharansky provides a fascinating insight into the return to Judaism of large numbers who had long been considered lost to the Jewish people in the former Soviet empire. Granting the importance of the quest for better economic opportunity and more political freedom in this emigration movement of Biblical proportions, we are reminded by Sharansky and other Refuseniks of the Biblical truth that "man does not live by bread alone" (Deut. 8.3). Sharansky's discovery of the reality of spiritual power and his transforming experience of the presence of God may have been heightened by isolation in his prison cell. Comparable opportunities for a religious awakening occur for anyone in the free world who, after his material props have been knocked out from under him, suddenly comes to recognize a power other than his own that can uphold him. Sharansky's case duplicates the psalmist's turn to God, "Out of the depths I have called you, Oh Lord" (Ps. 130.1) or, as the adage goes, Man's extremity is God's opportunity.

The best source on the life and spiritual development of Sharansky is in his autobiography, *Fear No Evil* (Random House, New York, 1988). We spoke in Sharansky's office in the Soviet Jewry Zionist Forum, in Jerusalem, November 18, 1991.

Q: Near the end of your imprisonment, your little book of Psalms was taken from you by the Soviet Guard as you were going to cross a bridge. You threw yourself on the ground and would not move until it was given back to you. Was this little booklet of Psalms a means of demonstrating defiance, a symbol of Jewish identification? Or did you actually read it because you wanted to express yourself religiously?

SHARANSKY: It had many different meanings. I was developing my relation with religion, my Judaism, during the time I was in prison. The book of psalms was received, sent to me by my wife, Avital, shortly before my arrest. There was a note from her, "This book of Psalms has been with me for a year and now I feel the time has come to send it to you." It was very nice to get this souvenir from my wife, but at that time it was only a souvenir for me. My life was full of struggle with the KGB, the times were exciting, and I put it aside. And then it was confiscated together with all my things when I was arrested. Then, being in prison, lacking any contact with the world, I began fighting for the return of my personal things and, then, I discovered this little book among my things. At the end of a long struggle, I received it on the day when I found out my father had passed away. Then I decided, coincidently, that I should read the Psalms as I had no other way to have any ceremony in connection with the death of my father. I spoke a little Hebrew, but it was only colloquial Hebrew. It was very difficult, at first, for me to understand the psalms, but when I concentrated on it, and compared one psalm with another, I began to understand. Avital's book came to me, and King David himself came to me to support me and God came to me to support me. Then it turned into a very important spiritual experience not only of my connection with Avital and with my culture but with that spiritual world which was giving me the strength and purpose to survive.

When, at the end of my imprisonment, they took everything from me before sending me away and when they took me to the airfield, I understood that almost all my strength in all those years came from that little book and I can not leave it. That's why I threw myself into the snow, because I was afraid if I now gave up, I would lose all my world. It summed up my resistance to the KGB not to let them take away from me all these values.

Q: Were there any psalms in particular, that have become the most important to you?

SHARANSKY: Well, the one from which I took the title of my book *Fear No Evil*.

Q: That is from the twenty-third psalm, "The Lord is My Shepherd."

SHARANSKY: The other is the one which says, "When my father and my mother leave me, then God will take me up (Ps. 27:10)." It is like *atta imadi*, "You [God] are with me" (Ps. 23:4). Even when you are left all alone, there is still a Force upholding you.

Q: So those became the most important ones to you?

SHARANSKY: I connected these various sentences. I cannot separate them. In fact, all the words from the psalms, some I understood better than others, spoke to me.

Q: How do you describe yourself now, not only as an Israeli, but as a Jew? Is religion simply a background or is it something that you try to understand and practice? Are you a Jew in theory or in practice, or both a thinking *and* a practicing Jew?

SHARANSKY: I don't like definitions, especially with reference to religion, Judaism, and our heritage. You mention thinking Jews. Are there *non*thinking Jews? Are they not looking, searching for a way, even if they don't realize exactly what they are searching for?

Q: We have many different Jews. We have forgetting Jews. We have hidden Jews.

SHARANSKY: Yes, but everybody is thinking. So you see why I don't like definitions. I am a Jew, which means that I realize myself as part of Jewish history, and that realization came to me in my struggle in the Soviet Union, as one who wanted to return to a specific culture and a specific tradition. That is how I began looking back and thinking my way back to the Jewish religion. I reached that realization in my last years in prison. I found that there are powerful spiritual roles which are much stronger than material goals and which were dictating to me the way I behaved much more than material needs. That is how I, as one who was so far from this tradition and didn't believe in forcing upon himself what was not natural for him, came to understand and to feel God. I am now moving back to this world with my own speed, in my own way. My children shouldn't have that kind of a gap between themselves and their people. That is why I chose a religious school for them.

Q: It has been said that man's extremity is God's opportunity. When we are stripped of everything, we have nothing else to lean on, we finally reach out to the ultimate. That may have been true at the time of your imprisonment. Now you are a free man, free to choose, free to neglect. Do you have as much desire to explore the Jewish religion, the basic elements of faith, at this point as previously in your life?

SHARANSKY: When I came back to my people and to my God, my life became so much more meaningful and interesting. After the prison, I had no desire to go back to that life which I had before. On the other hand, life out of prison is in danger of becoming more shallow because of a lot of obligations, a lot of pressures, a lot of meetings, a lot of interviews, and all that. Inevitably, you are left with less time to think, to analyze. And so, I have come to rely more and more on external things. You are choosing your way of life by educating yourself, by deciding what kind of school your children will go to, and by deciding with what kind of people you spend Shabbat. We prefer to spend Shabbat having some kind of discussions, but life is losing some of its depth or essentiality. It is a pity. Yes, I am interested, I'm very curious what kind of Judaism will develop for my life.

Q: Is there any Jewish belief of which you can say, *ani ma'amin be'emunah sh'lemah*, I believe this with complete faith?

SHARANSKY: I believe that there is God and that the Jewish people have a special mission which is influencing our history and our lives. I believe, as I said before, that there is a spiritual world. If you go beyond your material goals and live in accordance with your spiritual goals, there will be much more meaning to your life. I believe that the more you live according to Jewish tradition, the more natural and easier your life will be. I believe that the way back to your tradition and to your God must be a very natural way, not something you force yourself to do, things which you don't understand or don't accept or don't feel as an absolute mandate. I realize that this contradicts the Orthodox view that whether or not you understand you must follow the practice. I practice Shabbat and I am enjoying it very much.

Q: Are you satisfied with what your children are learning in their school?

SHARANSKY: They are in kindergarten. I know so little that even what my children are learning in kindergarten is so much more than what I was learning when I was a child. So, when I am reading the *parashat ha-shavua* [the weekly Bible portion] and my five-year-old daughter is telling me about some kind of commands which I didn't know and she knows, I can say that I am very satisfied.

Q: Is there any historic personality, thinker, writer, a figure in the Bible or in literature, that especially appeals to you?

SHARANSKY: Because of what I told you, King David. I am not a specialist in Judaism. I read some articles by Rav Soloveitchik and his *The Lonely Man of Faith* which impressed me; also the book of *Nine Questions People Ask About Judaism* by Joseph Telushkin and Dennis Prager. This type of book was very helpful, on the level I could appreciate, basic Judaism.

Q: What comes to your mind as you think about God?

SHARANSKY: God is a power and a spirit. Now, there is a world of moral values, and when you try to interpret these values in practical ways, why you should behave this way or that, it sometimes makes no sense. When I was in prison, I was given a very simple choice: "Agree to say what we ask you to say, and you can go to Israel." And for all the pragmatic reasons which they were feeding me they thought I would do it. They felt if I'd do it, I would lose that which I had found for myself and I would again be a slave and again live the kind of life which I was not interested in. There is a God of moral values which simply was not part of their culture, a God who really exists objectively and dictates to you the way to live if you choose it. Of course you have freedom of choice. I was lucky, I had a chance to compare both ways of life, life without God, a fully materialistic life, and the kind of life when you are doing what you feel will satisfy your sense of what ought to be. And that is how I came to God. I don't think about God as a person who is the chief producer. I think of God more as a spirit.

Q: Is your God a source of ideas and of power?

SHARANSKY: Does God exist objectively or does a person within himself develop that idea? That is the question which makes the difference between theology and humanism. As for this question, I have no answer and that doesn't matter.

Q: It doesn't matter because you have the strength of experience. Experience is stronger than any argument. You found yourself driven by an absolute power. There is one small book in the Bible that expresses this sense of the irresistible mandate, the force of the world that ought to be: Amos. It is the most powerful statement of exactly the attitude that you expressed. A person who cannot but act in a certain way. I must speak—God has spoken, who can be silent? (See Amos 3.8.) You cannot resist the force that moves you. Can you imagine that God gave the Jews a mission? Can you imagine God favoring one people against another?

SHARANSKY: You can look at the Jewish mission as a favor or a burden, a task. There are always people who take upon themselves some kind of burden and others who condemn them as crazy or suspect that they want more than others. Or they are simply regarded as unfortunate victims who must suffer. Twenty years ago, when the first Jews were leaving the Soviet Union, other Jews were looking at them as though they were crazy or failures. Now, the same people that come here think how clever and smart were those who came before.

Q: Do you think history will bear out the Jews as being on the right path, having a superior system of beliefs, or a superior vision of society and human relations?

SHARANSKY: Yes. Take the pure light of Jewish philosophy, of Jewish ideas, or visions of society. But the picture is complicated. How many Jews themselves believe in the Jewish way of life?

Q: Aside from your prison experience, have you had any other experience which experientially would influence your belief in God? Do you believe it is possible to experience God?

SHARANSKY: In some moments my wife Avital and I, when we were worried, we felt inspired. We felt that our wildest dreams were becoming true. Our prayer has come to God, whether it was the moment when our daughter was born or whether it was the moment when the Soviet empire collapsed. They say that at such moments you are feeling the presence of God, or the presence of spirit, or the presence of justice or whatever. I wouldn't overestimate the importance of such single moments because the experience which I went through in prison was much deeper. It was not one moment of revelation, but years of revelation. In those years I gained the realization that life, the principles of life, are dictated by some higher authority. The single moments of revelation can always be explained through one's own mood or inner state of mind.

Q: You said beforehand that there is a contrast between the religious believers who think their inspiration or their ideas come from God, and the humanists who believe that whatever we think, our moral values were developed in centuries or millennia of human experience. It is possible to say both. One can say, God speaks *to* man, and one can say, God speaks *in* man. The problem is how to distinguish which voice is mine and which is God's?

SHARANSKY: And whether there is a difference at all. Maybe the difference is only definitions. I did a lot of thinking about these things in prison. In all my past, my ethical and scientific thinking was strictly materialistic. I had been taught that that's the way I developed, through the experience of my own life and the lives of many generations. But my state of mind and my behavior were telling me that there are some things beyond me and the more I realized it, the more I became a free person.

Q: You said that you went beyond materialism, that you discovered the power of the spiritual dimension. Does that include the idea of immortality, of the soul?

SHARANSKY: Whether the soul of King David exists or not, King David, three thousand years after his death, came to me with his Psalms to my prison cell and gave me a lot of strength, and that is what is important for me. And that is why the question of his soul, whether it physically exists or continues in some other way, is not important for me. It is not important. It is very difficult for me to understand what it means, maybe because of my materialistic background.

Q: In the last two hundred years there has been a fierce debate on the question of the Messiah in Jewish theology. Do you have any views on the Messiah?

SHARANSKY: No, I don't have a place for it in my thinking. Our human desire for perfection, our desire to improve the world is something in us. Even Jews who are forgetting about Judaism, have this driving force inside themselves for the improvement of this world. That shows me that there is some kind of direction in this world. There is movement from the past to the future; things don't move in a circle.

Q: There is a linear development in history.

SHARANSKY: There is a direction, progress. But it is not the scientific progress of my younger years. I am looking for moral improvement of the world which is a most difficult process. So in this way I can see the Messiah like an idea of perfection.

Q: You are now an Israeli. If you had the power to create a Jewish state, what kind of country would it be? Would it be strictly secular? Would it be a theocracy? Or would it be a combination of both?

SHARANSKY: I am not Messiah; I am not God. I don't have the chutzpah to create an ideal state for Jews. Whatever formula we might apply now, it will not be stable because Jews are in the midst of a process and it is a very difficult process of constant change and adjustment in their return to Zion. Also we face the crises of many secular beliefs and remain vulnerable to assimilation. Despite all that, the Jewish people is building a Jewish State for everyone. The formula that I thought was so simple when I was in Russia, that is, the idea of a democratic, pluralistic state, becomes much more difficult the moment when all these people come together. Given the formula of a democratic pluralistic state like America, you can see that the specifically Jewish challenge, all the beliefs and values that you were talking about, would simply disappear. You can talk about an Orthodox Jewish State but then it will not be the State of the Jews because the majority of the Jews, even those who are trying to find their way back to religion, wouldn't fit into such a State.

I think there must be some basic democratic principles with enough room for people to search for their own ways, to create a State which has not yet been built. I don't mean "built" in terms of territory or borders, or from the point of view of their main institutions. What I mean is that there is a need to build a formal, basic consensus. If you were to say, let us write a constitution, it would be practically impossible, under these circumstances, to write this constitution. We need more time to develop our system. But somehow things have to be done already. We are talking about religion. From my point of view, one of the biggest mistakes is that religion becomes more and more involved in party politics.

Q: You would separate religion from politics?

SHARANSKY: The fact that religious parties are playing such an important role in day-by-day political affairs undermines their real role in Judaism as the force which should unite the Jewish people in their historical way. So I would leave politics to politicians. Politicians can themselves be religious persons. I'd like to see more of them with *kippot* [skullcaps], but not as representatives of their religious movement.

Q: You are saying that the State is in the process of building: we need a democracy in which the different forces and different opinions can be expressed; but you deplore the politicizing of religion. It becomes part of the struggle of the marketplace.

SHARANSKY: Exactly right. What is happening now is undermining and weakening the opportunities of religion to influence Israelis. Many Israelis today feel that they are Jews simply because they live in and are citizens of the State of Israel. They feel that to be religious means to fight for your part of the budget and to favor one political agenda against another.

Q: When you are in politics, you make deals, you compromise your moral principles.

SHARANSKY: Then your real message is not listened to by the people.

Q: You are a diaspora Jew who came to Israel. Would you like to see all Jews to come to Israel if it were possible? Or do you think it is important that there be a Jewish State *and* a Jewish people, international and global?

SHARANSKY: Judaism has developed, connecting the Jews of the diaspora, and the Jews of the world, with the land of Israel. It would be unnatural to expect changes in world Jewry that would make them all Zionists. On the other hand, history is pushing more and more Jews to go to Israel and what is happening these days proves it. People who never dreamed nor cared about Israel, who thought that they were no longer Jews, feel themselves endangered in the diaspora. They find out that there is no place in the world for them, not even in the *goldene medina*, America. We are ready to accept them. I think in the future the majority of the Jewish people will live in Israel. I think that diaspora Jewry will diminish. If diaspora life is tough, our people will be leaving. If their life is soft, many Jews will be simply disappearing. I see the future of the Jewish people, that is the majority of Jews, in Israel. I am talking about the next century; I'm not talking about the time of the Messiah.

Q: Imagine that you had time, let us say, two or three days a week to do what you want, read what you want, study what you want—what would you want to learn about Judaism?

SHARANSKY: I shall have to disappoint you because, in fact, I am a beginner in the world of Judaism. I am studying Torah. I have a teacher once a week and we are going slowly through the Chumash [Pentateuch] and some of the commandments. We have been doing this for more than two years and I have still not finished Chumash. If I had much more time, I would like to finish it, with all the commandments, and then study the other books of the Tanakh [Bible], not just reading but studying the text with Rashi and the other commentators and consider command after command. In the normal traditional Jewish family, people have gotten their basic Jewish education in school and I never could do it. Eventually, I would like to read books by ha-rav Kook and ha-rav Soloveitchik who have both had a profound influence on the people around me. Also, from time to time I like to go to the seminars of ha-rav Steinsaltz.

Q: What do you think of him?

SHARANSKY: I think that he is a great man. There is need in the world and also in Judaism for people who can cross the borders of their own group and he is one of the most impressive persons I ever met for whom there are no borders in any area in the world of science, religion, and specifically in the world of Orthodoxy. He crosses all bridges.

Adin Steinsaltz

Rabbi Adin Steinsaltz, now in his mid-fifties and the world's best-known Talmudist, was raised in a secular home. He read Marx before the Torah and Freud before the Talmud. While still a socialist teenager, he had planned a career as a mathematician and physicist, but he turned to Orthodox Judaism to fill a void in his life. As a former agnostic who turned religious when he began to doubt his own doubts, Steinsaltz understands the mind of the skeptic and has the spark that can kindle religious faith in nonbelievers. He thus serves as a bridge between the world of the religious and nonreligious Jews.

Steinsaltz heads two yeshivot in Israel, and he created a Jewish research center in Moscow. Among the various branches of Judaism, Hasidism is the one to which he feels closest, "the only brand of Jewishness that made any sense to me." Most recently a Fellow at the Woodrow Wilson Institute in Washington, he was honored in 1991 by his own country's highest award, the Israel Prize.

Steinsaltz seems like a man who has found a hidden treasure and can't wait to tell the others about it. The treasure is the Jewish religious heritage, the indispensable source of meaning without which life remains an emptiness.

The wisdom he discovered in rabbinic literature, the insights he gained from encounters with great philosophic minds, and the illumination drawn from Jewish mystical writings, are fully integrated in his mind and are related to the various sciences and interests which we characterize as "modern." What comes out of his mouth are not strings of quotations, but fresh and original ideas, rooted in deep learning and reflection, sparkling answers to questions such as: Can God be experienced? What is meant by God's voice: Is it possible to know anything about God?

If only a lighted match can kindle a fire, Steinsaltz may be said to be ablaze with the fire of faith and enthusiasm, and with the power to spark that flame in others.

Choosing a life of a Talmud scholar, he has so far translated into modern Hebrew most of the thirty-six volumes of the Babylonian Talmud, and recently undertook an English edition of that monumental compendium of Jewish Law and tradition. In addition, he has published several books on Jewish spirituality, mysticism and Biblical interpretations, including *Biblical Images: Men and Women of the Book, In the Beginning* and *The Long Shorter Way,* both subtitled "Discourses on Hasidic Thought," *The Strife and the Spirit* and *The Thirteen Petalled Rose.* We spoke in Rabbi Steinsaltz's study in Jerusalem, November 20, 1991.

Q: What was it that most influenced you to move from the secular world view of your youth into a religious pathway?

STEINSALTZ: I cannot point to any particular event or person that did it. I found very few Jewish converts who, according to Willam James's description, experienced an overnight conversion.

Q: That was not the case with you?

STEINSALTZ: That was not the case with me, but, generally speaking, it is very rarely the case with anybody, with any Jew that I know. I thought about what there is in Judaism that makes it hard or next to impossible to make such a conversion. It must be in our nature. We are, as a people, quite obstinate, which means changes and shifting positions are not by any means easy for our people. I found very few that could claim an overnight conversion. In most cases, it was a prolonged process. In my case, my role models were either not religious, or half-religious. The religious ones I knew were not very tempting. My move was prompted by a basic lack of belief in the tenets of the secular world in which I lived. In my teens, there began a search for understanding the world and finding my place, instead of following the general view. I felt the need to think for myself. This may be a bit unusual. Independent thinking clearly is a disappearing art, but there were all kinds of personal reasons why it wasn't so unusual for me. It was possibly an attitude of not caring very much about society's opinion.

Q: Independence of mind?

STEINSALTZ: Independence of mind. For my late father, I put on his tombstone a quotation: *ahavta tzedek v'tisna resha* [You have loved righteousness and hated wickedness. Ps. 45.8]. This, and just his name. And for my mother I put four words: *ahavat chesed v'hatz-ne-a lechet* [Love kindness and walk humbly. Micah 6.8].

Q: Was your father, from your point of view, a moralist aware of the *t'nuat ha-mussar* [the Mussar movement]?*

STEINSALTZ: Oh no. Morality, in our family had nothing to do with theory or theology. This was part of my upbringing, of life in the family. The only brand of Jewishness that made any sense for me was Hasidic. You might say it is in the genes.

Q: Do you come from a Hasidic family?

STEINSALTZ: Oh yes. I come from several rebbes; so it is possibly in the genes . . .

Q: What were you searching for in your reading?

STEINSALTZ: To define myself and the world.

---

*Mussar means "morality" or "ethics." The Bible's strong emphasis on moral conduct which inspired numerous ethical works in the post-Biblical era gave rise to a systematic movement for Jewish ethical advancement in the nineteenth century. At a time when Talmudic learning and Hasidic pietism competed for supremacy in Jewish life, Rabbi Israel Salanter (1810–1853) founded the Mussar movement to include ethics among the highest priorities of Judaism.

Q: How old were you when you could say, now I know where I am?, now I have found myself?

STEINSALTZ: I read a story by Kafka about a person who wakes up and finds that he is a cockroach. Finding myself religious was almost the same thing for me.

Q: It was a surprise?

STEINSALTZ: It was more than a surprise. If one wakes up and finds himself an angel, it is different. But when you find yourself a cockroach? The most frightening and hardest point to get over and the biggest obstacle in Judaism are the Jews. The theory is so much superior to the people. Part of this trouble is belonging to a group of people that one does not particularly admire. I knew them and I didn't particularly admire them. Incidentally, since then my point of view has changed very much. The change in my attitude came about like in the story of *Avraham avinu* [Abraham, our patriarch], rather than any of those conversions which are traumatic and dramatic; very gradual, and by way of making friends and observing them.

Q: Would you say that you were, then, one of the *mevakshe derech* [seekers of the way]?

STEINSALTZ: I was not one of the mevakshe derech in the sense as that term is understood today, i.e., seekers of spirituality. I did not search for spirituality. I was really searching for something to place me in this world, in existence.

Q: Orientation?

STEINSALTZ: Yes, orientation. As I said about Avraham avinu's quest, questions such as, who made it?, how does it work?, from where did it come or where does it go?

Q: Looking for truth?

STEINSALTZ: More like a person who is going for a stroll and looks at the scenery.

Q: Perhaps like a person who goes traveling and sees new pictures, new landscapes?

STEINSALTZ: Just imagine that you are packing something with no particular purpose in mind except you are aware you want to go somewhere.

Q: Then your greatest pleasure must have been the adventure of discovery?

STEINSALTZ: It was discovery. It was not a systematic search, nor was it in the nature of a revelation, a bright new light that is shining.

Q: Not a sudden illumination?

STEINSALTZ: Not a sudden illumination.

Q: How do you react to a message that says *d'var ha-Shem*, "This is the word of God"? Do you understand it as something given to a person, or is it something that speaks out of us and is identified as the word of God?

STEINSALTZ: Well, I was never a great believer in what the Christians call the still, small voice. I always suspected that what one hears may be any kind of voice, from a grandmother to whoever, but not God. If one may again use strong language, I would say there is an even chance that it is the devil who speaks in this still, small voice. By the way, you know that *kol d'mamah dakkah*, the so-called still, small voice (1 Kings 19.12) should be translated "a small voice of stillness." *Dakkah* is an adverb and it might be translated in this context "a voice of stillness (or silence) which is 'small'."

Q: What does that mean?

STEINSALTZ: What is the voice of silence? How does silence become noticeable? In many ways silence speaks louder than an audible voice. What the text *wants* to say is that God was not in the visible and audible things, earthquake, fire, storm. Then came stillness.

Q: But what would be the point of that context? Elijah was looking for some sign of God. It was not in the earthquake, it was not in the fire, it was not in the storm. And then came silence. What's the meaning of that?

STEINSALTZ: You want to see the glory of God, something tangible, and the text says, all these things are ephemeral and incidental. The highest point that you can reach is the absolute void, the emptiness, the stillness. From there comes a voice, not a still, small voice. You perceive it standing against the Infinite, something beyond comprehension. It is the voice of the void, like the void before Creation.

Q: Would you say perhaps, that in that absolute stillness and silence, the curtain is lifted, all the obstacles and the in-between things are removed, and you come as close as you can to the perception of God?

STEINSALTZ: We are told that Moses and Isaiah both saw God. Isaiah through glasses, so to speak, but Moses, directly. Isaiah's vision was blurred; he described God in all kinds of images. Moses' vision was clearer.

Q: More profound?

STEINSALTZ: He saw beyond what everyone else could see. Moses' and Elijah's revelations were very much alike, a lot of parallels. People can be divinely guided, knowingly or unknowingly. It is different from anything clear cut, from any other kind of knowledge. When we speak of the Godhead, we are, to use a philosophic term, referring to "the absolute other." The Midrash says Samuel was a *tiron*, a beginner in prophecy.* (See I Samuel 3.) The point is, he was not given the thing-in-itself to perceive.

Q: Is it possible for a person to be greatly mistaken and misjudge the so-called revelation or to believe he has the revelation when he has not? But in the case of Samuel, we have the unusual situation where it *really* was a revelation, but he did not understand it.

STEINSALTZ: The mistakes of those who imagine they *have* revelations are perhaps more dangerous, because they are prone to act upon them. You know I am not sure about the *Rambam*'s [Mai-

---

*Biblical theology (see Deut. 34.10), as well as Midrashic literature (rabbinical commentaries), elevates Moses above all other prophets. Compared with him, the prophet Samuel was a mere beginner.

monides] notion of a prophet as one who is either connected with or comparable to the notion of a philosopher. This description of a prophet may be just a very nice person, but he doesn't seem to be a prophet. Something else is moving him. The danger comes in when the prophet is feeling something, and the more strongly he feels it, the more I might suspect that he's really hearing his own voice, an echo of himself.

Q: So for that reason you would be suspicious of anyone saying that he has heard the word of God?

STEINSALTZ: I would be extremely suspicious.

Q: Is it impossible?

STEINSALTZ: I don't think it is impossible.

Q: How do you judge, then? What would be a criterion?

STEINSALTZ: I see a kind of double problem. On the one hand, the person himself is not sure until some time has passed. On the other hand, an outsider is in a much worse position. Take the story of Gideon: *V'asita li ot she-ata m'dabber immi*, "Show me a sign that you are talking with me" (Judges 6.17).

Q: He is looking for a sign, for evidence.

STEINSALTZ: He had a revelation. But he was suspicious. He wondered, which voices are these? Do I hear myself amplifying my own voice?

Q: If you had to judge a prophecy or revelation, not one from the Tanakh [Bible], but from a contemporary person who is serious, who has followers, what would be your criterion for judging? Or would you not want to judge?

STEINSALTZ: Oh, I had to. There is someone in the States who declared himself as the Messiah. He clearly has some kind of ESP. I met him. He spoke about revelation, a serious person. He was brought to me by a person who was then professor at a university. The only way of judging is to make assumptions. One of these assumptions is that a person, claiming to have received a revelation, shouldn't be speaking stupidities.

Q: So that would be your test?

STEINSALTZ: Absurdities, stupidities are for the most part what we hear from all kinds of people who proclaim a revelation. The basic problem is that what they hear and what they reveal is so unimportant. For example, would you believe me if I said that the Almighty told me to smoke only so many cigarettes?

Q: That brings us to the question of what we can finally know. Is it possible to have a *da-at ha-Shem*, a knowledge about God? What kind of knowledge is meant in *b'chol derakhekha da-ehu*, "In all your ways you shall know him" (Proverbs 3.6.)?

STEINSALTZ: It depends on what kind of knowledge we are talking about. For some people, knowledge is intellectual. And for others, knowledge is emotional. There are people who are "attuned"; it is neither intellectual nor emotional.

Q: Do you mean connected?

STEINSALTZ: They are connected! Some people will know in a certain way, because of a natural grace. They know "this is the right way." They feel somehow that they are moving in the right way and they will react rightly.

Q: They have a sense of intimacy with God?

STEINSALTZ: They have a closeness that is not conscious. It is an instinctive awareness; when I say he is "attuned," I mean a resonance to God. With some people it is more intellectual. For example, the notion that somebody is writing *b'ruach ha-kodesh* [in the holy spirit], refers to an intellectual involvement. Is he writing revelations? Revelation implies an "otherness" and one of my ways of testing it is to ask, is it really so "other"? And if it is not, if, e.g., it merely repeats what friends in school already told me, I would suspect it. I would suspect it among other things, when it is not "individual," i.e., when it is not something new and different.

Q: You would expect a revelation to be not the common knowledge available to everyone, but different, new, unexpected?

STEINSALTZ: In order for a revelation to be credible, it needs to be an individual's distinctive resonance to God! If I had two or three whose statements are exactly alike, then, these two or three are lying!

Q: They are lying if their statements are identical?

STEINSALTZ: Yes. See, if people tell the same basic story in different styles, then their veracity stands higher. A genuine personal account, something you saw with your own eyes, has to be colored by your personality. Now, if you are just repeating what somebody told you, it will conform to what others are saying. It may be a lie; it will not have your identity; it will be just a copy. Let me suggest an analogy for the relationship of the prophets and prophecy: there is *one* melody rendered by different instruments, violins, cellos, flutes. It is the same melody, or you might say, the same truth, but it sounds somewhat different on each instrument.

Q: It will have each instrument's characteristics.

STEINSALTZ: It will be exactly the same melody. Can there be knowledge of God? I would say such knowledge comes out of being attuned and resonating to God. With some, it's a matter of pure instinct, a first reaction. They do good, not because they are particularly religious. They act without being particularly conscious of the goodness of their action.

Q: Would you say this is the case of a person who walks with God wherever he is?

STEINSALTZ: Yes, without even knowing it!

Q: Resonating to God's presence?

STEINSALTZ: Some people have a very high aptitude, whether they are playing golf or doing mathematics. They are always making the right turns. You possibly know about some people's sense of direction? Some people are natural in their sense of direction; others will always get lost. "Knowing" may be something purely intellectual, or instinctive and natural.

Q: What can a person do to experience God?. Can God be experienced, or are we referring to various events from which we deduce the power of God?

STEINSALTZ: It is a practical question often ignored by theologians. They write books about God but they are not necessarily bothered by any of it in a personal sense. But, clearly, for many people this is a bothersome problem. It is tantalizing for some people. Did you know Buber?

Q: Yes, I met him.

STEINSALTZ: Buber "played" the prophet, which he was not, but he had a wonderful, good mind. Buber said there were quite a number of people who had experienced seeing the pillar of fire, not an actual external fire, but a revelation. The difference between them and Moses was *what* they learned from it. One of the points that has always bothered me is the possibility of the senseless or stupid revelation. Let's say you have a wonderful experience, you feel reborn and, then, what you hear is that a pound of meat can be bought cheaply in this or that store.

Q: Are you saying that a revelation that ends with triviality is no revelation?

STEINSALTZ: It is a matter of what you are expecting. You need to be prepared for an experience to gain the right thing from it. What I am saying is that a person may be looking and searching and unless he has some idea of what he's looking for and a notion of what to expect, he may end up with some foolish thing, a discovery or revelation of absurdity. In one of Andersen's tales, a group of people who never saw a nightingale or heard his voice are looking for him. They search and search, and suddenly, for the first time in their lives, they hear a bull and because of its powerful sound they say, let's get him; it must be the nightingale. Then, they hear a frog, and still other sounds. And each time, they are sure it must be the nightingale's voice. When you search for something you really don't know, you may end up with nothing. That is the risk of listening to your so-called revelation, it may be no more than the voice of a frog.

Q: You may totally misjudge your experience?

STEINSALTZ: Yes, one may misjudge one's experience. Also, it may be the other way around, one may have a genuine experience of God but not understand it. I don't believe a person can identify with God, perhaps because my God is so much bigger. I don't think one can become very "friendly" with God. Quite to the contrary of certain Hollywood films in which the hero becomes God's "pal" and performs miracles with His help. I'd call that *goyim naches* [gentiles' pleasure]. We Jews don't relate to God on such terms. There are in our mental hospitals any number of Messiahs but, as far as I know, not one that is imagining he is God.

Q: Your explanation, then, of *ta-amu u'reu*, "experience [taste] and see" (Ps. 34.9), is that experience is possible but that it also takes more than experience to understand it. We must have knowledge, we must prepare the mind.

STEINSALTZ: We must prepare, but remember you are likely to see what you expect to see, but whatever it is, it won't be God. Some people fantasize about a huge white cloud, and sitting there is God on a golden throne. If that is what they want in a revelation, they might see it, but it surely won't be God.

Q: The value of the experience is conditioned by the expectation and knowledge beforehand.

STEINSALTZ: Yes, that is true. But sometimes the opposite is true. The experience may come to you unexpectedly. I remember, once on a trip, having a casual conversation with a woman during a transatlantic flight to the U.S.A. Toward the end of the flight I learned that the purpose of her trip was to meet me. She was totally surprised when she found out that I was the man. I was not at all what she had expected. Similarly, we may be taken by surprise in an experience of revelation altogether different from what we would expect.

Q: You referred to the "Messiahs" in insane asylums. Let us now think of the Messiah seriously as a major article of faith. Do you foresee a personal Messiah? Do you believe Jews must cling to this belief in light of the Holocaust? Has not the Messianic faith turned into a forlorn hope, a wish or dream?

STEINSALTZ: First of all, the Messiah is clearly not a deus ex machina: "Now I am in trouble, and the Messiah will rush to my rescue." He is not a rescue squad. At times, I may prefer a different kind of existence, and wish the Messiah's coming will make a change for the better. But, if I am happy and satisfied with my life, any kind of a disruption would be frightening. So I don't think about the Messiah. But, if I am living a miserable life, then a change for the better is something that I would be thinking about quite a lot. The basic notion of the Messiah is related to the riddle of the world. Somehow there must be an answer to our quest for meaning.

Q: It is like the piece of a puzzle that needs to be put in.

STEINSALTZ: It is a piece of the puzzle. It is also the idea of getting out of a maze.

Q: What kind of Messiah do you believe in?

STEINSALTZ: Oh, a very personal one. Now, in our time, the chances for communication are enormous. We are living in a world that is so unstable that we are losing all certainty; we are losing all kinds of fixed adherence to anything.

Q: Rigidity and self-confidence have been badly shaken.

STEINSALTZ: Certainly; on the other hand, people are still searching for them. Some people were talking with me about the Messiah. I said, if the Messiah had come forty years ago, Ben-Gurion would have called out the *Palmach* [Israel's elite fighting force] to fight him.

Q: Then to you, Messiah is the principle of a divine response to human impotence.

STEINSALTZ: The world is far more ready today for any kind of a move, because huge, dramatic changes are now easier since the world is far less rigidly fixed in any position. This means that you have now such a loose combination of things that rearranging them is much easier than it was forty years ago.

Q: In other words, the Messianic agenda of overcoming oppression and bringing peace and security to the world is more doable now by a great person than it was in the past?

STEINSALTZ: It is more doable. Our ability to make big changes is much greater. I also believe that, great as our problems may be in this world, the human condition does not have to be a tragedy. I believe there are solutions, maybe terribly difficult to find and apply. But there is a formula.

Q: Assuming the Messiah has a job to do and the ability to do it, must he be a person, endowed with supernatural powers?

STEINSALTZ: I don't know that supernatural powers are needed. I don't see in any basic source the necessity for supernatural powers in the Messiah.

Q: Do we still need to believe in the Messiah at all?

STEINSALTZ: The Messiah is the answer to the world's unsolved and unsolvable problems. If you believe that you are not just going around in a purposeless, useless way, you have to believe *b'viat ha-mashiach* [in the coming of the Messiah], namely, that eventually there is a solution.

Conclusion:
What Jews Still Believe
in Spite of Everything

The teenage girl Anne Frank who wrote in her diary, while hiding in an attic in Amsterdam, "in spite of everything I still believe that people are really good at heart," may well have been the last Jew to affirm the essential goodness of humanity. Faith in the inherent nobility of man, a doctrine of the Enlightenment rather than of Jewish theology, had been evaporating for generations until the savagery of two world wars and the Holocaust put an end to it. Amazingly, that chamber of horrors we call history, which stripped us of our native trust in man, left the Jewish faith in God largely intact. In spite of everything, Jews still believe in God and, more or less, still cling to age-old doctrines derived from their monotheistic faith. This is one of the more remarkable conclusions one may draw from our inquiry into the new condition of Jewish beliefs.

I make no claim that the fourteen eminent Jews—rabbis, philosophers, scientists, novelists, and other intellectuals—whom I involved in religious dialogue constitute a statistically correct sampling of the religious thinking of Jews throughout the world, even though they represent the full rainbow of religious diversity

from Orthodoxy to near agnosticism. Yet, because of their promi-
nence and intellectual stature, these fourteen men and women
may be considered indicative of newly emerging patterns of Jewish religious thought. In reviewing their dialogues, one cannot
but sense a general mood of confidence in Judaism as a religion.
There is no hint of religious decline, no lamentation over the loss
of faith which so often marked previous reports about the Jewish
religious condition.

One can point to several signs of a religious upturn. Popular
American Jewish magazines* have lately been publishing feature
articles about the new quest for Jewish spirituality. Dozens of new
books are expanding upon Jewish theology and most conspicu-
ous among them are those that focus on God.

If Daniel Bell were to republish his 1977 lecture "The Return
of the Sacred?,"† he would now probably put an exclamation
point after the title instead of a question mark. The 1970s witnessed a radical shift from social activism to preoccupation with
one's individual self in defining one's identity. The countercul-
ture historian Theodore Roszak called it "the longest introspec-
tive binge any society in history has undergone"‡

Roszak was not referring to a pietistic movement or a rage for
religious contemplation, but to a narcissistic kind of introspec-
tion, an obsessive fixation upon one's self. Having had our fill of
finding ourselves, asserting ourselves, esteeming ourselves and
fulfilling ourselves, we wound up with the discovery that at the
end of the exhaustive exploration of our identity was nothing but
a yawning emptiness within. The deeply felt need now is to reach
beyond ourselves for a larger context of meaning, for insights of
faith to take us beyond the limits of knowledge. The recovery of
the sacred is propelled by a craving for purpose which outlasts
our mortal self, by the quest for higher meaning to redeem us
from seemingly pointless existence, by the need to break out of

---

*I refer to magazines such as *Moment, Tikkun*, and *The Jewish Spectator*.
†"The Return of the Sacred?" delivered as the Hobhouse Memorial Lecture at the London School of Economics, March 1977, and published in *The Winding Passage*, essays in
sociological journeys 1960–1980, by Daniel Bell, ABT Books, Cambridge, MA.
‡Ibid., p. 348.

our existential loneliness to connect with the Ultimate in transcendence—and that is God.

Many of the religious beliefs voiced in our dialogues respond
to the anxieties of a generation despairing in its sense of insignifi-
cance and frightened by the abyss of nihilism. My question,
whether it is thinkable that the ultimate Power of the universe
could be aware of all the myriads of living beings and be concerned about a single person, a mere speck of dust in the cosmos,
was repeatedly answered with the affirmation of the God of Israel
as a God who cares.

Norman Lamm said simply: "It all depends on how big a God
you believe in . . . I believe in a very big God who can be concerned with everything, even a speck as apparently insignificant
as my own life in this vast universe." Steven T. Katz believes in
God's personal and impersonal aspects, neither of which can be
explained: "As for the mystery of God . . . If I could understand
God, *I* would be God. The Kotzker Rebbe once said: 'A God that
any Tom, Dick or Harry can understand, phooey, I don't need
such a God.' "

Our conception of God as a personal being is not a statement
of fact but, according to Katz, a reflection of our desire for "a
sense of security and meaning. By security I mean that human
life is not a random thing, that it is not meaningless, that there is
some kind of ultimate purpose into which we fit in some oblique
way that is not clear to us. That our actions do matter, and that
ultimately there will be a kind of squaring of the circle, that a
divine personal being, God, knows how it all fits together. Meaninglessness is the ultimate enemy of Judaism."

For Katz, belief in a personal God who cares is an expression of
our faith that: "Our life counts and that the world counts and that
it's not Sisyphus, pointlessly rolling the rock up the hill only to
have it come back down again and crush us. That there is something redemptive, something salvific, something meaningful,
that's what this personal aspect of God supplies."

The astrophysicist Arno Penzias declares God to be the source
of purpose in the universe: "By looking at the order in the world,
we can infer purpose and from purpose we begin to get some
knowledge of the Creator, the Planner of all this. This is, then,

how I look at God, I look at God through the works of God's hands and from those works imply intentions. From these intentions, I receive an impression of the Almighty."

Penzias is fully aware that his concept of a purposeful Creator may just be a "security blanket," but to believe otherwise, he finds impossible: "How can I face the world?"

Rachel Cowan is not alone in the sudden discovery that her social idealism has run out of steam. The will to do good must be empowered by a sense of obligation to something higher than one's own mood or personal preference. She finds that higher reality in the experience of genuine prayer which, for the first time in her life, gave her this "sense of intensely personal communication with God, the sense of being in the presence of God." When she wondered how she could sustain this feeling, the late Rabbi Wolfe Kelman wisely instructed her—and readers who are also on the entry level of the religious life might well take his advice to heart: "No person of faith lives on that level. You create a spiritual discipline so that between this moment and the next something carries you along and you are sort of ready and you are speaking to God when these moments happen."

In other words we need a religious structure, patterns of religious practice, to preserve our sensitivity for those precious moments of inspiration. It follows that we must not hastily write off the synagogue even if, admittedly, the service at times is dull and there is no sense of God's presence. Everyone in our dialogues who criticized the synagogue for its frequently uninspiring worship services, acknowledged also occasional prayer experiences of genuine awe, moments of a soaring sense of sanctity and luminous visions of the world's perfection. Cynthia Ozick credits the prayerbook for an occasional sense of the numinous presence of the deity: "It sometimes comes flying out of the text . . . although at times . . . it stirs me to intense tedium."

Norman Podhoretz, a fairly rare visitor to the synagogue, finds that: "A lot of the prayers are inferior. Still there are moments in the Machzor [High Holy Day prayerbook] which have given me a sense of connection with God."

Arno Penzias likewise reports: "Standing there, mumbling for an hour really bothers me." But, as the worship service proceeds it "does more than just identify me with our people and our history. It brings me closer with something that has sanctity so that, sometimes, I am able to feel that sanctity."

Much can be learned from our dialogues about the so-called God-experience. For the longest time I yearned for such experience. I coveted the ecstatic visions of the mystics who encountered God. Why could I not share in such experiences? The poetess Else Lasker-Schüler voiced my longing in her poem "Oh God":

> *If only once I could grasp*
> *God's hand . . .*
> *Oh God, oh God, how far am I*
> *From Thee!*

How does one get in touch with God or, as the poem puts it, "grasp God's hand"? Where is "the mountain top on which God is seen?" (Gen. 22.14).

Did my partners in dialogue report anything like an experience with God? I made a surprising discovery. Those strongest in faith and most devout in observance were least likely to have had a God-experience. All sorts of religious experience, yes. But not a God-experience. Only two persons in the group, the sophisticated editor of *Commentary*, Norman Podhoretz, and the Soviet dissenter, Natan Sharansky, claim to have had such an experience—and oddly, both describe themselves as rather unobservant. This finding caused me to reconsider the meaning of "God-experience." What is it really, and how crucial is it for religious faith?

England's leading Jewish theologian, Rabbi Louis Jacobs, said to me: "I never had anything like a mystical experience." Then he added: "My belief in God has very little to do with experience." Moreover, he found the words "encounter" or "dialogue" with God rather meaningless.

The staunchly Orthodox Professor Yeshayahu Leibowitz can make no sense out of an "encounter with God" except in the context of religious observance: "encounter with God is the fulfillment of the mitzvot." To illustrate his point, he adds: "If I washed today at half past six in the morning and went to the synagogue to fulfill the prayer duty, that was my encounter with God."

In view of Hasidism's emphasis on the immediacy and accessibility of God, I expected Rabbi Levi Yitzhak Horowitz, known to his Hasidic followers as the "Bostoner Rebbe" to attest to experiences of God, or at least affirm their possibility. But he, too, quickly distanced himself from the notion of a God-experience: "Torah and mitzvot represent in this world the elements of ha-Shem (the name, i.e., God), the elements of faith. These are the instruments by which we are able to experience what ha-Shem means." He clinched his point with an example which he thought would be especially appealing to me as a resident of Washington. Referring to the public tours of the White House, he said:

> A Jew can certainly not drop in on the inner sanctum of God, no more than, when in the White House, one would go into the president's living quarters. . . . Such a person would have *chutzpah*. That is not where you belong.

The Bostoner Rebbe affirms that through various ritual acts one gains "that special feeling of being connected, of being linked up." But clearly, this feeling of being "connected" with God is far less than a God-experience.

The philosopher Emil Fackenheim helped me make a breakthrough in my thinking about the God-experience. During our long discussion in the kitchen of his apartment in Jerusalem, I asked, "Do you think that the word 'experience' is meaningful or applicable to God? In what sense does a human being experience God?" His answer—"the word 'experience' is a slippery word"—made me realize how hazardous it is to speak of a God-experience. What is an experience? It has a subjective meaning and in that sense it refers to one's own feelings aroused by whatever cause, which may be imagined or objective reality. We can never be sure that *God* is the cause that triggers our feelings, images, ideas and illusions. The ideas and feelings aroused in us in consequence of the religious experience surely say something about our own psyche and state of mind, but whether they disclose anything about God is open to question.

Fackenheim points out that many synagogues have a Talmudic quotation inscribed above the ark, "Know before Whom you are standing." "Standing before God" does not mean that you have to experience God's presence. When I asked if knowing, the mere knowledge, the inner certainty, of being in the presence of God is all that we can experience, Fackenheim answered "yes" and warned "all this emphasis on experience can lead you very badly astray."

Although I now attach far less importance than previously to the so-called "God experiences" or "encounters" with God (whatever that may mean), I would not dismiss them out of hand. Each case needs to be judged on its own merit. Podhoretz describes such an experience: "I sort of apprehended in the flashes . . . the nature of things . . . What I had was a blazing experience of illumination." Podhoretz does not call it exactly an experience of God, but a "mystical religious experience." What he gained from it was some kind of intuitive knowledge, "a sense of understanding." He then specifies: "And what I understood . . . was what the Bible tells us about God and about the nature of the world and about law."

In his prison cell, the Soviet dissident Natan Sharansky, who was raised in the spirit of Marxist atheism, had a powerful religious experience in connection with his reading of the psalms. He discovered a spiritual reality for which his materialistic ideology had made no allowance: "God came to me to support me . . . Even when you are left alone, there is still a force upholding you." He was puzzled by his inability to make pragmatic compromises with his oppressors which might have eased the conditions of his imprisonment. Prudence would have persuaded him to yield, but an inner force commanded him to resist. He discovered, as he put it, "that spiritual world which was giving me strength and purpose to survive." In response to my question, "Do you belive it is possible to experience God?" Sharansky recalled certain moments of exaltation when one is supposed to feel the presence of God. However, with a healthy dose of skepticism, he pointed out that he "wouldn't overestimate the importance of such single moments." He then explained:

The experience which I went through in prison was much deeper . . . It was not one moment of revelation, but years of revelation. In these years I gained the realization that life, the principles of life, are dictated by some higher authority. The single moments of revelation can always be explained through one's own mood or inner state of mind.

Whether this new insight was given to Sharansky directly by God or was the outgrowth of his own thinking is an unanswerable question. I prefer to believe that both are true, or that the presence of God, as perceived by Sharansky, and his own mind were interactive, which is not so far-fetched if you believe, as I do, that the human creature is never totally separated from its Creator.

Whenever God makes a "comeback," the new religious upsurge registers not only in worship attendance but also in Bible study. Our dialogues document the centrality of the Bible in the religious consciousness of the Jew. The reader who cannot decide whether the Bible is a fully human or divinely inspired book might well turn from the theological arguments on the question to Professor Katz's phenomenological approach to the Bible as reading experience. It's the show and tell approach or, read and see how it feels:

> There seems to me to be some awareness, some disclosure of authority, of exceptional power, that is more persuasive than any alternative explanation of the text. And that overwhelming sense that the Torah is always more than we understand, that it transcends our effort to make it into something merely of our own design, that it is always an incarnation of a mysterious presence, is the compelling, or should we perhaps say more cautiously, the near compelling, evidence in itself.

I write these closing lines on the porch of my apartment in Jerusalem while watching thousands of adults and children walk up the winding road around Mount Zion to the Western Wall in celebration of the unification of Jerusalem. The crowds of youth singing in the streets on their way to the wall fulfill Jeremiah's prophecy that "yet again there shall be heard in this place . . . the voice of joy and the voice of gladness" (Jer. 33.10). It is indicative of the wondrous continuity and unity of the Jewish people. As certain as we can be of anything, we are sure about three things: The State of Israel will grow and flourish; diaspora Jewry will survive, even if diminished in number, to play a significant role in the life of many nations; and the Jewish religious heritage of distinctive beliefs, celebrations, and ethical norms will remain the common source of Jewish consciousness around the world.

In the 1960s, *Commentary* published a symposium entitled "The

Condition of Jewish Belief" in which thirty-eight rabbis and theologians presented their views on major Jewish doctrines. It was then noted that there was "far less theological unrest among Jews than among Christians today, and—for better or worse—few new ideas about Judaism." Now, a generation later, our dialogues confirm a common core of faith despite diversity in the formulation of Jewish beliefs. The uncompromisingly monotheistic God concept, however nuanced, remains the foundation of contemporary Judaism as it has since Biblical times. Neither the challenge of modernism nor the shock of the Holocaust have turned the Jew godless. Belief in the chosen people and Messianic redemption suffered some erosion, but not even all of the skeptics would categorically reject these doctrines. And so the Jews today remain in covenant with God.

Index of Biblical References

Index of Names

Names of the fourteen persons featured in this book appear in this index only if cited outside their respective chapters.